McGraw-Hill Social Studies

Cleo H. Cherryholmes
Lynn Cherryholmes
Gary Manson
Peter H. Martorella
Rosemary Messick
Anna Ochoa
Joyce Speas
Jan L. Tucker
June Tyler
George Vuicich

PROGRAM CONSULTANTS

LAURENCE W. ARONSTEIN
Principal, Memorial School
Millis Elementary Schools

MADGE BARNETT
Social Studies Consultant
Minneapolis, Minnesota

JOANNE BUGGEY
Social Studies Consultant
Minneapolis, Minnesota

GEORGE W. FRENCH
Director, Social Studies
Philadelphia Public Schools

RITA IRONS
Educational Consultant
Westport, Connecticut

MARK LYTLE
Department of History
Bard College

JOHN D. McAULAY
Emeritus of Education
Pennsylvania State University

ANTHONY PETRILLO
Director of Instruction
Jefferson County Schools

VINCENT PRESNO
Department of Curriculum and Instruction
Wright State University

PETER R. SENN
Department of Economics and Social Science
Wilbur Wright College

BARBARA VORNDRAN
Career Education Specialist
Teachers College, Columbia University

BETTY J. WICKRE
Countryside Elementary School
Edina, Minnesota

CONTENT CONSULTANTS

FELIX D. ALMARAZ, JR.
Associate Professor of History
The University of Texas of San Antonio

J.G. BRADLEY
Department of Education in the Social Sciences
McGill University

JOANNE CHANCEY
Consultant on Early Childhood Education
Florida State Department of Education

KAREN L. MOHR CHAVEZ
Department of Sociology and Anthropology
Central Michigan University

MARIO R. daCRUZ
Education Specialist
São Paulo, Brazil

JOSEPH DECAROLI
Department of Curriculum and Instruction
Newark, Delaware

RAMIRO GARCIA
Bilingual Consultant
Los Angeles City Unified School District

JUDY GILLESPIE
Social Studies Development Center
Indiana University

JOHN T. GULLAHORN
Department of Sociology
Michigan State University

JOHN HOSTETLER
Department of Anthropology
Temple University

MARI-LUCI JARAMILLO
American Ambassador to Honduras
American Embassy, Tegucigalpa

JANET LOPE
Administrator
Bureau of Indian Affairs
Shiprock, New Mexico

IAN M. MATELY
Department of Geography
Michigan State University

C.W. MINKEL
Principal Representative of Michigan State University at the Brazilian Ministry of Education
Brazilia, D.F. Brazil

ALFRED E. OPUBOR
Center for African Studies
Michigan State University

LOUISE SAUSE
Department of Early Childhood
Michigan State University

ENID SCHILDKROUT
Department of Anthropology
The American Museum of Natural History

HARRIET SKYE
Office of Public Information
United Tribes Educational Technical Center
Bismarck, North Dakota

EDOUARD TAPSOBA
Ministry of Planning and Rural Development
Republic of Upper Volta, Africa

JACK F. WILLIAMS
Department of Geography
Michigan State University

CLASSROOM CONSULTANTS

JANE KANNE
Logan Elementary School
Los Angeles, California

ANN WILSON
Garfield School
Elgin, Illinois

NANCY PINNELL
New Pitman School
Kirkwood, Missouri

VIRGINIA FRIDDELL
Meadowbrook Elementary School
Norfolk, Virginia

MARY LINLEY
Western Avenue School
Geneva, Illinois

KENNETH SHERWOOD
Kings Highway Elementary School
Westport, Connecticut

ANN PITSTICK
Swift Elementary School
Arlington, Texas

Understanding the United States

BY
George Vuicich
Department of Geography
Western Michigan University

With the assistance of
Joseph P. Stollman
Department of Geography
Western Michigan University

SENIOR AUTHORS
Cleo Cherryholmes
Department of Political Science
Michigan State University

Gary Manson
Department of Geography
Michigan State University

WEBSTER DIVISION, McGRAW-HILL BOOK COMPANY

New York   St. Louis   San Francisco   Auckland   Bogotá   Düsseldorf
Johannesburg   London   Madrid   Mexico   Montreal   New Delhi
Panama   Paris   São Paulo   Singapore   Sydney   Tokyo   Toronto

Editorial Development:

Senior Editor:	Paul Hastings Wilson
Project Director:	Len Martelli
Editors:	Marlena M. Baraf, Mary Ann Demers, Cathy Kellar
Editing and Styling:	Sal Allocco, Diana Ober, Patricia L. McCormick
Design Supervision:	Lisa Delgado, Bennie Arrington
Photo Research:	Suzanne Volkman, Cecile Brunswick
Production Supervisor:	Karen Romano
Consultant:	Alma Graham, Founding Member, Textbook Committee, NOW-NY
Design:	Graphic Arts International
Cover Photo:	Bill Weems/Woodfin Camp

Library of Congress Cataloging in Publication Data

Vuicich, George.
  Understanding the United States.

  (McGraw-Hill social studies)
  Includes index.
  SUMMARY: A fifth grade social studies text dealing with the history and people of the United States and threaded with the themes of cultural pluralism, equality, and social justice.
  1. United States—Juvenile literature. [1. United States] I. Stollman, Joseph P., joint author. II. Title.
E178.1.V85   973   78-1491
ISBN 0-07-011985-6

Acknowledgments are an extension of this copyright page and are found on page 384.

Copyright © 1979 BY McGRAW-HILL, INC. All Rights Reserved. Printed in the United States of America. No part of this publication may be reproduced, stored in a retrieval system, or transmitted, in any form or by any means, electronic, mechanical, photocopying, recording, or otherwise, without prior written permission of the publisher.

ISBN: 0-07-011985-6

CONTENTS

UNIT ONE — THE UNITED STATES TODAY

1 OUR NATURAL ENVIRONMENT 10
The Continent of North America 11 ■ East and Central Regions 14 ■ Other Regions of North America 17 ■ Climates of North America 21 ■ North American Rivers and Lakes 23

2 OUR COUNTRY AND ITS NEIGHBORS 26
The United States Today 27 ■ Where Do Americans Live? 30 ■ Canada Today 33 ■ Mexico Today 37 ■ Sharing a Continent 40

3 LEARNING ABOUT PEOPLE OF THE UNITED STATES 43
Cultural Groups in the United States 44 ■ Sharing Behavior and Language 46 ■ Sharing Beliefs 50 ■ How Are People of the United States Alike? 53 ■ UNIT REVIEW 56

UNIT TWO — THE BEGINNING OF A NATION

1 SETTLING A CONTINENT 60
The First Americans 61 ■ Cities of the Sun 64 ■ Other Early American Cultures 68 ■ Europeans Discover a New World 71 ■ Spaniards Arrive 76 ■ The English and Other Europeans 80

2 THE ENGLISH COLONIES 85
Jamestown and the South 86 ■ Plantation Life 91 ■ Early Settlers of New England 94 ■ The Puritan Church 97 ■ Education and Trade 101 ■ The Middle Colonies 105 ■ Philadelphia 109 ■ Amish People in the Middle Colonies 113

3 A CULTURE FROM COLONIAL TIMES 117
Amish People Today 118 ■ Values and a Way of Life 122 ■ Cooperation among the Amish 126 ■ Making Decisions 129 ■ Benefits and Costs of Deciding 132

4 THE AMISH AND CHANGE 135
Growing up Amish 136 ■ "When I Grow up" 140 ■ Choosing New Things 142 ■ The Problem of Change 145 ■ UNIT REVIEW 148

UNIT THREE A NEW NATION

1 FREEDOM FROM GREAT BRITAIN 152
Trouble with Great Britain 153 ■ Revolution 156 ■ Fighting for Independence 159 ■ Fighting for Independence II 162 ■ Leaders: Helping People Decide 166 ■ Leaders: Lending Faith and Courage 169 ■ Why the Americans Won 173

2 A NATION IS BORN 177
Early Government 178 ■ The Constitutional Convention 181 ■ Rules for a New Government 184 ■ The Bill of Rights 187

3 THE NATION GROWS 191
Moving West 192 ■ Life on the Frontier 195 ■ Beyond the Mississippi 199 ■ Oregon and the Southwest 203 ■ The Gold Rush 207 ■ Mexican Americans in the Southwest 210

4 SPANISH-SPEAKING AMERICANS 213
Se habla Español 214 ■ Mexican Traditions and the Roman Catholic Church 217 ■ The Morelos Family 222 ■ At Home 224 ■ Learning in Two Languages 227

5 PLANNING A TRIP 229
Planning the trip to Allende   230   ■   Scenes Along the Way   234   ■   Crossing Borders   236   ■   Into Mexico   240   ■   Allende, at Last!   244   ■   UNIT REVIEW   248

UNIT FOUR — THE NATION CHANGES

1 A DIVIDED NATION 254
Slavery   255   ■   Blacks Against Slavery   260   ■   Who Shall Rule?   264   ■   Civil War   271   ■   After the War   276

2 THE INDUSTRIAL REVOLUTION 282
The Beginnings of a Modern Nation   283   ■   Immigration   288   ■   Problems of Immigrants   292   ■   Big Business and Industry   296

3 THE PASSING FRONTIER 299
Settling the Great Plains   300   ■   The People of the Plains   303   ■   Whose Land?   307

4 NATIVE AMERICANS TODAY 310
Reservations   311   ■   Native American Contributions   314

5 BETWEEN TWO CULTURES 317
Who Are the Navaho?   318   ■   How People Learn   321   ■   Navaho Teachers and Models   324   ■   Confusing Models   328   ■   Two-Culture Schools   332   ■   UNIT REVIEW   334

UNIT FIVE — THE MODERN WORLD

1 INTO THE TWENTIETH CENTURY 338
The United States at the Turn of the Century   339   ■   The Reformers   341   ■   Women Get the Vote   345

2 A CHANGING WORLD 349
The 1920s   350   ■   World War II   353   ■   The Home Front: Effects of War   358   ■   The Atomic Age   361   ■   Justice for All   363   ■   Challenges for the Future   368   ■   UNIT REVIEW   374

UNIT ONE
The United States Today

1
OUR NATURAL ENVIRONMENT

How are the regions of North America different from one another? What are the climates like? How are the rivers and lakes of North America important to people?

The Continent of North America

You are one of the people living in North America. Your ancestors may have come here sometime in the last 400 years. During that time, many people from all parts of the world came to North America. Native Americans lived here even before that time. If you are a Native American, your people have lived in North America for thousands of years.

Have you heard the song that begins "Oh beautiful, for spacious skies"? Do you remember the rest of the words? This song is called "America, the Beautiful." It tells about the beauty of North America. It tells how big the land is, how wide the skies are, how rich the crops are.

North America is a *continent*, or large land mass, on Earth. There are three large nations on the continent of North America. They are Canada, the United States, and Mexico.

Because North America is so large, it has many different *landforms*, or kinds of land. In some places, the land is as flat as a tabletop. In others, it is as jagged as the edge of a saw. Some land in North America is covered with thick forests. Some land is covered with drifting sand. How do we study a land with so many differences?

We can begin by dividing the continent into seven *regions*. These regions are large areas where the landforms are similar. The seven regions are:

- the Atlantic and Gulf coastal plain
- the Appalachian (ap′ ə lā′chən) Mountains
- the Central Lowlands and the Great Plains
- the Rocky Mountains
- the Great Basin
- the Pacific Coastal Ranges and Lowlands
- the Canadian Shield

Find each of these regions of North America on the map on the following page.

The *elevation* key on the map tells how high some of these regions are. The color green stands for the lowlands. This

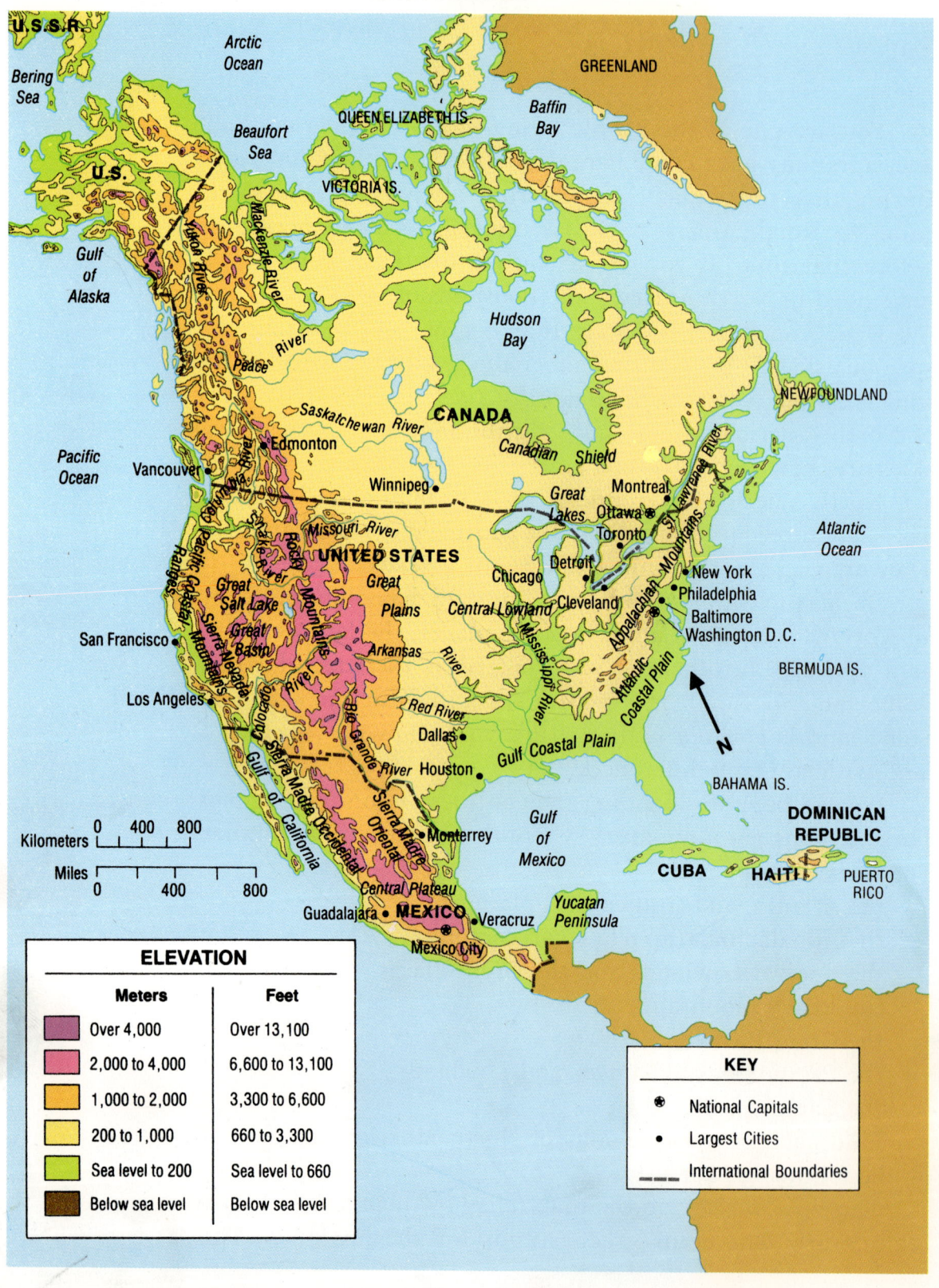

land is usually found along seacoasts. The highest land is colored in purple. Look at the key. How many meters high is this land? Now look at your map and find the areas in purple. What regions of North America have the highest land?

The other key on your map gives the *symbols,* or small drawings, that stand for national capitals, largest cities, and *international boundaries.* Find the symbol for national capitals. Then, find the national capital of the United States.

International boundaries are the lines on a map which divide one nation from another. They show where one nation ends and another begins. Find the symbol for international boundaries on your key. Now look at the map. With your finger, trace the international boundary between Canada and the United States. Then find and trace the international boundary between the United States and Mexico.

Notice that the land regions of North America do not stop at international boundaries. Landforms do not change suddenly as you go from one country into another. For example, the Great Plains extend from Canada through the United States and into Mexico. The coastal plains lie along the seacoasts of both the United States and Mexico.

In the next few lessons, you will learn about the land and resources of the seven main regions of North America.

Choose the best answer:
1. North America is (a) a landform, (b) a nation, (c) a continent, (d) a region of the United States.
2. An international boundary separates (a) one land region from another, (b) Mexico from the United States, (c) the Great Plains from the Rocky Mountains.
3. An elevation key is useful because it tells you (a) how high land regions are on a map, (b) where nations are located, (c) how far one place is from another.

4. Look at the map on page 12. Try to find the general area where you live. What large city is nearest to the place where you live?
5. In which region of North America do you live?

East and Central Regions

Along the east coast of North America is a narrow plain. This plain begins far up the coast and becomes wider as you travel south. On the map on page 12, trace with your finger the coastal plain. Notice that the coastal plain extends all along the Atlantic and Gulf coasts of the United States.

The coastal plain is low and flat. In some places, there are large areas where the land is covered with shallow water. These areas are called *swamps* or *wetlands*. The swamps are thick with plants, and there are many wild animals.

Much of the coastal plain is fertile land. In the north, farmers grow vegetables and raise dairy cattle. In the south, they grow crops such as oranges and rice.

Some of the largest cities in North America are found on the coastal plain. Many of the cities on the plain are near important or famous waterways.

West of the coastal plain are the Appalachian Mountains. These mountains begin in Canada. They reach all the way to Georgia and Alabama. The Appalachians are old mountains. This means that they were formed millions of years ago. Since

Swamps are important areas for wildlife.

Compare this picture of the Appalachians with the picture of the Rockies on page 17.

then, they have been worn down by the wind and the weather. Today, most of these mountains have rounded tops. The valleys between them do not have steep sides.

In parts of the Appalachians, the land is not good for farming. People have farmed thin strips of land in the valleys where it is flat. But farmers here barely grow enough for themselves to eat. Much coal, however, is found in these mountains. Coal is black and rocklike. It is used for fuel and is very valuable today.

Stretching across the center of North America are the Central Lowlands and the Great Plains. This is one of the largest areas of flatland in the world. It stretches from northern Canada to the Gulf of Mexico.

The plains east of the Missouri River are called the Central Lowlands. Here is some of the most fertile land in the world. On these plains, the farmers grow corn, soybeans, and wheat. More of these crops are grown here than all the people of North America can eat. The Central Lowlands is also rich in oil and natural gas.

Many of the large cities in the United States are located in the Central Lowlands. Cities are often built on level land because transportation there by road or railway is fairly easy. Find Chicago, Detroit, and Cleveland on the map.

The combines are harvesting wheat on the Great Plains.

To the west of the Missouri River is the Great Plains. Less rain falls here than on the Central Lowlands. Much of the land is covered with grass. Great herds of cattle and sheep graze on these plains. They provide most of the meat, wool, and leather used by the people of North America. Great amounts of wheat are also grown on the Great Plains.

TO DO

1. Imagine that you are in Philadelphia and are traveling west to the city of Winnipeg. Number the following regions in the order in which you would cross them: (a) the Great Plains, (b) the Appalachian Mountains, (c) the coastal plains, (d) the Central Lowlands.
2. Match the following regions with the goods they produce:
   - a. Northern Coastal Plain
   - b. Central Lowlands
   - c. Appalachian Mountains
   - d. Great Plains

   1. herds of cattle and sheep
   2. coal
   3. vegetables and dairy cattle
   4. corn and soybean crops

ON YOUR OWN

3. Look at the coastal plain on the map. Name the cities you see. Why do you think many cities on the coastal plain were built near waterways?

Other Regions of North America

West of the Great Plains of North America are the Rocky Mountains. These are high mountains with jagged peaks and steep valleys. The Rocky Mountains were formed later than the Appalachians. Compared to the Appalachians, the Rockies are new. Some of the people living in the Rocky Mountains earn their living by mining and logging. The Rocky Mountains also attract visitors who come for sports and vacations.

West of the Rockies in the United States is a large area of high land called the Great Basin. This land receives little rainfall. Much of it is desert. Find this area on your map. The rivers here do not flow toward the sea. Many flow into the Great Salt Lake. There are few big cities in this part of North America.

The land near the Rocky Mountains is good for grazing cattle.

On the left are sand dunes in the desert. On the right is the Great Salt Lake.

Along the Pacific Coast of North America, we find mountains, valleys, and coastal plains. Some of these mountains are close to the ocean. They are called the Pacific Coastal Ranges. Other mountains separate the Pacific Coastal Ranges from the Great Basin. Find the names of these mountains on your map on page 12.

The plains are narrow along the Pacific Coast. But look at the map closely. Between the mountain ranges are some large valleys, especially in California. These lands are heavily farmed. Some of the important crops of these valleys are grapes, oranges, and lettuce. What large cities are found along the Pacific Coast of North America?

Two mountain ranges similar to the Pacific Coastal Ranges and the Rockies continue down into Mexico. They cover much of Mexico's land. Mexico can be divided into four areas by its mountains. Find these areas on the map on page 12 as you read about them.

The central plateau (pla tō′) is the part of Mexico where most people live. It is the high, flat land between Mexico's two mountain ranges. The soil is fertile. Farms there grow much of Mexico's food. Mexico City, the capital of Mexico, is found in this area.

The southern area is mostly mountains and swamplands. But the Yucatán (ū′kə tan′) Peninsula in the south is low and flat. A *peninsula* is an area of land surrounded by water on three sides. Many of Mexico's Native Americans live in the Yucatán. It is a poor area with few roads and fewer factories. Most of the people live on small farms. The main city here is the port of Veracruz (ver′ə krüz).

The western area, except for Baja California, is much like the central plateau. It has good farmlands. It also has many mines and factories. Tourists from all over the world visit the beaches along the Pacific Coast.

Orange groves in a California valley.

Ruins of an old civilization can be found in the Yucatán.

Baja California is a peninsula about 1,223 kilometers (760 miles) long in northwestern Mexico. It separates the Gulf of California from the Pacific Ocean. It consists mostly of high mountain ranges. On the Pacific side, there are two large coastal plains. The land is generally too dry and poor for cultivation. Its seacoast is popular with tourists, and the land is rich in silver, lead, copper, and gold.

The northern area borders the United States. This is much like southwestern United States. Large areas of northern Mexico receive little rainfall. Cattle ranches are found here. So are iron, lead, and silver mines. Irrigation has made some of the land into good farmland.

The last main region of North America is called the Canadian Shield. This is a large area of rocky hills covered with forests. It is also known as the Laurentian Plateau. It forms the central land mass of North America. It has the shape of a giant shield. It extends from Newfoundland, in the east, to the Beaufort Sea, in the northwest, and south through Wisconsin and Minnesota. Few people live in the northern region. But the land is rich in minerals such as nickel, copper, and silver. There are also many streams and lakes in the Canadian Shield. These waters attract many Canadians and Americans from farther south, who come for vacations.

1. Which of these regions are rich in forests and minerals? (a) the Great Basin, (b) the Canadian Shield, (c) the Rocky Mountains, (d) the Yucatán Peninsula.
2. Where are the most fertile land areas in Mexico? (a) in the central plateau, (b) in the northern area, (c) in the western lands, (d) in the south.

3. In your opinion, which are the three most important regions to all North Americans? Give your reasons.
4. What regions of North America would you like to visit? What would you do there?

Climates of North America

Look outside. Is the sun shining? Is it raining, windy, or cloudy? Is it cold or warm? When you answer these questions, you are describing the *weather*. The weather is the condition of the air at any one moment or on a particular day. *Climate* is something different. *Climate* means the weather on an average day or over a long period of time. For example, in Miami the climate is usually hot and wet in the summer and mild and wet in the winter.

When we talk about weather or climate, we are talking mainly about two things. First, we are talking about the *temperature,* or how much heat is in the air. Second, we are talking about the amount of *precipitation*, or water, that falls from the air. This water can be rain, snow, sleet, hail, or fog.

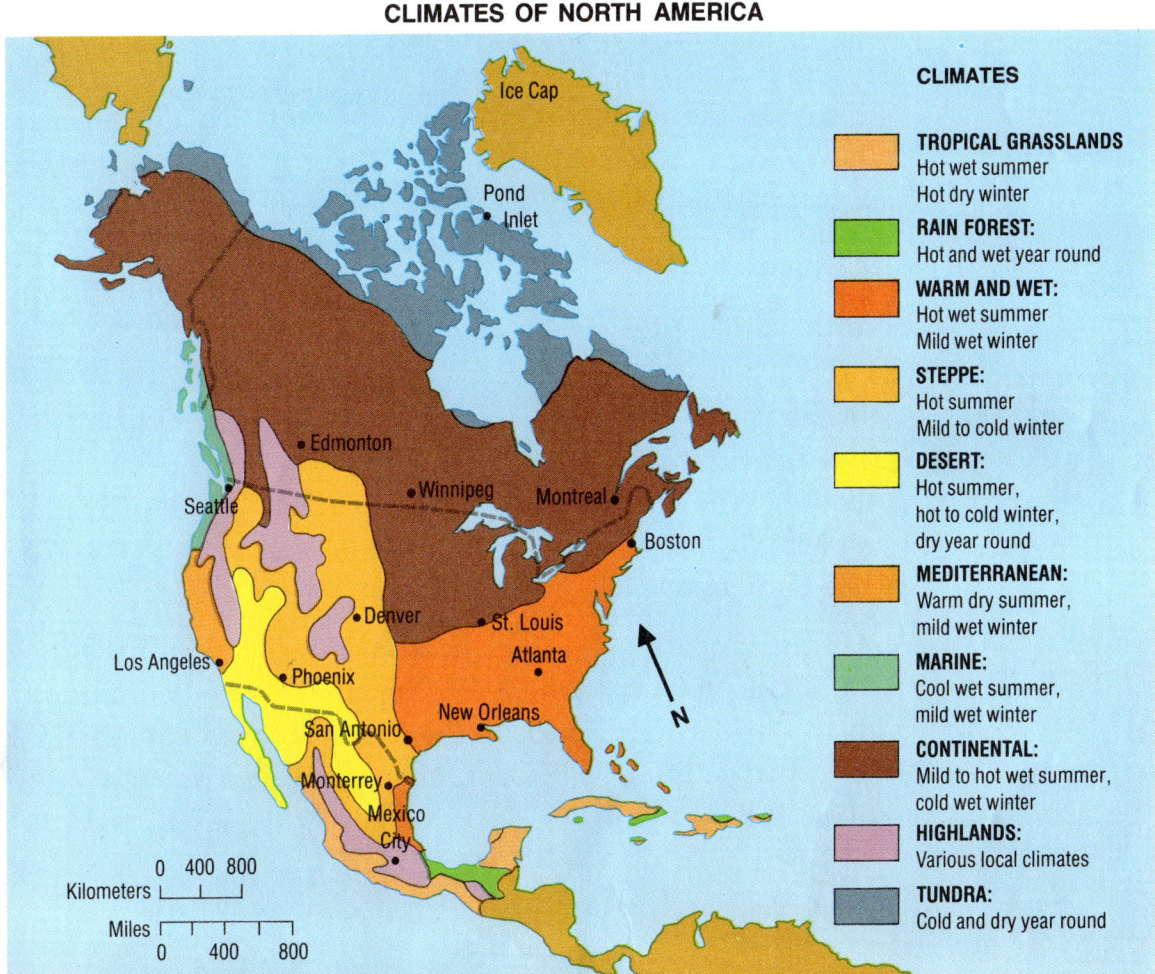

People enjoy the warm, sunny climate found in Hawaii.

When you describe the weather, you tell people about temperature and precipitation. You might say "It's cold and snowy." Or, "It's hot, and the sun is shining." When you describe the climate, you are saying what the weather is like during a season of the year. You might say "The winters here are not very cold, but it rains a lot." Or, "The winters are very cold, and it snows a lot."

Look at the climate map of North America on page 21. It shows eight different climates. Look at the key for the map. Notice that the climate is described for both winter and summer. It is not described for spring and fall. The weather in spring is partly like summer and partly like winter. How could the climate for fall be described?

TO DO

1. What is the weather like today? Tell about it, using the words *temperature* and *precipitation*.
2. Look at the climate map of North America. Find Seattle, Phoenix, and New Orleans. How does the key describe the climate of each of these cities?

ON YOUR OWN

3. On the climate map, find the area in which you live. How does the map describe the climate of your community? Is this a good description of the climate of your community?
4. In which climate of North America would you prefer to live? Tell why.

North American Rivers and Lakes

Rivers carry water from the land to the oceans. They are very important to people. River valleys often have much fertile land. Here, people farm and often build cities. Rivers also provide a way to go from place to place. Before many roads were built, rivers were one very important means of transportation.

You have probably heard of the Mississippi, the Missouri, and the Ohio rivers. You may know about the St. Lawrence, the Colorado, and the Rio Grande (rē′ō grand′). These are just a few of the rivers that flow in North America. Find these rivers on the map of North America on page 12. These rivers *drain* a large part of North America. When a body of water drains a land area, it carries all the extra water away from that area.

Find the Great Lakes on your map. They are the largest group of *freshwater* lakes in the world. This means the water in these lakes is not salty like the ocean. The Great Lakes are very deep. They are connected to the Atlantic Ocean by the St. Lawrence River. Many ships travel these lakes, carrying passengers and goods. There are many important cities on the Great Lakes' shores.

The Mississippi River begins far in the interior of North America. This picture was taken in Wisconsin.

Lakes provide many opportunities for recreation, such as sailing.

Notice that many rivers of North America flow into one another. The Missouri River flows into the Mississippi River. The Ohio and the Arkansas (är′ kən sô) rivers also flow into the Mississippi. Such a group of rivers is called a *river system*. The land area drained by a group of rivers is called a *drainage basin*. Much of the rain or snow that falls in a drainage basin is caught and carried away by its river system. Some drainage basins are very small. Others are very large.

The landforms in each area determine which way the rivers flow. The mountains are like divisions of the land. Rivers on different sides of mountains will flow in different directions. Find the rivers that begin in the Rocky Mountains. Into what bodies of water do they flow?

Climate also plays a part. Where rain or snow is heavy, rivers are usually larger. There are probably more rivers in such places, too. Do you remember where the dry areas in North America are? Check your climate map. See how many of the largest rivers are located in the dry areas.

LARGEST RIVERS IN NORTH AMERICA

RIVERS	LENGTH IN KM	LENGTH IN MILES
Mackenzie	4,216	2,530
Mississippi	3,757	2,254
Missouri	3,704	2,222
St. Lawrence	3,040	1,824
Rio Grande	3,016	1,810
Yukon	2,880	1,728
Arkansas	2,320	1,392
Colorado	2,320	1,392
Columbia	1,942	1,165
Saskatchewan	1,928	1,157
Peace	1,912	1,147
Snake	1,661	1,032
Red	1,629	1,012

1. Look at the list of rivers on the chart on this page. Find these rivers on the map on page 12.
2. Where does most of the water in rivers come from? Where do rivers take this water?

3. Is there a river close to your community? Do you use this river? Tell how.

1. Name the seven regions of North America. Describe the landforms and important resources of two of them.
2. On your map on page 21, find Montreal, Atlanta, and Los Angeles. Then describe the climate of each of these cities.
3. Name three important rivers in North America. Into what bodies of water do they flow?

2

OUR COUNTRY AND ITS NEIGHBORS

What do people in this country have in common? How are they different from one another? How can the United States and its neighbors work together for a better future?

The United States Today

United States citizens live in a large nation of 9,519,622 square kilometers (3,675,547 square miles). There are more than 216 million people in the United States. Only three countries on Earth have larger populations. They are China, India, and the Soviet Union.

The United States is also a powerful and rich nation. It has a large Army, Navy, and Air Force. It has more factories and businesses than any other nation in the world.

The system of transportation in the United States reaches even the smallest town in the nation. It is fairly easy for its people to move from place to place. There are waterways, highways, railroads, and airlines connecting all parts of the country.

Large, divided highways have different names in different parts of the United States. In Los Angeles, this road is called a freeway.

Each large United States city has a distinctive skyline. Above is Seattle.

The United States also has a very good communications system. Telephones, radios, televisions, newspapers, and magazines are all part of this system. These things make it possible for most people in the United States to know what is going on in the world. They help people here keep in touch with and learn about one another.

People in the United States are like one another in many ways. They share many beliefs. You will read about some of these beliefs later. Most share a common language, which is English. They share a common government and are expected to follow the same laws.

The people also use many of the same objects. They drive the same kinds of cars. They use the same brands of toothpaste, soft drinks, soups, televisions, jeans, and bicycles. You could drive all around the country and find most of the things you see every day.

But the people of the United States are also different in many ways. They are different in the amount and kinds of things they have. The poor, the wealthy, and the in-between do not live in the same way. The people have many different interests and abilities.

They have come from different parts of the world. Some are still arriving. They have brought different ways of living, talking, and thinking with them. They have settled in different parts of the country. Where they live sometimes makes the way they live different. The kinds of jobs people do are often unlike jobs in other parts of the country. The way people have fun and the kinds of music they enjoy are often different.

Some people say that these differences are among the things that make the United States great.

---

1. Which of these statements are *not* true about the United States? (a) There are about 216 thousand people there. (b) Its people are like one another in many ways. (c) The United States has more businesses than any other nation.
2. Name at least three ways in which information moves from place to place in the United States.
3. Name three ways in which the people of the United States are different from one another.

---

4. Why are good roads important to the people of the United States?
5. In your opinion, what are the three most important things about the United States?

Where Do Americans Live?

Below is a *political* map of the United States. The word *political* has to do with government. The map shows the District of Columbia, which we call Washington, D.C. Washington, D.C., is our nation's capital. This is where our national government is located. The divisions shown on this map are our country's fifty states. Also shown is the capital of each state. A state government meets in a state capital. Political maps can show many different divisions. They can show how a continent is divided into nations, or how a state is divided into counties.

THE UNITED STATES – POLITICAL MAP

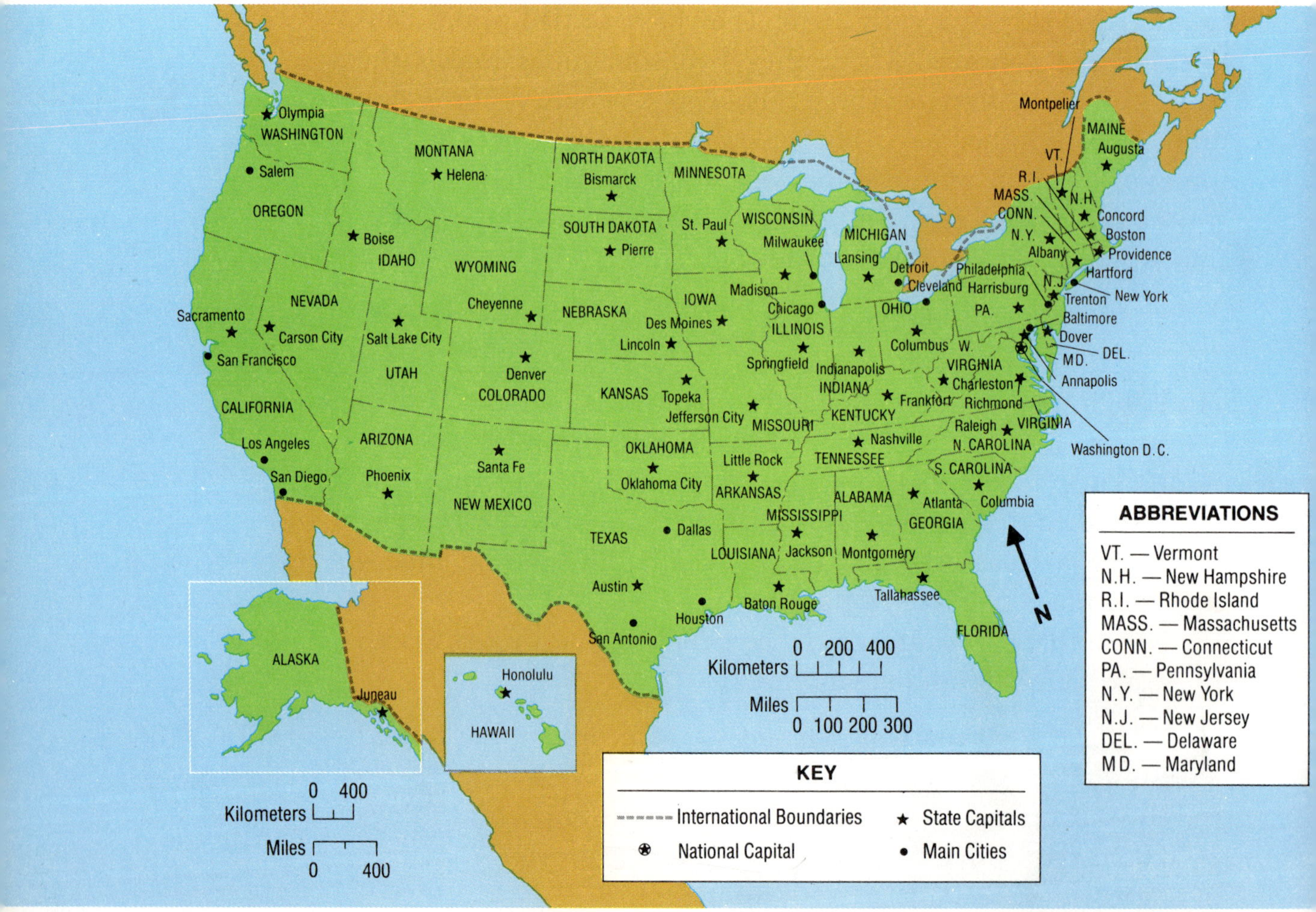

ABBREVIATIONS

VT. — Vermont
N.H. — New Hampshire
R.I. — Rhode Island
MASS. — Massachusetts
CONN. — Connecticut
PA. — Pennsylvania
N.Y. — New York
N.J. — New Jersey
DEL. — Delaware
MD. — Maryland

KEY

- - - - - International Boundaries ★ State Capitals
⊛ National Capital • Main Cities

Today, 75 of every 100 people in the United States live in *urban areas*. Urban areas are towns and cities with more than 2,500 people in them. *Rural areas* are towns, villages, or farms in the country with fewer than 2,500 people. Twenty out of a hundred Americans live in country towns or villages.

Look at the *population-density* map of the United States on page 32. It shows where the people lived in the last census. Every ten years, the government takes a *census*, or counts its population. Examine the map. Study the map key. The color red stands for the most crowded areas. Notice that the Northeast is one of the most heavily populated regions. Few people live in the areas colored light green. Much of this land is in the Western United States.

The center of population for the United States is marked with a circle on your map. A north-south line and an east-west line cross on that spot. As many people live north of that place as live south of it. As many people live east of that place as live west of it. The center of population moves from year to year, as people move from place to place. Since the early days of our country, the center of population has been moving farther west.

The center of population shown on your map is only for the mainland of the United States. It does not include the states of Alaska and Hawaii. It does not include the island of Puerto Rico.

Few people live in mountainous areas, but people use these areas for recreation.

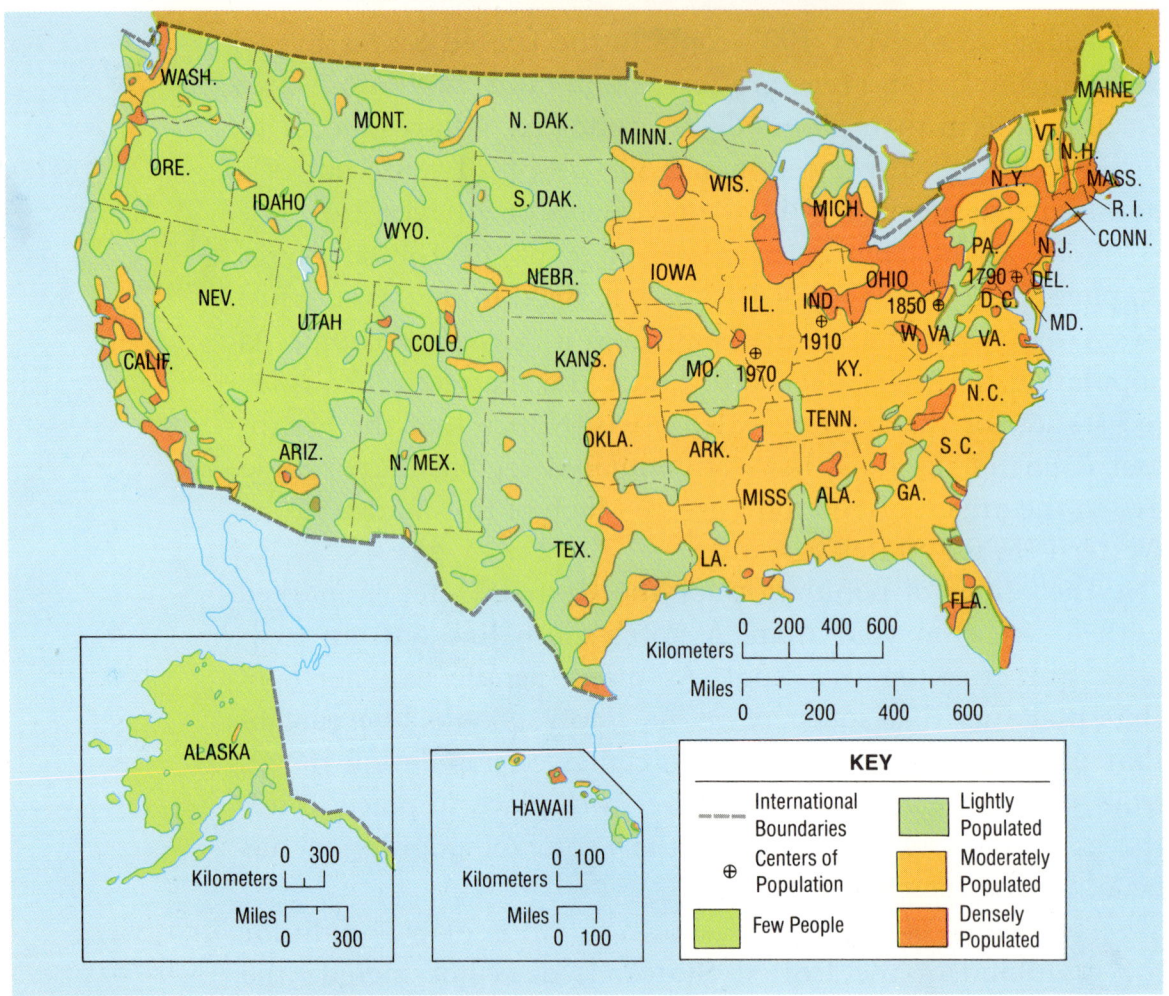

THE UNITED STATES – POPULATION DENSITY

TO DO

Choose the best answer:
1. A political map shows (a) landforms, (b) how a nation is divided into states, (c) where people live.
2. Most people in the United States live (a) in rural areas, (b) on the West Coast, (c) in urban areas.

ON YOUR OWN

3. How often does the government of the United States take a census? When was the last census taken?
4. What is the most densely populated western state?
5. Is your community in an urban or rural area? How can you find out?
6. What is the name of your state? Using the map above, describe the population density of your state.

Canada Today

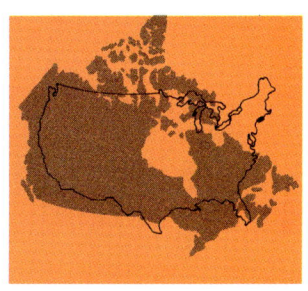

The nation of Canada shares the North American continent with the United States. Canada is slightly larger than the United States. It has 9,976,139 square kilometers (3,851,809 square miles). About 216 million people live in the United States. How many do you think live in Canada?

If you said about 200 million for Canada, you guessed wrong. Canada has about 22 million people. It is a wide open country. It has a small population for such a large country. Look at the population density map of Canada. Find the areas where most people live. Notice that few people live in northern Canada. The climate here is very cold.

CANADA-POPULATION DENSITY

KEY
- Few People
- Lightly Populated
- Moderately Populated
- Densely Populated

As in the United States, there are many differences within Canada. The Rocky Mountains are in the west, the Great Plains in the center, and the Laurentian Highlands in the east. In the far north is an area called the Arctic. Ways of living are different in each of Canada's regions.

Many of Canada's 11,000 Eskimos live in the Arctic. The Eskimos of North America are called the Innuit. *Innuit* is the Eskimo word for "people." The Arctic is one of the coldest parts of North America. In the winter months, it can get as cold as −39°C (−40°F).

About 240,000 people in Canada are Native Americans. Many of them live on reservations. Some, however, live and work in Canada's cities.

CANADA—POLITICAL MAP

Innuit sometimes build snow houses, called igloos, as protection against the cold.

Most Canadians, like most Americans, have European backgrounds. About half have English ancestors. One-third have French ancestors. English and French are the two official languages of Canada. All documents published by the national government are written in both languages. In some *provinces* where most French Canadians live, there are both English and French schools. There are also schools where both languages are taught.

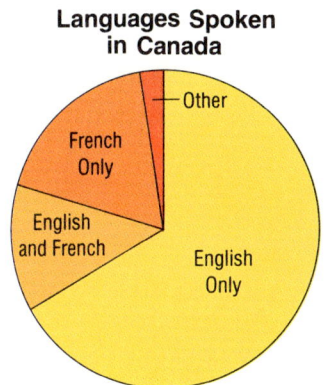

Languages Spoken in Canada

Canada is divided into ten provinces and two territories. Each province has its own government, which is something like the governments of our states. The national government of Canada meets in Ottawa (ot′ ə wə). The lawmakers in Ottawa form the *Parliament*, just as in Washington, D.C., where the lawmakers form the *Congress*. A *prime minister* directs the government of Canada.

Canada has many natural resources. Among them are minerals, timber, fertile land, oil, and natural gas.

People in the United States own more than half of all Canadian factories. Money from the United States has helped to build many businesses in Canada. Canadians are not so sure this is a good thing. They are an independent nation. They want to have greater control over all the resources of their country.

Above: Lumber, an important Canadian resource.

Right: The French language in Quebec.

Canada and the United States are friendly. The International Peace Garden is one of the monuments built in honor of this friendship. The people of Manitoba and North Dakota gave the land for the garden.

TO DO

1. Name two different groups of people who settled in Canada.
2. Canada is divided into _____ provinces and _____ territories.
3. The capital of Canada is _____. Find it on your map on page 12.

ON YOUR OWN

4. Name some ways in which Canada is like the United States.
5. Name some ways in which Canada is different from the United States.
6. Compare the population-density map for Canada with the similar map for the United States on page 32. In what ways is the population distribution similar in both countries? In what ways is it different?

Mexico Today

Mexico is the third country which shares the North American continent. It covers 1,972,546 square kilometers (761,604 square miles). About 50 million people live in Mexico.

Of every 100 Mexicans, 30 are Native Americans. Their ancestors lived in Mexico thousands of years ago. Another 15 of 100 have Spanish or other European backgrounds. The

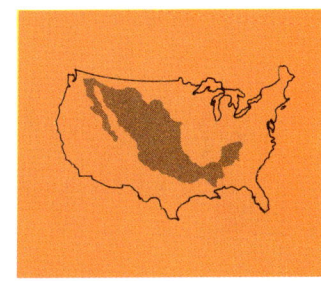

MEXICO-POLITICAL MAP

KEY
- ––––– International Boundaries
- ⊛ National Capital
- • Main Cities

STATES AND TERRITORIES OF MEXICO

1. Baja California
2. Territorio de Baja California
3. Sonora
4. Chihuahua
5. Coahuila
6. Nuevo León
7. Tamaulipas
8. Sinaloa
9. Durango
10. Zacatecas
11. San Luis Potosí
12. Nayarit
13. Aguascalientes
14. Veracruz
15. Jalisco
16. Guanajuato
17. Querétaro
18. Hidalgo
19. Colima
20. Michoacán
21. México
22. Puebla
23. Distrito Federal
24. Tlaxcala
25. Guerrero
26. Morelos
27. Oaxaca
28. Tabasco
29. Chiapas
30. Campeche
31. Yucatán
32. Territorio de Quintana Roo

37

Both traditional and modern ways are found in Mexico. Above, on the right, is a traditional Spanish building. The other pictures show modern Mexico.

ancestors of most of these people came to Mexico during and after the 1500s. The remaining 55 out of 100 are *mestizos* (mə stē′ zōz). Mestizos have mixed backgrounds. They have both Spanish and Native American ancestors. Most people in Mexico speak Spanish.

Sixty out of every hundred Mexicans live in urban areas. Most of them live in central Mexico. One of the reasons is climate. Look at your map on page 21. What is the climate like in this part of Mexico?

In a market, many different prepared Mexican foods are sold.

Mexico is divided into twenty-nine states, one federal district, and two territories. It has a president and a congress. The people of Mexico elect their government leaders, just as the people of the United States and Canada do.

Mexico and the United States have not always been friends. Much of the southwestern part of the United States once belonged to Mexico. Later, you will read about a war between Mexico and the United States in the 1840s.

Today, Mexico and the United States have grown friendlier. Many Mexicans have relatives in the United States. The two countries now help each other in many ways.

1. Which of these statements is true? (a) More people live in Mexico than live in Canada. (b) More people live in Mexico than live in the United States.
2. What is the capital city of Mexico? Look on your map on page 12. Where is Mexico's capital located?

3. Name some ways in which Mexico is like the United States.
4. Name some ways in which Mexico is different from the United States.

Sharing a Continent

It is important to know about our neighbors. What happens in Canada and Mexico affects the United States in various ways. Neighboring countries also share many things.

Canada, the United States, and Mexico share many physical features. For example, all three countries have long ocean coastlines. Look at your map on page 12. Notice that the Rocky Mountains run down the length of the continent. The Great Plains is also shared by all three nations. Notice that Canada and the United States share the Great Lakes. The United States and Mexico share the Rio Grande and the Colorado River. Sharing physical features means that the countries are alike in other ways. Ocean coastlines, for example, mean ocean ports. All three countries have port cities. Canada, Mexico, and the United States can send ships loaded with goods to each other.

Great industries are located along the St. Lawrence Seaway.

Neighbors like Canada, the United States, and Mexico can work together to make things better for their people. Canada and the United States built the St. Lawrence Seaway together. This seaway opened up the St. Lawrence River to oceangoing ships. Now ships carry goods from the Atlantic Ocean to any city on the Great Lakes. They can go to Toronto, Detroit, or Chicago. The two nations also built dams on the Columbia River. These dams produce electric power for both countries.

Canada and the United States trade with one another. Canada has resources the United States needs. Some of these resources are oil and lumber. The United States makes things Canada needs. Of the goods Canada buys from other countries, over 80 percent come from the United States. Among them are cars, appliances, and other machines.

Neighbors share problems, too. Pollution is one problem Canada and the United States share. Pollution of the Great Lakes is a common problem. Big factories along the shores dump waste water into the lakes. Lake Erie is so dirty that swimmers can't go into the water in many places. The Chicago River is so clogged with waste that, a few years ago, it actually caught fire.

In 1909, Canada and the United States started the *International Joint Commission*. It is the commission's job to clean up the lakes. Today, United States and Canadian scientists are working on the problem of pollution together.

The American Southwest and the northern part of Mexico are dry. The Rio Grande flows along the border. Together, the United States and Mexico have built dams on the Rio Grande. The dams prevent flooding when there are heavy rains. They also hold back water in lakes called *reservoirs* (rez′ ər vwärz′). This water is used to irrigate farmlands. It is also piped into cities and towns. Mexico and the United States finished one of these dams, Amistad (am′ i stad′) Dam, in 1969. The reservoir behind this dam stores water for the use of both countries.

United States and Mexican scientists have worked together to save animals that are in danger of being killed off forever. They helped save the birds on Raza Island in Baja California. In 1964, Raza Island was set aside for wild animals only. Elephant seals, Guadalupe fur seals, and grey whales are also protected by both countries.

Another way Mexico and the United States help one another is in industry. United States businesses want workers. Mexicans need jobs. So "twin factories" have been set up in border cities. Mexicans do the work in their factory. Products are then taken to the United States twin factory. There they are packaged and sent away to be sold.

The two nations also trade with one another. The United States buys cattle, minerals, and farm products. Mexico buys machinery. Mexico also has many United States visitors. Tourists are important to Mexico.

Canada, Mexico, and the United States work together to protect wild animals. Together they try to solve water problems. They can help clean polluted air and water. They trade with one another. These are ways in which nations can share a continent and help one another.

1. Which of these features are shared by the United States and Canada? Which are shared by the United States and Mexico? (a) the Great Lakes, (b) the Rio Grande, (c) the Columbia River, (d) the St. Lawrence River, (e) the Colorado River.
2. Name two problems that people of Canada and the United States are trying to solve.
3. Name two problems that people of Mexico and the United States are trying to solve.

CHAPTER REVIEW

1. Name some ways in which Americans are alike. Name some ways in which they are different.
2. What are the two official languages of Canada? Why are these the main languages of Canada?
3. What are the three main groups of people in Mexico? In what part of Mexico do most people live?
4. Name several ways in which the United States, Canada, and Mexico are working together.

3
LEARNING ABOUT PEOPLE OF THE UNITED STATES

What is a culture? What do members of cultural groups share? What beliefs do many people of the United States share?

Culture Groups in the United States

People have come to the United States from all parts of the world. They have arrived at different times in our history. Some groups have kept closer to their original ways of living than other groups.

Some people in the United States may not be like you in certain ways. They may wear clothing or eat food that is different from yours. They may not speak the same language that you do. They may not believe in some of the things in which you believe.

We usually like people who are like us. We understand

Most people in our country came to the United States on immigrant ships like this one.

them. We feel comfortable with them. It is sometimes difficult to understand people who are different from us. Sometimes, we dislike them just because they are different.

But learning about people who are not like you is important. It is useful to learn about different ways of doing things. Also, by comparing different ways with your own ways, you can learn more about yourself. Comparing is an important way of learning.

One way to learn about different groups of people is to study their way of living. When you study a group's way of living, you are studying its *culture* (kul'chər). Culture means the behavior, beliefs, and language that are shared by the members of a group.

People who share the same culture form a *culture group*. In the United States, there are many culture groups. Because they live in one country and are subject to the same laws, together they form a society. The *dominant*, or major, culture group in the United States is British American. The minor culture groups are called *subcultures*. Among them are Italian Americans, Japanese Americans, Navaho, and Cuban Americans. What other groups can you name?

Later in this book, you will learn about several United States cultural groups. You will also learn a great deal about yourself and your own culture.

TO DO

Choose the best answer:
1. A culture is (a) a group's way of living, (b) the language shared by a group, (c) a national monument.
2. A cultural group is made up of (a) people who share the same race, (b) people who live together in a nation, (c) people who share the same behavior, beliefs, and language.

ON YOUR OWN

3. Can you think of something you would like to learn from someone who is very different from you? What is it?
4. Where did your ancestors come from? Find out from your family.

Sharing Behavior and Language

Many people in the United States retain customs from their original countries. How many likenesses and differences can you find among these family meals?

Many United States families still celebrate special occasions from their original countries. Above is a Ukrainian folk dance. On the bottom left, a Norwegian parade. On the right, the Chinese New Year celebration.

People in culture groups do things in ways that are alike or similar. They prepare food in similar ways. They raise their children in similar ways. They make decisions and solve problems in ways that are alike. These are all kinds of *behavior*. People's behavior is how they act or what they do.

You share many kinds of behavior with others in your culture group. Suppose you are talking to someone you don't know very well. How close would you stand to that person?

You would choose a distance that is comfortable for you. Did you know that this distance is influenced by your culture?

In some cultures, people stand very close to persons they don't know very well. Sometimes, they almost touch each other. In other cultures, strangers stand far apart. Each culture shares a different kind of behavior. Now what would happen if a member of a "closer" culture tried to talk to a member of a "farther" culture? Probably each would feel that the other person had bad manners.

Usually, we do not think about our own ways of doing things until we see someone who behaves in a different way. Suppose you were given a prize in front of the whole school. What would your classmates do? If they clapped their hands, would you clap your hands with them? Probably not. But in some cultures, it is the right thing to do. Clapping along with your audience shows that you appreciate them, too. This does not mean that everyone in a group does exactly the same things all the time. Each person does things in his or her special way.

Languages Most Used in the United States Other Than English

1. Spanish	8. Norwegian	15. Dutch
2. German	9. Slovak	16. Chinese
3. Italian	10. Greek	17. Russian
4. Polish	11. Czech	18. Lithuanian
5. French	12. Hungarian	19. Native American Languages
6. Yiddish	13. Japanese	20. Ukrainian
7. Swedish	14. Portuguese	

To get an idea of the number of people who speak these languages, look at the top three. Spanish is spoken as a first or second language by about 11 million Americans. German is spoken by about 4 million Americans. Italian is also spoken by about 4 million persons in this country. At the bottom of the list, about 300,000 persons speak different Native American languages. About 200,000 Americans speak Ukrainian.

Do you speak or understand any of the languages listed above?

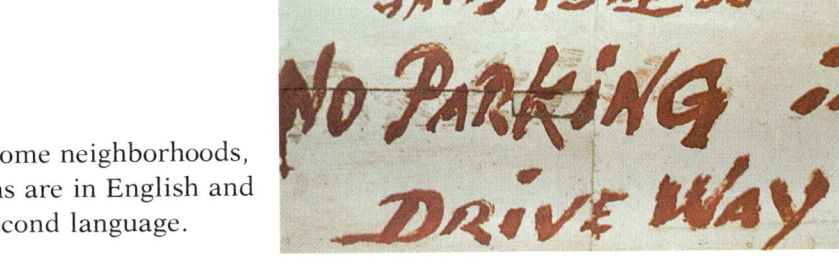

In some neighborhoods, signs are in English and a second language.

People in culture groups also share a common language.

The language you learn as a child lets you talk to other members of your group. You can communicate with them. But language does more than that. It also shows what is important in a culture. It shows how the people of a culture think. One culture, for example, does not know about war. The people do not understand these ideas. Their language has no words for *war* and *weapon*.

1. Which of these statements is *not* true? Members of a culture group (a) do things in similar ways, (b) do the same things all the time, (c) share a language, (d) communicate with others in their group.

2. Find out what the comfortable talking distance is for you and your friends. Talk with a classmate at a distance of 30 centimeters (1 foot). Then move closer, to about 15 centimeters (6 inches) from each other. Which distance was more comfortable? Experiment with other distances. How do the different distances make you feel?

3. Do you or members of your family speak a language other than English? Which language? When is this language used? At home? With your friends?

Sharing Beliefs

People in culture groups share many beliefs. Sharing a belief means that you agree with other people about what is true, good, or right.

People in cultures or groups usually agree on what behavior is right or wrong. Such an agreement about behavior is called a *norm*. A norm is a shared belief about how the members of a group should behave.

Most norms are not written down. But almost everyone in a group knows what they are. In many cultures, telling lies is wrong behavior. Do you know how children learn not to lie to other people? They learn from their parents, who tell them that lying is wrong. They also learn by watching what others do. If other people who are important to the children lie, the children may lie. If these people don't lie, the children probably won't. Children learn the norms of those around them.

People in culture groups often share beliefs about what

Freedom of religion is an important value. These are Episcopalian monks.

is important or not important. Beliefs about what is important are called *values*. When you believe that a thing, a person, or an idea is important, you value that thing, person, or idea. If you have a choice, you will try to choose the thing, person, or idea that is most valuable to you.

Words like *good, best, bad,* or *worse* are often used when people talk about their values. Other words showing values are *nice, pretty, beautiful, ugly,* and *evil.* There are many more. When you use these words, you are saying how valuable something is to you. You may say, for example, that detective movies are "better" than sports movies. This means that you value detective movies more than sports movies. If you have a choice, you will watch a detective movie instead of a sports movie. If you can, you will choose what you value more. You will give up what you value less.

Different cultures often have different values. Some groups value people who spend large amounts of money. Other groups value people who save money or don't waste anything. Some groups value winning and trying to be best. Other groups value working together and sharing.

This family is celebrating the Jewish holiday of Sukkoth.

United States citizens value the right to peaceful protest and the right of each person to get an education.

ON YOUR OWN

1. Which of these statements tell about a *norm*? Which ones tell about a *value*?
   (a) You are not allowed to chew gum in class.
   (b) He's my best best friend!
   (c) A good meal is the most important thing in life.
   (d) In the United States, people are expected to obey the law.

TO DO

2. Think of one norm shared by the members of your class or your culture group. How did you learn this norm?
3. Are there values that many people in the United States share? What are some of these values?

How Are People of the United States Alike?

When a country contains many different groups, we say that it has *cultural pluralism*. Cultural pluralism means that different kinds of behavior, different languages, and different beliefs are found within the same country.

The United States has many different culture groups. But the people of the United States are alike in many ways, too. Some important beliefs are shared by many of them. Here are some examples. Do you share any of these beliefs?

Every person should have an equal chance for education and jobs.

Every person should be free to do and say what she or he believes is right within the law.

Everyone should be treated fairly and should treat others fairly.

People in the United States share a national government symbolized here by the White House, the home of the President.

Citizens of this country share interests in sports, recreation, and in learning.

United States citizens have always been willing to defend their country when it became necessary.

TO DO

1. Look up the word *pluralism* in a dictionary. Can you think of another word that means almost the same thing?
2. Look carefully at the pictures on pages 53 and 54. Then list five things you think most people of the United States have in common.

ON YOUR OWN

3. With your classmates, make a master list of all the things you think people of the United States share.

CHAPTER REVIEW

1. List as many different culture groups in the United States as you can. Try to name at least four.
2. Define *culture*, using the terms *behavior*, *beliefs*, and *language*.
3. Choose the best answer. Sharing a belief means that you agree with someone (a) about the weather, (b) about what is true or good, (c) about the best way to do something.

UNIT REVIEW

What Do I Know?

1. Here are some of the land regions of North America: *the Central Lowlands, the Rocky Mountains, the Canadian Shield, the Great Plains, the Pacific Lowlands,* and *the Appalachian Mountains.* Match one of these regions to each of the following statements:
   (a) It is one of the most fertile plains in the world.
   (b) Large valleys here are heavily farmed. Important crops are grapes, oranges, and lettuce.
   (c) Here herds of cattle and sheep provide most of the meat, wool, and leather used in North America.
   (d) This is a chain of old mountains that reach from Canada to Alabama.
   (e) It is a cold region rich in minerals and forests.
   (f) These mountains have jagged peaks and steep valleys. They separate the Great Plains from the Pacific regions.
2. The numbers on this map stand for important bodies of water in North America. Match these numbers to the bodies of water listed below.

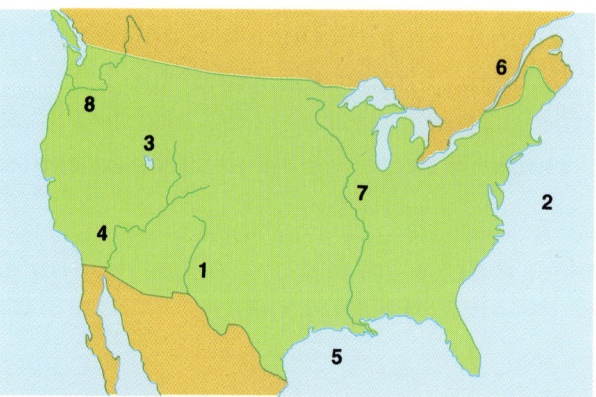

Mississippi River
Gulf of Mexico
Atlantic Ocean
Columbia River
Rio Grande
St. Lawrence River
Great Salt Lake
Colorado River

3. Which are the most populated areas of each of these North American nations? Match the nations on the left to the correct answer on the right.
   Canada   (a) eastern half
   the United States   (b) central area
   Mexico   (c) southern area

What Can I Do?
1. What do these symbols stand for on your map on page 12?
   (a) •   (d) — - —
   (b) ✪   (e) ▬ ▬ ▬
   (c) ★
2. Below is a pie graph showing the different groups of people who live in Mexico today. Look at the graph. Then answer *true* or *false* to the statements that follow.

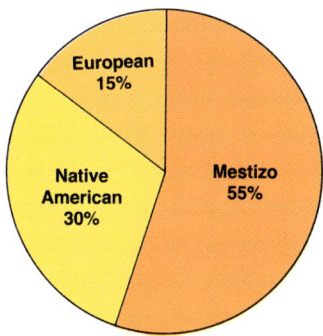

   (a) Half of all Mexicans have European backgrounds.
   (b) Most Mexicans are mestizo. This means that they have both Spanish and Native American ancestors.
   (c) About 30 of every 100 Mexicans are Native Americans.
3. Use the pictures on pages 50 to 55 to help you answer these questions:
   (a) Find a picture that shows people sharing behavior. What kind of behavior does the picture show?
   (b) Find a picture that shows people sharing a value. What value is being shared?
   (c) Find a picture that shows cultural pluralism in the United States. Why is this an example of cultural pluralism?

What Is Important?
1. What are some beliefs that many Americans share?
2. Why is it important to learn about people who are different from us?

UNIT TWO
The Beginnings of a Nation

1

SETTLING A CONTINENT

Who were the first Americans? What were some early Native American cultures? Why did Europeans explore and settle the New World?

The First Americans

All people have a past. This is true for groups as well as individuals. People study their past for many reasons. They want to know where they came from. They want to know how they got to be the way they are. They hope that if they know themselves better, they can make better plans for their future. A famous American once said, "Those who do not study the past are doomed to repeat it." The speaker meant that if we do not learn from our past mistakes, we may make the same mistakes again. On the other hand, we can learn something from our past successes, too.

When people tell about real events that happened in the past, they are telling *history*. In this book, you will study the history of the American people.

Time lines can help you learn history. They are lines which show important events in the order in which they happened. Time lines give you an idea of what happened over a certain period of time. As you read about important events in American history, see where they fit on the time lines in your book.

Here is a time line of some early events in North and South America.

TIMELINE 40,000 B.C. — A.D. 1300

B.C. 40,000	8000	4000
Arrival of first Americans	Farming begins in South America	Copper Culture in North America makes early use of metals

A.D. 100	250	1300
Hopewell Mound Builders flourish in North America	Maya build great cities of stone	Aztecs conquer central Mexico

61

ROUTE OF THE FIRST NORTH AMERICANS

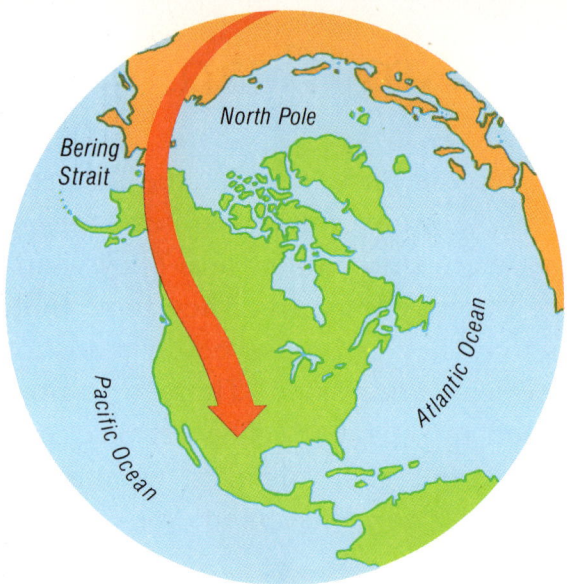

It is thought that the first people in North America came from Asia sometime between 30,000 and 80,000 years ago.

Look at the map on this page. Notice that the northwest tip of Asia is only about 80 kilometers (50 miles) from the northern tip of North America. People may have crossed from Asia to North America by raft or by boat. Or they may have walked across when the level of the ocean was much lower. They probably came in small groups over a period of many thousands of years.

These early people were daring hunters and good stone-cutters. Their tools were made of chipped stone. Some pieces were beautifully carved. With axes and spears, these early Americans hunted wild animals. Some of the animals they hunted were larger than any now living on this continent. In Texas and New Mexico, stone and ivory spearheads have been found sticking in the bones of animals. Some of these animals died more than 10,000 years ago.

As the early people moved south and east, they kept themselves warm and protected at night by gathering around campfires. Remains of their campsites have been found. They lived on the animals they caught and on the wild fruits and vegetables they picked along the way. They also fished in the rivers and along the seacoasts. Some of these people found places they liked in North America. They decided to stay here. Others moved on to Central and South America.

About 10,000 years ago, some people in South America learned to plant crops. They liked this better than picking wild fruits and vegetables, which were not always easy to find. These people became farmers. They planted beans, corn, cotton, and potatoes.

Farming meant that these people had a fairly steady supply of food. So they could settle in one place. People living in one place often learn special kinds of things. Usually, they learn to herd certain animals for food or skins. They learn how to make baskets. They learn to make pots out of clay. Some learn to make cloth from cotton, from other plants, or from the hair of animals. Sometimes, they learn how to melt down soft metals, such as gold or copper, to make jewelry and tools.

About 3,000 years ago, some of the people in South America learned to do these things. They traded their goods with people in other places. Sometimes, they traveled great distances to carry on their trade. In this way, the knowledge of how to grow corn and to work with metals may have been carried into what is now Mexico and the United States.

These early people from Asia were the ancestors of today's Native Americans.

1. Choose the best answer: History is (a) a story about the present, (b) a story about real events in the past, (c) the events on a time line.
2. When did the first Americans come from Asia?
3. What were their tools and weapons made of?
4. Name four crops that these early people learned to plant.

5. Draw a time line of your personal history. You can begin the time line on the day you were born. If you prefer to do a shorter time line, pick one year or one day of your life. Write down the important things that happened to you during that period.

Cities of the Sun

More than 3,000 years ago, a people called the Maya (Mä′yə) settled in the rain forests of what is now the country of Guatemala (Gwä′tə mä′la). In the following years, many went to live on the Yucatán Peninsula in Mexico. They built great cities out of stone. More than 800 Mayan cities have been found in Guatemala and the Yucatán.

At the center of each Mayan city was a very high temple. It was shaped like a pyramid with a flat top. Steep steps were cut into the stone leading up to the altar at the top. Mayan priests held their religious ceremonies there.

The Maya learned many important things. They studied the stars and became good *astronomers*. They became excellent mathematicians. Mayan people used the zero 1200 years before it was used in Europe. They developed a calendar as accurate as the one we use today.

The Maya were also fine stonecutters. They carved many beautiful statues of their gods and their way of life. They carved large stone calendars for their temples. They used a complicated kind of picture writing called *hieroglyphics* (hī′ər ə glif′iks).

This is the Temple of Warriors found in the Yucatán.

Yet the Maya did not use metals to make tools. They did not use animals to work for them. They carved in stone without metal tools, and they moved large stones without the help of animals. We do not know how their government was organized. But they had an organized religion with many priests. They were a very peaceful people. They grew corn, potatoes, and tobacco. And they developed a great culture.

Mayan Society lasted peacefully until about the year 1100. Then the Maya were conquered by another people from central and southern Mexico. These people were the Toltec (Tol′tek). The Toltec were stonecarvers, too. They carved huge heads out of stone. Many of these heads have been found in the middle of the jungle. No one knows how the heads were brought there or why they were made.

The Toltec and Maya people had an influence on each other. Together, they built cities with high temples like pyramids. Some of their most beautiful cities are near the middle of the Yucatán.

A stone carving now in Mexico City.

The Toltec and the Maya liked to play sports. A ball game, something like kickball or rugby, was very popular among them. Each team would try to score points by kicking the ball through loops high up on opposite walls of the court. The court was about the size of our football field. A raised, stone platform was built at each end of the field. The heads of the teams and the referees sat on those platforms to watch the game. One of these courts is still standing at Chichén Itzá (Chə chen′ ət sä′).

In the 1300s, or possibly later, the Toltec were conquered by fierce Aztec warriors. The Aztec built a large empire and ruled several million people. They made beautiful objects of gold and precious stones. They also built great stone temples, like pyramids, where people worshiped the sun and other Aztec gods.

The capital city of the Aztec was Tenochtitlan (Tā nöch tē′ tlän). Tenochtitlan was a large city built on an island in a shallow lake. It was located where Mexico City is today. Tenochtitlan was built mostly of stone. It was shaped like a wheel, with four wide roads. The roads connected the island city to the land around the lake. The roads had open spaces, so that canoes on the lake could pass through. The open spaces were crossed by wooden bridges.

The city had many squares where markets were held and trading was carried on. All kinds of goods made in the countryside were sold here. These included food products, jewelry made of gold and silver, lead, brass, copper, bones, shells, and feathers. The Aztec also sold spun cotton in all colors, pots, pitchers, tiles, and vases of glazed and painted clay.

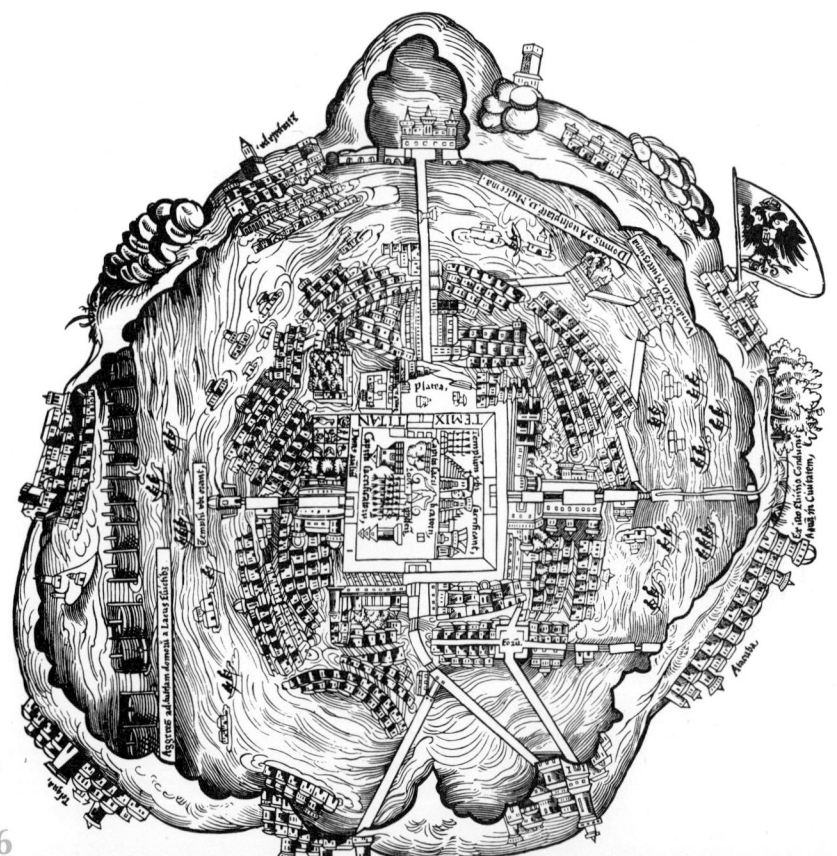

A simple map of Tenochtitlan.

An Aztec stone clock.

The Aztec empire lasted about 200 years, until the Spanish arrived in Mexico in 1519. A small Spanish army conquered the Aztec. The Spanish had guns and cannons. The Aztec did not have weapons like these. The Spanish conquest marked the beginning of the end of the great Native American nations in the New World.

1. Match the societies, on the left, with the things they did, on the right.
   Maya   (a) With the Maya, they built a beautiful city in the Yucatán.
   Toltec   (b) They developed a very accurate calendar.
   Aztec   (c) They carved huge stone heads.
                (d) They ruled several million people.
                (e) They invented the zero long before it was used in Europe.
                (f) They made beautiful objects from gold and precious stones.
2. What three products were grown by Mayan farmers?

3. Name some ways in which the Maya, Toltec, and Aztec people were similar.
4. Name some ways in which they were different.

Other Early American Cultures

In the area that is now the United States, there were many ancient peoples. *Evidence,* or signs, of their cultures has been found throughout the country.

One ancient group of people is known today as the Old Copper Culture. They lived 5,000 to 7,000 years ago near the Great Lakes, where Wisconsin is today. Copper spearheads and tools have been found in this area. They show that these early people knew much about working with metal. They are some of the earliest examples of metal work anywhere in the world.

In the Southwest, in the desert where Arizona, New Mexico, and Mexico meet, there was once a great lake. The Cochise (Kō′chēs) people lived there for thousands of years, from 9,000 to 6,000 years ago. The Cochise used stone bowls and *pestles,* or grinding stones. With these tools, they ground wild grains and seeds into food. Descendants of the Cochise people were planting corn about 2,000 years ago. They dug irrigation ditches to water the surrounding area in order to grow crops. These people were probably the ancestors of the modern Pueblo people. The Pueblo built large apartment houses of *adobe* (ə dō′bē), or sun-baked clay. Their houses can still be seen.

Also about 2,000 years ago, another culture began to develop in the Ohio and Mississippi Valleys. It came to be known as the Hopewell Culture. It started as a community of farmers. Slowly, it grew into several communities that agreed to help and protect one another. The Hopewell communities eventually reached from the Gulf of Mexico to Wisconsin, and from New York to Kansas.

The Hopewell people built large, high mounds of earth. We are not sure what these mounds were for. But they contain burial sites and may have served some religious purpose. The Hopewell were also great traders in art objects, sea shells, wood, copper, and different kinds of food.

Another mound-building people, called the Temple Mound Culture, developed about 500 years ago. These people

Native Americans still live in pueblos in New Mexico.

The Great Serpent Mound found in Ohio.

lived along the Mississippi River Valley. Their villages were surrounded by high wooden fences. They built temples 33 meters (100 feet) high that were shaped like pyramids with flat tops. They had many things in common with the earlier Maya people in Mexico. They may have been influenced by the early cultures in Mexico through trade.

One of the best examples of an early culture that survived into modern times is the Natchez (Nach′ez). The Natchez lived in Mississippi near where the city of Natchez is today. Their king and high priest was called Great Sun. The king's mother, if she was alive, or his sister, was the Woman Sun. She chose the king's successor from among her sons or brothers when the king died.

There is a story told about the Spanish explorer, Hernando De Soto (Hər nän′dō Də Sō′tō), when he came to the land of the Natchez. De Soto sent word to the Natchez that he was the Sun's younger brother. De Soto meant to impress them, because the Natchez were sun worshipers. He thought that, in this way, they would be easy to conquer. The Natchez people answered, "If you can dry up the Mississippi River, we will believe you." Of course, De Soto couldn't do that. So, the Natchez drove him out of their lands.

1. Name four ancient societies that lived in what is now the United States.
2. Complete the following sentence: Some of the earliest examples of metal work in the world were produced by _____ .
3. What people dug irrigation ditches in the Southwest desert?
4. How were the Hopewell people and the Temple Mound Culture like one another?

5. What evidence of early American cultures can you find in the pictures on pages 64 to 69? Make a list of all the signs or proofs that you see.

Europeans Discover a New World

"Wednesday, October 10th, 1492. Steered west-southwest day and night, and made 59 leagues progress. Here the men lost all patience. They complained of the length of the voyage. But the Admiral encouraged them the best he could. He told them their voyage would make them rich. And he added that they had come so far, they could not turn back. They had no choice but to go on.

In this painting Columbus lands on the island of San Salvador.

"At two o'clock on Friday morning, land was discovered. They found themselves near a small island, where they saw people on the beach. The Admiral landed in a small boat with a party of his men. They found very green trees, many streams of water, and many kinds of fruit. The Admiral planted a flag on the beach and claimed the land for the King and Queen of Spain."

The "Admiral" in this story was Christopher Columbus. The story comes from his diary. This voyage, in 1492, was the first recorded discovery of the New World by Europeans.

There is evidence to show that people from Africa, Asia, and Europe may have come to the New World long before Columbus. Many of these Old World people were great sailors. Probably the first European visitors to North America were the Norwegian (Nôr wē′jən) Vikings. They had reached Iceland and Greenland in the 900s. Led by Lief Ericson, they explored the northern coast of North America in 1003. Years later, some English sailors might have come as far as the Grand Banks, a rich fishing area off the coast of Nova Scotia (Nō′ və Skō′ shə). They might have come to catch fish that fed there. But for the next several hundred years, Europe had no interest in exploring the New World.

In the 1400s, Europe began to change. Nations such as France, England, Spain, and Portugal had begun to form. Scientists had developed tools that helped sailors cross the oceans. These tools, like the compass, helped sailors know where they were and in what direction they were going. They no longer had to stay close to land to keep from getting lost. Still, sailing out of sight of land was very frightening to sailors in such small ships.

Trade had grown quickly with the nations of Asia. Europeans wanted the silk, spices, and gold objects that were made in India and China. In the 1400s, the trade routes were over land. It took many months, and even years, to carry goods over mountains, deserts, and plains. The goods were often damaged along the way or stolen by robbers. Nations in Europe wanted to find better trade routes by sea.

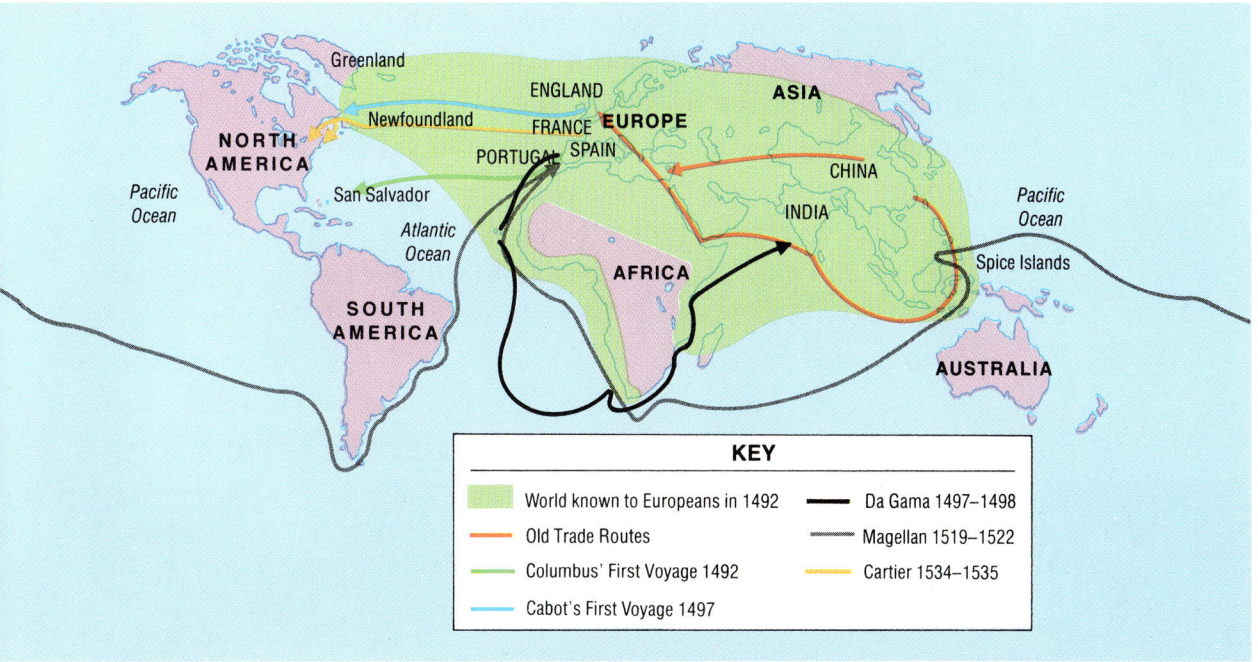

EUROPEAN DISCOVERY AND EXPLORATION

Kings and queens provided ships and money to explorers. The Portuguese were the first Europeans to encourage exploration overseas. Prince Henry "The Navigator" opened a special school to train sailors, navigators, and mapmakers. The Portuguese looked for a route east around Africa.

Christopher Columbus, the son of an Italian weaver, believed he could find a shorter route to the riches of Asia by sailing west instead of east. He shared the belief of many that the world was round. But he also thought the world was much smaller than it is. Many people thought Columbus was a fool. But Queen Isabella of Spain was more farsighted. She gave him the support he needed. She agreed to pay for Columbus's voyage.

In 1492, Columbus set sail with three ships—the *Nina* (Nē′nə), the *Santa Maria* (Sän′tə Mə rē′ə), and the *Pinta* (Pin′tə). He and his sailors traveled thirty-three days across the Atlantic Ocean without seeing land. Finally, on October 12, they arrived at San Salvador. They also explored the islands of Hispaniola (His′pən yō′lə), Puerto Rico, and Cuba.

The people whom Columbus found on these islands were the Taino (Tī′nō). But Columbus called them "Indians," because he thought he had arrived in the Indies. He returned to Spain with some of these peaceful Taino people. He also brought tobacco and a little gold. Queen Isabella and King Ferdinand were not satisfied with this cargo. Columbus made three more voyages to the New World, but he never found the riches he was looking for. Columbus died in 1506, poor and unhappy. To the end, he believed he had found the best route to India.

This is a reproduction of Columbus's cabin on the Santa Maria.

Over the next 100 years, many other explorers followed Columbus. In 1497, another Italian, John Cabot, sailed from England to Newfoundland. He hoped to find a northern route to India, but he failed. Amerigo Vespucci (A mer′i gō Ves pü′chē) traveled to the New World in the years that followed. He was one of the first to realize that Columbus had discovered a new world—large and wonderful, and even rich. He wrote stories about this new land. A German mapmaker drew maps of this new world in 1507. The information that the explorers had brought back was used to make the map. The mapmaker called the new world America, after Amerigo Vespucci.

Then, in 1519, an expedition led by Ferdinand Magellan (Mə jel′ən) did what Columbus had hoped to do. Magellan found a sea route to the Indies. He was an explorer paid by the Spanish king. Magellan sailed around the southern tip of South America. He then crossed the Pacific Ocean to the Spice Islands in the East. He had started out with five ships. All but one were destroyed during the voyage. Magellan was killed in the Philippines. In 1522, the remaining ship arrived back in Spain. It was the first ship to sail all the way around the world. The goods it brought back to Spain were worth more than enough to pay for the whole voyage. They also gave the king a large profit.

TO DO

1. When did Columbus discover the New World?
2. When did the Norwegian Vikings come to the New World?
3. Who was the first explorer whose ship sailed all the way around the world?
4. Name two or three reasons why Europe became interested in exploration in the 1400s.

ON YOUR OWN

5. Are there places that you would like to explore? Tell about them. What do you expect to find there?

Spaniards Arrive

The news of a new world to explore spread quickly throughout Europe. Spain was the first nation to seek gold in the Americas.

The Spaniards heard about a rich empire in North America where Mexico is today. Hernando Cortez (Hər nän′ dō Kôr tez′) went to Mexico with only 500 people. Between 1519 and 1521, he conquered the great Aztec Empire. The Aztec were great warriors, but the Spaniards had many advantages. They had guns and cannons, iron armor and swords, and horses. The Aztec had never seen these things. The Aztec also had enemies among the people they ruled. These people thought Cortez would free them from having to pay taxes to the Aztec Emperor, Montezuma (Mon′ tə zü′ mə). So they helped the Spanish soldiers.

TIMELINE 900's-1565

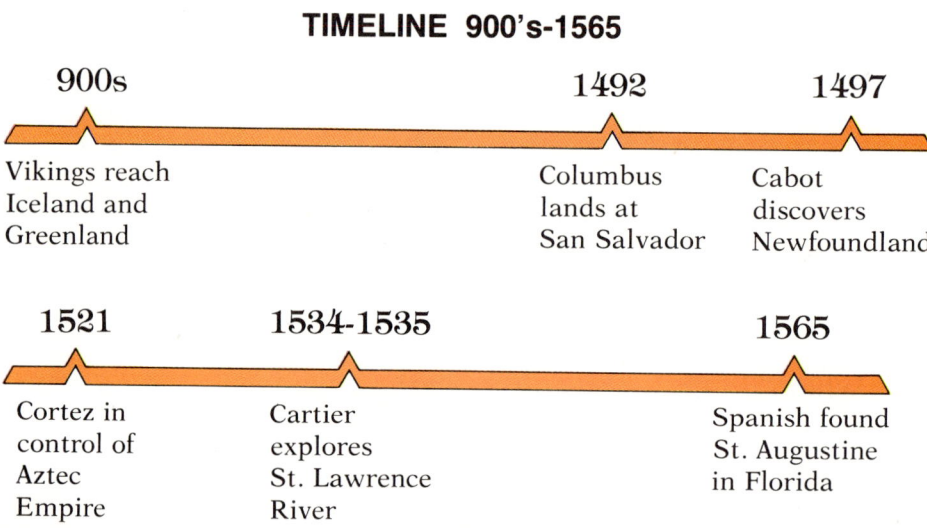

900s	1492	1497
Vikings reach Iceland and Greenland	Columbus lands at San Salvador	Cabot discovers Newfoundland

1521	1534-1535	1565
Cortez in control of Aztec Empire	Cartier explores St. Lawrence River	Spanish found St. Augustine in Florida

Probably the greatest disadvantage the Aztec had was a story that had been handed down from generation to generation. According to this story, the ancestors of the Aztec were ruled by white gods. These gods had gone away hundreds of years before. But they had promised to return one day in great white birds that flew over the water. Then they would rule the Aztec again. When Montezuma heard that whites had come to Mexico in big ships with sails like white wings, he was not sure what to do. He though the Spaniards might be the ancient rulers of the Aztec. Montezuma waited. In the end, he decided to fight. The Aztec fought well, but it was too late.

Over the next fifteen years, Spanish conquerors took over rich empires in South America. From all these places, the Spanish sent gold and silver back to Spain. This made Spain the richest nation in Europe.

Spanish explorers were eager to find other rich Native American empires. So they traveled north from Mexico into what is now the United States.

Panfilo de Narvaez (Pän'fi lō də När vä'ās) explored Florida in 1527. Afterwards, he sailed his ships along the Gulf of Mexico. There, near what is now Galveston, Texas,

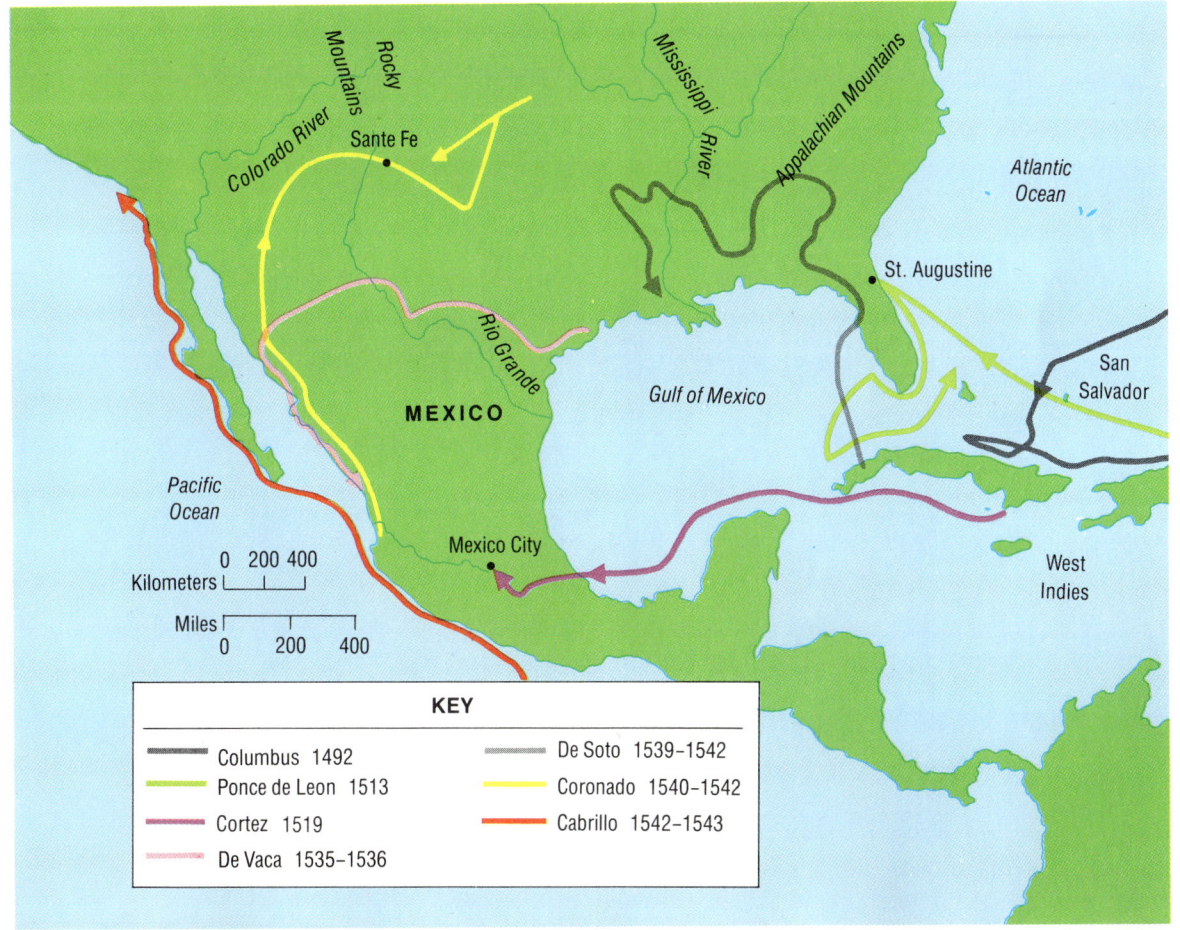

SPANISH EXPLORERS IN NORTH AMERICA

his ships were wrecked. Four men—Cabeza de Vaca (Kə bā′ zə də Vä′ kə), two other Spaniards, and a black man named Estevanico (Es′ tə vä′ ni kō)—survived the wreck. For six years, these men wandered across Texas. Finally, they reached Mexico City. They had walked at least 1,600 kilometers (1,000 miles). They brought with them Native American stories of seven rich cities called the "Cities of Gold."

St. Augustine, Florida, was the first Spanish settlement in what is now the United States.

Beginning in 1540, Francisco Coronado (Fran sis′kō Kôr′ə nä′dō) spent two years exploring parts of Texas and Kansas. He was looking for a rich empire like that of the Aztec. Some of his explorers discovered the Grand Canyon. But Coronado found no cities of gold.

In 1541, Hernando de Soto explored Florida and what are now the states of Alabama, Arkansas, and Mississippi. He discovered the Mississippi River, which the Native Americans called "The Father of Waters." He got as far north as the present site of Memphis, Tennessee. De Soto died near the great river he found.

Spanish Catholic priests were important to the Spanish settlements in all these places. They came to the New World to teach Spanish beliefs and culture to the Native Americans. They built *missions,* or religious communities, where they lived and taught the people. Much later, large cities grew around some of these missions.

Spanish soldiers, priests, settlers, and governors changed half of the New World. They brought to it Spanish laws, language, religion, and ways of living. In Lima, Peru, and in Mexico City, universities were built in 1551. The first printing press in North America was set up in Mexico City in 1539. When the governor of Mexico sat down to dinner in the 1540s, he and his guests ate in a palace. The richness and elegance there was not to be matched anywhere else in North America for at least 200 years.

TO DO

1. Why did the Spanish want to conquer the New World?
2. Name two products of the New World that were shipped back to Spain.
3. List three Spanish explorers. Next to their names, write down the parts of the New World they explored.

ON YOUR OWN

4. Explain in your own words the changes the Spanish made in the New World.

The English and Other Europeans

By the late 1500s, other European countries began to discover riches in the New World. The French, the Dutch, and the English began to explore and settle North America.

The French explored the St. Lawrence River and the Atlantic coast near the Grand Banks. They founded settlements

The expedition of La Salle, a French explorer.

Some Native Americans of the Northeast lived in villages like this one.

in Quebec and Montreal. They traveled in canoes along the Great Lakes region and down the Mississippi River, setting up small trading posts along the way. The French traded for furs with the Native Americans, who trapped the animals in the great forests which covered much of the continent. In the Grand Banks, the French caught huge amounts of fish. They dried the fish in the sun. Then they took them back to France. These activities brought the French a good profit.

The Netherlands sent explorers to the middle Atlantic coast. One Dutch captain, Henry Hudson, discovered the fine harbor that is now known as New York. He also explored the Hudson River. Soon, the Dutch began founding settlements in that area and making a lot of money in trade.

NORTH AMERICAN SETTLEMENTS 1630

Many English nobles and merchants became interested in the New World. They had heard of the great amounts of gold being shipped to Spain. They knew that the French and Dutch were making money in the New World. The English rulers wanted a share of these riches. They also wanted some of the products that could be gotten in the New World, especially timber and tar for building ships. They wanted to start farms and plantations in the New World to grow crops that could not be grown in England.

Merchants and nobles asked the English king to grant them land to settle. The king gave them land south of the Dutch claims in North America. The merchants and nobles then formed companies that outfitted ships to carry settlers to the New World. There, they meant to start English colonies.

A *colony* is a group of people who settle in a distant land. In that land, they are still ruled by their parent country.

In the following years, many English people settled in North America. Yet, the trip to North America was hard and dangerous. And life in the colonies was hard and dangerous, too. Why were so many English people willing to face these dangers? For one thing, England had too many people. Most were poor. John Winthrop, who later became a leader in the colonies, said that in England, a human was "of less value among us than a horse or sheep." Work was hard to find. Food, land, and shelter were getting very expensive. In the New World, land could be had for almost nothing. People who worked hard could make a living.

Many people came to the colonies from English prisons. Some of these prisoners had been criminals. Others had been put in prison because they could not pay back money they owed. The English authorities were glad to be rid of them. The colonies needed workers.

Many *orphans* were also sent to work in North America. Hundreds of these children were taken from London streets and put on ships bound for the colonies. The children had nothing to say about this. But most people did not think it was wrong. They thought the children should be glad to make themselves useful.

Some people left home for religious reasons. The Puritans wanted to "purify" the Church of England, which was very powerful. They said the church should get rid of its rich buildings and ceremonies. It should be plain and simple. The church gave the Puritans a great deal of trouble. Some were thrown into prison. As a result, many of them left England. Other religious groups left for similar reasons. They wanted to worship and live according to their beliefs. At that time, nations did not allow citizens to worship as they pleased.

Many of the people who wanted to come to the colonies could not pay for their trip from England. So they came as *indentured* (in den′chərd) *servants*. They signed a contract, or indenture, with a company or a wealthy person. The servant agreed to work without pay for a set time. This was usually about seven years. In return, the company or master paid for the voyage and provided food and shelter for the servant. At the end of the seven years, the servant was free.

Some English people came to North America in search of more freedom. Others were trying to escape poverty in England. For most, the hardship was worth the risk.

1. What is a colony?
2. Choose the best answer: Why did the English start colonies in North America? (a) They wanted adventure, (b) They wanted to make money, (c) They wanted to get rid of prisoners.
3. *Indentured servants* (a) were servants for life, (b) agreed to work for a set time, (c) worked until they had enough money to be on their own.

4. Look at the map of early European settlements on page 82. Examine the key. Then list one Spanish, one French, one Dutch, and one English settlement.

1. Number the following events in the order in which they happened: Vikings explore Iceland and Greenland.
   Mapmaker names the New World "America."
   Asians cross the Bering Strait into North America.
   Columbus lands in San Salvador.
2. Name two of the early Native American societies. Then describe several of their achievements.
3. List at least four reasons why the European nations explored and settled the New World.
4. Orphan children and merchants were two of the groups that came to the English colonies. Can you name two other groups?

2
THE ENGLISH COLONIES

How was Jamestown started? Who settled in New England? How did people make a living in the Middle Colonies?

Jamestown and the South

In 1607, the Virginia Company founded a colony at Jamestown, Virginia. Jamestown was to be the first successful English colony in North America. One hundred and twenty people had signed on with the Company to establish this colony. Some practiced trades, and some were gentlemen. The tradesmen knew how to do things that would be useful, such as carpentry and blacksmithing. But the gentlemen were not used to working. There were no women in the colony at first.

Jamestown did not begin well. The colonists chose a swampy spot about 48 kilometers (30 miles) up the James River. The place was full of mosquitoes carrying diseases. The water was salty and dirty. To add to these problems, winter was coming. The colonists had to have shelter and food. What food the colonists had brought from England had quickly run out. But most of the men wanted only to search for gold. They did not want to clear fields, plant crops, or build homes. In the end, a few colonists did most of the work. They built a small fort, some shelters, and a storehouse.

Among these colonists was Captain John Smith. He made friends with the Powhatan (Pou′ə tan′) people through Pocahontas (Pō′kə hon′təs), the daughter of a chief. The Powhatan

A drawing of Jamestown.

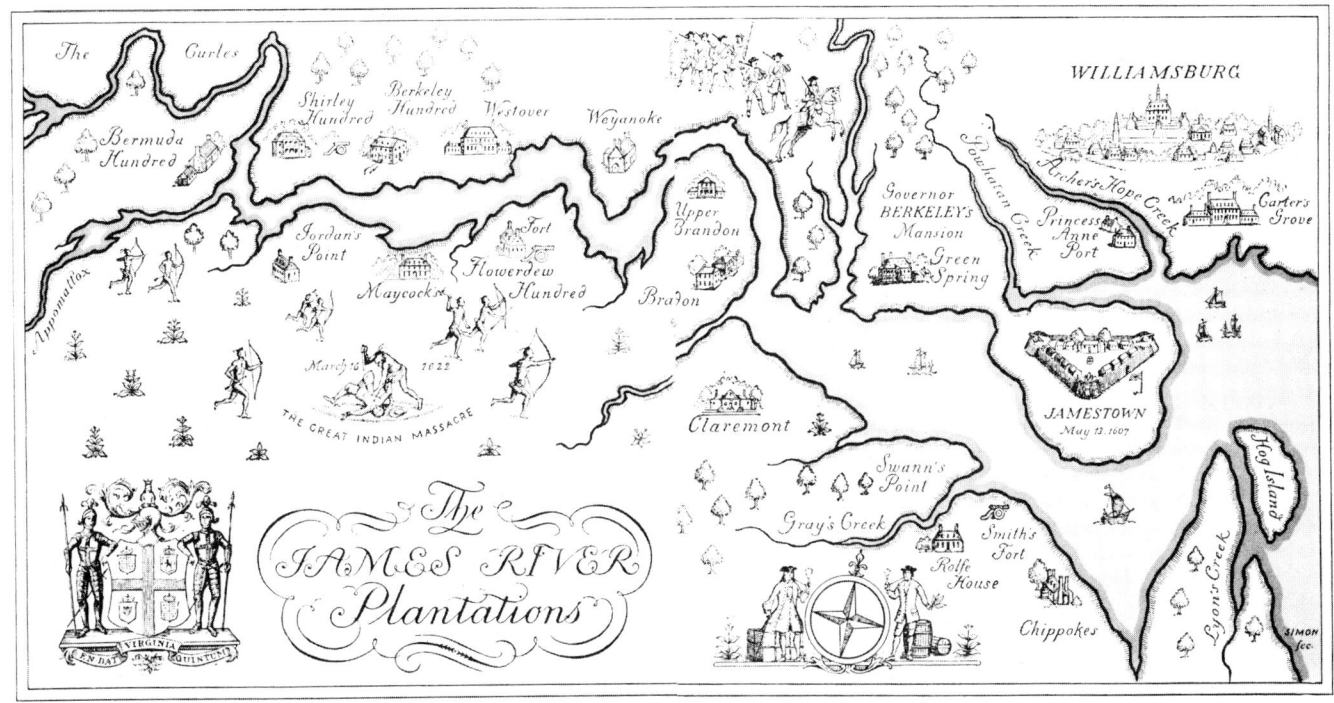

Note the names of the plantations along the James River in this old map.

supplied the colonists with food that first winter. Otherwise, they all probably would have died. Even so, when spring came, only 40 of the original 120 were still alive.

The following year, Captain Smith became the leader of the colony. More settlers also arrived. Among them were the first two English women in America. Captain Smith made sure that everyone did his or her fair share of the work. He told the colonists, "He who will not work, will not eat." Soon the colonists put up more buildings and planted good crops. But Smith had to go back to England. While he was gone, the settlers fell to quarreling again. People stopped working. And so the winter of 1609 caught the colonists with little food. Over 400 colonists died in that "starving time."

A new governor arrived in the colony. Over the next few years, he made the colonists live under strict military rules. They were marched to the fields by the beat of a drum. Twice a day, they were marched to church in the same way. People who broke the rules or did not work were punished. In this way, the colony managed to hang on.

Life in Jamestown finally did change. There were several reasons for this. The Virginia Company decided to divide its land among the colonists. Each was given land to farm. Once they were landowners, the colonists were willing to work very hard. There was no longer a need for such strict rules.

Then, in 1613, the colonists found a way to make money. John Rolfe, a colonist who later married Pocahontas, planted a new kind of tobacco. His tobacco was very popular in London. Soon, England was buying all the tobacco Jamestown could produce. It was so valuable, it was even planted in the streets of the colony! This new source of wealth pleased the owners of the Company. It also brought more settlers to Jamestown.

Among these settlers were women. Most were already married to male colonists. But in 1619, ships began to bring

TIMELINE 1607-1681

1607	1619	1619	1620	1630
Jamestown settlement is begun	First Africans arrive at Jamestown	House of Burgesses starts self-government in colonies	Pilgrims found Plymouth Plantation	Puritans form Massachusetts Bay Colony

1635	1638	1664	1675-1676	1681
Rhode Island is founded in search of religious freedom	Harvard College is founded	English get New Netherlands from Dutch	War between Indians and Puritans. Indians defeated	William Penn's Colony is started

THE ENGLISH COLONIES

As the English colonies developed, the people found many different ways to make a living. Refer to this map as you study the English colonies.

unmarried women to Jamestown. They were given a place to live and work until it was decided whom they would marry. Then the bridegroom paid the cost of his new wife's voyage. As more women came, family life became stronger. Settlers began to think of the colony as home.

Another thing that changed life in Jamestown was government. In 1619, the Virginia Company gave the white male landowners a voice in running the colony. These men could elect *representatives* from among themselves. Representatives are people who are chosen to speak or act for a group. The Virginia representatives, called *Burgesses* (bėr′jis əz), formed an assembly that made laws for the colony. This assembly was called the *House of Burgesses*. It was the start of self-government in America.

Life in Virginia was still hard. Disease killed hundreds of people every year. Other colonists were killed by Native Americans, who were becoming more and more angry as Europeans took their land.

In spite of these dangers, the colony of Virginia began to flourish. Other colonies were founded in the South, beginning with Maryland in 1634. In the years to come, the colonies of North Carolina, South Carolina, and Georgia would be firmly established.

1. Number the following events in the order in which they happened:
    Colonists suffer through the "starving time."
    John Rolfe plants a new kind of tobacco.
    Jamestown is started.
    Self-government begins.
2. Which of the following is *not* true? Jamestown had a bad start because (a) most of the settlers did not want to work, (b) the Native Americans were unfriendly, (c) the settlers chose an unhealthy spot.
3. List at least three reasons why life in Jamestown became better.
4. A *representative* is (a) any person who can vote, (b) someone chosen to speak or act for others, (c) a land owner.

5. Why do you think the colonists at Jamestown did not realize that they had to work hard in order to have food for the winters? Where would the food come from?

Plantation Life

In the South, the main way of making a living was raising crops to sell. The South had large areas of rich soil. It had a mild climate. There were many months between the last frost of spring and the first frost of fall. These conditions made it possible to produce large crops to sell to other countries, especially to England. Tobacco was the main crop in the South. Other crops were rice and *indigo* (in'də gō), a blue dye taken from various plants. Much later, cotton became important.

Most planters who raised these crops were small farmers. They had little money and only a few workers to help them. A few were wealthy planters who owned great amounts of land. They were able to raise huge crops on these large farms, which were called *plantations*. To run their plantations, planters needed many, many workers.

In the beginning, plantation workers were indentured servants, white as well as black. The first Africans to arrive in Jamestown, in 1619, had been indentured servants. They worked until their contracts were over and then became free.

This old drawing shows what a plantation was like. High on the hill is the owner's house. Below are other plantation buildings.

Slaves, both men and women, worked long hours in the fields. Here they are picking cotton.

Some became landowners, themselves. But as time passed, planters stopped using indentured workers. It became cheaper to use the Africans who were being brought to the colonies as slaves.

These people were captured in parts of western Africa. There, they were put in chains and sold to slave traders. The slave traders brought them to America in ships. When they arrived, they were sold in slave markets. Then they became the buyer's property. Usually, the buyer owned them for life.

After 1640, the colonies began to pass laws concerning slavery. Some laws declared that the children of slaves were also slaves. Some laws made it more difficult for any blacks to live as free men and women. By the 1700s, most blacks in the Southern colonies were slaves. They did most of the work on the plantations.

The planters tried to make or grow almost everything they needed on the plantation. A small part of the land would be used to plant food for the planter's family and slaves. The rest would be planted with tobacco, rice, or indigo to be sold for cash. After the harvest, the cash crop was prepared for sale on the plantation. Most plantations were near rivers and had their own docks. In this way, the crop could be loaded directly onto boats and sent to market.

In many ways, a plantation was like a small village. Life centered around the planter's house. Usually, this house was very grand. But there were many other buildings nearby. There were stables, a cook house, laundries, and rooms for weaving and spinning. There might even be a schoolhouse for the planter's children, or a mill for grinding corn. Farther away, often hidden behind trees, were slaves' cabins, storage buildings, and cattle pens.

George Mason, a Virginia planter, describes how his father's plantation worked.

"My father had among his slaves carpenters, barrel makers, blacksmiths, leather tanners, shoemakers, spinners, weavers, knitters, and even a distiller. His woods supplied timber for the carpenters and barrel makers, and charcoal for the blacksmiths. His cattle were killed for his own use and for sale. They supplied skins for the tanners and shoemakers. His sheep gave wool for the weavers and spinners. His orchards gave fruit from which the distiller made brandy. His carpenters built and repaired all the houses, barns, and stables on the plantation."

Slaves working in the fields brought in the crops. Slaves working at trades kept the plantation running smoothly.

1. Choose the best answer. The main way of making a living in the South was: (a) practicing a trade, (b) raising crops to sell, (c) being a merchant.
2. What is a plantation?
3. Choose the best answer. Most planters in the South were (a) rich owners of large plantations, (b) owners of small farms, (c) indentured servants.
4. Look at the map on page 89. Name three important crops in the South. In which colonies were they grown?

5. Describe how the status of blacks changed in the colonies during the 1600s and the 1700s.

Early Settlers of New England

In 1620, a tiny ship called the *Mayflower* sailed from England for the New World. Crowded together in the small ship were 102 passengers. Most were members of families. Thirty-one passengers were children.

Half of the *Mayflower's* passengers were *Pilgrims*. The Pilgrims were the first group of Puritans to settle in North America. They had suffered in England because of their religious beliefs. They were now headed for Virginia. There they hoped to worship as they pleased.

After the *Mayflower* sailed for six weeks, it ran into storms in the Atlantic. The ship was blown off course. Instead of arriving in Virginia, the Pilgrims landed on the rocky coast of Cape Cod. For four weeks, most of the people stayed on the ship while small groups set out to explore the area.

It was almost winter. The Pilgrim leaders knew that everyone's help was needed. Otherwise, the group would not survive. Since they were far from Virginia, they decided to set up their own government.

The Pilgrims wrote a now famous agreement called the Mayflower Compact. They agreed that all the male Pilgrims would make the rules and laws for the settlement. The group would govern itself. It would pick its own leaders and make "just and equal laws." Women had few rights and could not sign the agreement. Still, the drawing up of the Mayflower Compact was the first time colonists had made plans to rule themselves.

The Pilgrims now sailed to an area John Smith had explored some years before. Smith had named the place "Plymouth" on a map. There was a clearing in the land and a stream nearby. At Plymouth, the Pilgrims set up the first permanent English settlement in New England.

During the first icy winter in Plymouth, half the *Mayflower's* passengers died. Many others became sick. The food the settlers had brought with them was almost used up. Winter was no time to plant a crop. Then, in early spring, a Native

American named Samoset visited the Pilgrims. Samoset spoke English. He had learned the language from early explorers of the area. Samoset helped the Pilgrims communicate with the Wampanoag people who lived 64 kilometers (40 miles) away.

That spring, the Wampanoag showed the Pilgrims how to hunt wild turkey and deer. They showed them where to fish. They taught them how to plant corn and barley and how to get sap from the maple tree. The Pilgrims had a fine harvest of corn in the fall. And they were thankful. They made a feast and invited the Native Americans who had helped them. This was the first Thanksgiving.

The next group of settlers to arrive in New England were also Puritans. Like the Pilgrims, they came to live according to their religious beliefs.

The Puritans received a *charter* from the English king to start the Massachusetts Bay Company. This document gave the company the right to run the colony. It also listed the rules by which the company would govern. The Puritans voted to take their charter with them to the New World. The charter and the government of the company would be in

The first Thanksgiving included settlers and Native Americans.

For many years, Puritans carried their guns to church. They feared attacks by Native Americans.

Massachusetts. Then, the king could not easily tell the company what to do. So, from the very beginning, the Puritans had more freedom to govern themselves than most early colonists did.

The Massachusetts Bay Puritans were the largest expedition ever to leave for North America. Between 1630 and 1634, more than 10,000 Puritans came to Massachusetts. These Puritans were richer and better educated than the Pilgrims had been. They arrived in ships loaded with supplies, and they settled eight small towns. The largest group founded the town of Boston.

1. Choose the best answer: The Mayflower Compact is famous today because (a) it set up "just and equal laws," (b) it was the beginning of self-government in the colonies, (c) women were not allowed to sign it.
2. In one or two sentences, explain what a charter was.

3. In what ways were the Pilgrims different from the early Jamestown settlers?
4. In what ways was their experience similar?

The Puritan Church

John Winthrop, a Puritan leader, became the first governor of Massachusetts Bay. Winthrop had sailed for Massachusetts in 1630. Aboard the ship, he gave a sermon about his hopes for the new colony.

"We have joined together to find a place to live under a proper form of civil and church government. In cases like this, the group is more important than any individual. Our purpose is to improve our lives in order to serve the Lord.

"We have entered into a contract with God. Now if God should hear us and bring us in peace to the place we desire, then He has accepted our contract. And He will expect us to follow it strictly. If we sink into sinful ways, the Lord will surely break out in anger against us."

James Winthrop was a strong governor.

The Puritans wanted to set up a kind of holy city in the New World. In this model society, everyone would live according to the teachings of the Puritan Church.

The government of Massachusetts Bay was founded on these principles. The rules of the government and the church were closely tied. Only those who belonged to the Puritan Church could vote. Only Puritans could be elected to serve in government. No one could speak against the church. Yet everyone had to pay taxes to support it.

This made life difficult for some of the people who settled in Massachusetts Bay. People of other religious beliefs were sometimes called the "devil's agents." Even Puritans had problems. They could not speak out against a Sunday sermon, for example. Merchants were sometimes brought to court because, according to the church, they were charging an unjust price for some item. Many people who believed or lived differently were forced to leave the colony.

This painting shows Puritans at worship.

Roger Williams, a minister, was one such person. Williams said that the government should have no power over religious matters. Roger Williams had many followers. Governor Winthrop was afraid Williams' ideas might divide the colony. So he forced Williams to leave.

In 1635, Williams and his followers bought some land from Native Americans. Then they started the colony of Rhode Island. In Rhode Island, voters did not have to be church members. Colonists did not have to support any one church. Rhode Island became the first colony to have full religious freedom.

Anne Hutchinson was also one of the founders of Rhode Island. She, too, was forced to leave Massachusetts for her religious beliefs. Hutchinson arrived in Massachusetts with her husband and children in 1634. While living in Boston, she organized meetings for women. At these meetings, she discussed sermons that ministers had given.

Anne Hutchinson believed in religious freedom. She was sent away from Massachusetts.

She also introduced her own religious ideas into these talks. Hutchinson felt that each person should be free to think for herself or himself in religious matters. This was considered a dangerous idea in Massachusetts. Anne Hutchinson was taken to trial twice. She was found guilty of questioning the authority of the ministers. So she and her family were forced to leave the colony. She then started a settlement in Rhode Island.

Most of the first New England settlers had clustered around Boston. Later, people began to move inland. Some settlers moved to the fertile Connecticut River Valley. Another group of Puritans from London started a colony at New Haven. In 1662, the English king granted a charter that brought these two groups together as Connecticut. New Hampshire was also formed by colonists from Massachusetts Bay. By 1679, there were four New England colonies—Massachusetts, Rhode Island, Connecticut, and New Hampshire.

Choose the best answer:

1. The Puritans wanted to set up a society where (a) all people could worship as they pleased, (b) everyone would live according to the teachings of the Puritan Church, (c) the government and the church would be the same.
2. Roger Williams offered people in Rhode Island religious freedom because (a) he thought Puritans were evil, (b) he wanted to attract settlers, (c) he believed a government should have no say in religious matters.
3. Anne Hutchinson was banned from Massachusetts because (a) it was feared that she might cause others to stop listening to the ministers, (b) she never went to church services, (c) she refused to marry.

4. Do you know of any groups of people who have been forced to leave their homes recently because of what they believe? Do a project with your classmates to find out about some groups.

Education and Trade

The church was the center of life in New England towns. On Saturday afternoon, everyone started to get ready for Sunday. All work stopped. Even cooking was not allowed until sundown on Sunday. People spent much time in prayer. On Sunday, everyone went to hear long sermons in church.

On other days, the church was often used as the town hall. Villagers would meet there to pass laws, make decisions, or solve community problems.

The Puritans thought everyone should be able to read the Bible. Because of this, education was very important in New England. As early as 1647, public schools had been set up. Every community with more than fifty people had to hire a schoolteacher. In class, the children learned the Puritan religion along with their lessons. Here is part of the alphabet from the *New England Primer*, which was often the children's first school book.

Some Puritan women had schools in their homes. On the right is a horn book used by the children.

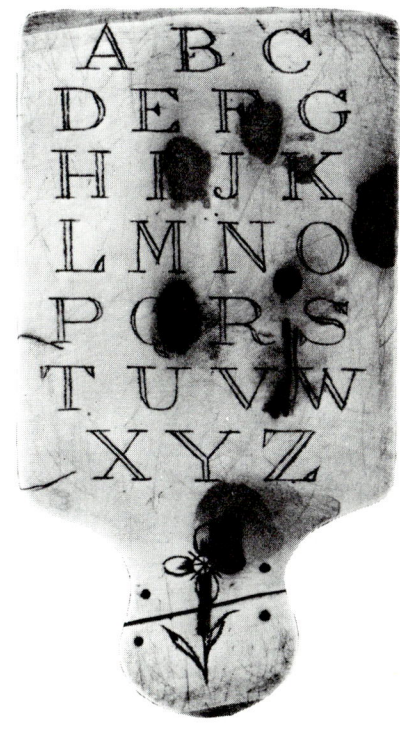

In *Adam's* Fall	A *Dog* will bite
We Sinned all.	The Thief at night.
Thy Life to mend	An *Eagle's* flight
This *Book* attend.	Is out of sight.
The *Cat* doth play	The Idle *Fool*
And after slay.	Is whipped at school.

Some women ran schools in their homes. Children would come to learn the alphabet, spelling, reading, and arithmetic. As the children studied, the teacher usually went about her household chores. Often, she was also looking after older girls who were learning to weave or spin. This was not unusual. It was said that New England people were used to doing "twenty different things well!"

The Puritans believed in hard work. And hard work was very necessary to live in New England. The soil was thin and rocky. The time between frosts, when crops could grow, was often short. These conditions made farming difficult.

In the spring and summer, farmers worked the rocky soil to raise wheat and corn. Sometimes there was a little extra to sell, but not often. The farmers also bred cattle and pigs. During the long winters, they trapped animals for fur and sometimes for food.

Because farming was so difficult, many New Englanders looked for other ways to make a living. Many turned to the sea. Thick forests supplied plenty of timber for building ships. At first, most of the ships were used for fishing. The Atlantic waters were some of the richest fishing grounds in the world. Many New Englanders made their living fishing in these waters. Soon, New England was selling dried, salted fish to other countries. Whale oil and whalebone also were important products.

Sometimes, New Englanders would sell their ships. With so much timber, they could easily build more. It was not long before shipbuilding became an important industry.

Most ships were used for trading. Merchants bought fur, timber, cattle, and some grain from the farmers. They bought fish from New England fishers. They shipped the food, especially the fish, to the West Indies. There, they traded for sugar. They sent the sugar to England, along with fur and timber. In England, they filled the holds of the ship with woolens, furniture, glass, and other manufactured goods. Then they set sail for New England. In New England and the other colonies, the merchants sold the manufactured goods. Then, they loaded their ships with goods to sell outside the colonies.

Sometimes New England merchants traded for molasses (mə las′iz) in the West Indies. This was a thick syrup which was made into rum, a popular drink. The rum was then used to trade for slaves in Africa. The slaves were sold in the West Indies and the Southern colonies.

This is a picture of the North Battery in Boston.

These men are packing salted herring into barrels for shipment.

Trade helped many other businesses to grow. Shipwrights (shəp′rītz) built ships. Other people made the ropes and sails for the ships. Coopers built barrels in which to ship grain and salted fish.

By the 1700s, New England was becoming a region of merchants, sailors, fishers, small farmers, and people who practiced trades. It was a region of many different occupations.

1. Why was education so important to New Englanders?
2. Why did many New Englanders turn to the sea to make a living?
3. Which of these products did New Englanders produce for trade? (a) dried fish, (b) gold, (c) timber, (d) furs, (e) ivory, (f) coal.

The Middle Colonies

The colonies of New York, New Jersey, Maryland, Pennsylvania, and Delaware were called the Middle Colonies. They were in the middle, between the older and more populated New England and Southern colonies.

New York and New Jersey first belonged to the Dutch. The Dutch claimed the territory when Henry Hudson explored it in 1609. They named their colony New Netherlands.

In 1626, the Dutch founded a fur-trading post on the island of Manhattan. They called it New Amsterdam. New Amsterdam was a good port. From it, Dutch ships sailed in all directions, trading goods.

The Dutch traded for furs with Native Americans in the north. Then they shipped the furs down the Hudson River to New Amsterdam. Dutch ships also sailed along the Atlantic coast. They picked up food and rum from New England. They took aboard tobacco from the Southern colonies. Then, ships filled with these goods sailed from New Amsterdam to Europe and the West Indies. From Europe, Dutch ships brought tea, cloth, and other goods. New Amsterdam quickly became a busy center of trade.

New Amsterdam in the 1600's. Today huge skyscrapers stand on this land.

To attract settlers to their lands, the Dutch set up the *patroon* (pət rün′) system. A patroon was someone who brought fifty settlers to New Netherlands. Such a person was then given a large piece of land. The patroon got a share of everything the farmers raised on the patroon's land. Patroons made all the laws. And a patroon acted as the final judge in almost all matters.

In 1664, the English captured New Netherlands. The Dutch settlers never fired a shot. Their governor, Peter Stuyvesant (Stī′və sənt), had ruled harshly. They were glad to be rid of him. New Netherlands now belonged to the Duke of York, a brother of the English king. The town of New Netherlands was renamed New York.

At first, few English people came to New York. Many did not want to go where there was no representative assembly. Without settlers, the Duke of York made little profit. Finally, the Duke allowed an assembly to meet. The assembly immediately passed a Charter of Liberties. It gave the colonists the same rights as all English citizens. These included *trial by jury*. Trial by jury meant that a person in court was found guilty or not guilty by others who were his or her equals.

The Duke of York gave what is now New Jersey to two friends named Carteret and Berkeley. The rules they made for their colony included religious freedom.

Maryland was founded in 1632, when 200 Catholic settlers landed at Chesapeake Bay. The Calvert family had received this colony from the English rulers. The Calverts were Roman Catholic. They made Maryland a safe place for Catholics and Protestants as well. The soil of the new colony was rich, and the climate mild. Tobacco soon became an important crop.

In 1681, an Englishman named William Penn was given a large parcel of land in the New World. He received it in payment for a debt that the king owed his father.

William Penn was a member of the Society of Friends. The Friends were called *Quakers* by others. They were a small group of Protestants whose beliefs caused them trouble wherever they lived. Friends believed that all people were equal

William Penn wanted a colony where all people would be free.

and good. They lived simply. They refused to fight in wars against other human beings. William Penn wanted a colony where people of all nations and religions could live together in peace.

With high hopes, Penn and other Friends sailed for his colony. It was a piece of land as large as England. There

Farms in the middle colonies were often prosperous.

were many rivers. The soil was rich. The new land was covered with trees. Penn called it Pennsylvania, which means "Penn's woods." Penn's colony included the land that is now Delaware.

William Penn sent pamphlets to Europe describing his new colony. He told about its religious freedom. He described its excellent farmland. Thousands of English Friends came to Pennsylvania. Many thousands of German farmers also arrived. There were Swedes, Finns, French, and Dutch settlers as well. Later, many people came from Scotland and Ireland.

Farms in Pennsylvania, New York, and New Jersey soon produced large amounts of wheat, corn, and oats. These were shipped to New England, the South, and the West Indies. The Middle Colonies became the "breadbasket" of the New World.

The Middle Colonies were much more mixed than the Southern or New England Colonies. They had many different kinds of people. They had some of the richest farmlands. Several of their towns became important centers of business and trade.

1. Which of these statements is *not* true? New Amsterdam became a center of trade because (a) it was located at the mouth of the Hudson River, (b) it was between the New England and Southern Colonies, (c) it had excellent farmlands.
2. Which of these colonies were started for religious reasons? (a) Maryland, (b) Pennsylvania, (c) New York.
3. *Trial by jury* meant that a person in court was judged by a) the patroon, b) the English king, c) representatives in the assembly, d) other people like himself or herself.

4. Name some ways in which the Middle Colonies were different from the New England Colonies.
5. Suppose you could go back to the 1700s in a time machine. Which of the English colonies would you visit? Why?

Philadelphia

In the 1700s, most colonists were farmers. But cities were growing quickly and bringing a new kind of experience to the colonies.

Philadelphia grew quickly under the English Friends. Like New York, it became a center of trade. Farmers sent their crops to Philadelphia. From there, merchants shipped them overseas. More and more people came to Philadelphia from Europe. Soon there were parsons, bakers, bricklayers, and well-educated teachers. Skilled workers designed clothes, furniture, and houses. Barbers cut hair off people's heads. Wigmakers found fancy ways to put hair back on.

This is Chestnut Street in Philadelphia in 1799.

Early printing presses were operated by hand.

Printing presses and bookstores appeared throughout the city. Women shared in this growth. Many colonial women edited newspapers. Cornelia Bradford owned and ran the *Philadelphia Mercury*. This was the third-largest newspaper in the colonies. Trade with Europe kept people in touch with European ideas. Newspapers printed news from the Old World. Imported books also let Americans know what learned people in Europe were thinking.

Growing cities like Philadelphia faced problems that people in towns and farms didn't have. Heavy traffic from horse-drawn carriages forced the cities to pave their streets with cobblestones. Otherwise, the streets became rivers of mud when it rained. Or, they became clouds of dust in dry weather. With so many people close together, cities needed sewers. And they needed rules to protect public health. Even so, diseases could spread easily. Epidemics of smallpox or typhoid (tī′foid) often killed thousands of people. Fires were yet another danger. Crowded wooden buildings burned quickly. A fire could destroy whole sections of a city. Fire companies were needed.

Bookstores in Philadelphia contained books printed both in the colonies and in Great Britain.

One important citizen of Philadelphia did much to help meet the needs of the city. His name was Benjamin Franklin. Ben Franklin was born in 1706 to a poor family in Boston. When he was 17, Franklin sailed to Philadelphia. There, he became a printer. Later, he owned his own newspaper. He also published *Poor Richard's Almanac*. This little booklet gave information about the weather, farming, and business. It often gave advice in a witty way.

Ben Franklin had a curious and practical mind. He developed a stove that could heat a room better than an open fireplace. It came to be called the Franklin Stove. He also invented *bifocal* glasses. With them, a person who needed glasses could read things up close and could also see things far away.

Franklin talked to people and wrote about the problems of the city. In this way, he helped bring street lighting and paving to Philadelphia. He organized volunteer fire companies. He also started the first hospital and lending library. In 1751, Franklin helped found the Academy of Philadelphia. Franklin also served as postmaster in Philadelphia.

This picture shows Benjamin Franklin studying a drawing of bifocals.

From Philadelphia, Franklin was able to learn a great deal about all the colonies and about Europe. He was loved and admired by many. Well-informed leaders like Benjamin Franklin would play an important role when the colonies broke away from England. Some years later, he became a representative for the colonies.

TO DO

1. Choose the best answer. Philadelphia (a) was a disorganized city, (b) had a good system of railroads by which farmers sent their crops to the city, (c) was an important center of trade.
2. Which of the following were problems in Philadelphia? (a) crowded wooden buildings, (b) diseases, (c) finding skilled workers, (d) letting the citizens know what was going on.
3. List some of the things Ben Franklin did for Philadelphia and the colonies.

ON YOUR OWN

4. In the mid-1700s, Boston, Philadelphia, and Charleston were among the largest cities in the colonies. Find these cities on your map on page 89. Then list the products that you think would be shipped from each of these cities.

Amish People in the Middle Colonies

One of the many groups that came to the Middle Colonies in the 1700s were a people called the Amish. The Amish were a small religious group in Europe. Most were German-speaking farmers. The Amish had strong religious beliefs. These beliefs were often different from the teachings of the main churches in Europe. Thus, the Amish were forced to move many times. There were few places in Europe where they were safe. Some of them were drowned, burned, or tortured.

So the Amish came to the New World. They came for the freedom to practice their religious beliefs. They wanted to lead a hardworking farming life. They would not dress in fancy clothes or live in fancy homes. They felt they were different from other groups. One of their favorite passages in the Bible was "Come from among ye and be separate."

Most Amish came to William Penn's colony. The first Amish arrived in Philadelphia on October 2, 1727. They had

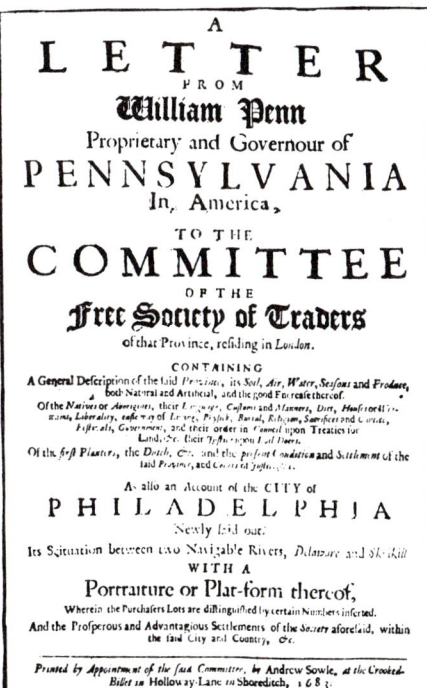

William Penn wrote letters to different groups in Europe inviting them to settle in his colony.

113

Amish today still plow the land as their ancestors did.

sailed aboard a ship called the *Adventure*. In Pennsylvania, Amish families started farms in an area called Lancaster County. Other Amish people settled farther west.

Over the years, Amish culture has changed very, very slowly. Today, many things the Amish do and believe have not changed since these people first came to North America.

In the next group of lessons, you will learn about Amish ways of living today. The Amish are an important people to study. They remind us of how most colonists lived in the early history of our country. On these pages are pictures of Amish people today. If there had been cameras in the 1700s, photographs of the Amish would not have been very different. There are no modern tools. There are few signs of modern American life. In these pictures, you can see how colonial families shared the work on a farm.

These Amish people are all doing work by hand. They do not use sewing machines or harvesters.

By studying the Amish, we can also examine some values that may have an important meaning for the people of the United States today.

Amish people lead a simple farming life. They are *self-sufficient*. They grow much of the food they eat. They build their own buildings. They sew their own clothes. For transportation, they use mostly horses. They could keep going even if somehow all the machines stopped. Their way of life depends on skills many people in the United States have now lost. Few Americans, for example, can make their own clothes or grow their own food.

Amish people waste very little. Their way of living does not harm the environment. It does not foul the air and the rivers.

The Amish help one another often. They believe in a close family and community life. They look out for one another in times of need.

The Amish have kept all these old ways. They have chosen to do so even though most of the world is changing around them.

TO DO

1. Can you name three other groups besides the Amish who came to North America seeking religious freedom?
2. Name two important Amish values.
3. *Self-sufficient* means that (a) you can meet most of your needs by yourself, (b) you do not harm the environment, (c) you try to change very, very slowly.

CHAPTER REVIEW

1. Answer *true* or *false* to each of the following statements: In Virginia, (a) women could vote for Burgesses, (b) servants could vote for Burgesses, (c) male landowners could vote for Burgesses.
2. List three ways in which the Puritan Church influenced the life of New Englanders.
3. What were two main ways in which the people of the Middle Colonies made a living?

3
A CULTURE FROM COLONIAL TIMES

In what ways are the Amish different from many other people in the United States? What is cooperation? How do people make decisions?

Amish People Today

The Amish are friendly people. But unless you are Amish, you probably won't get to see the inside of their houses. The Amish keep pretty much to themselves. They don't want too many ideas from the outside to change their way of life.

In Lancaster County, Pennsylvania, and in other places, the Amish stand out in many ways. There are no electrical wires going into the large, neat Amish farms. The Amish don't believe in using electricity or machines that run by electric power. They know what television is. They shop in stores that are brightly lit and air-conditioned. But they don't want such things for themselves.

This Amish kitchen could have existed 100 years ago on a prosperous Amish farm.

AMISH COMMUNITIES TODAY

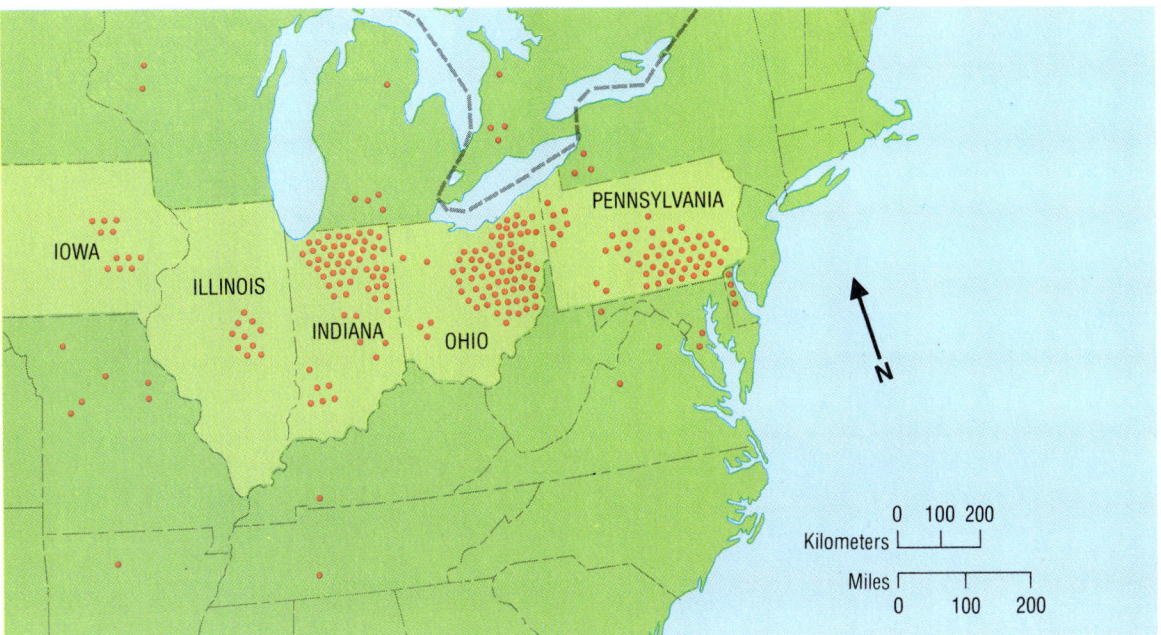

Amish people can be seen driving buggies, which are usually painted black. The buggies are pulled by horses. The Amish are surrounded by cars, trucks, buses, and tractors of modern America. They know all about them. Many Amish can drive tractors. Most Amish take rides in cars and trucks when it is necessary. They travel by bus or even by airplane when they visit a relative in another part of the country. But it is not proper for an Amish person to *own* a car, truck, or tractor. It you own something, it is usually because you want it. The Amish don't want motor vehicles.

Suppose you are Amish and have been invited by your neighbors, the Yoders, for dinner. Here is what might happen.

It is 5 P.M. You greet the family. There are eleven people in the family. There is Grandfather Yoder, who lives in a separate section of the house. Henry and Anna Yoder have eight children. The Grandfather Yoder and Henry Yoder have long beards. They wear dark clothes. Anna Yoder wears a white cap on her head. Neither she nor any of the girls wear makeup or jewelry. Instead of belts, the boys and men wear suspenders to hold up their pants. Their jackets have no collars or pockets. The Amish call such things "modern," or, sometimes, "English."

This Amish boy is learning farming from his father.

An Amish funeral procession.

There are no electric lights in the Yoder house. Light comes from a few large kerosene lamps. The dinner table is in the kitchen, near a coal-burning stove. The kitchen is the warmest room in the house.

The food is delicious, and there is plenty of it. There is a thick soup made with chicken and corn. Then come sausages, mashed potatoes, string beans, bread, apple butter, peach pie, and ice cream. Everything is homemade. Almost everything was grown on the farm.

At your end of the table, Katie, a fifteen-year-old girl, is talking to you in English. Others are speaking in Pennsylvania Dutch. This is the language that most Amish speak at home. It is similar to German.

Every now and then, you hear things like, "Eat your mouth empty once," and "Aunt Rachel is wonderful fat," and "The paper wants rain." These sentences are half-English and half-Pennsylvania Dutch. Can you guess what they mean?

It's now about 7:30 P.M. You have to leave. In the Amish country, everybody goes to bed early and gets up early. Work on the farm starts at sunrise or before.

1. Look at the population distribution map on page 119. In which three states do most Amish people live?
2. Which of the following are ways of living from the past: (a) Amish plain clothes, (b) tractors, (c) coal-burning stove, (d) television, (e) kerosene lamps, (f) suspenders, (g) buggies, (h) large families.

3. What electrical things do you have at home that the Amish wouldn't have?
4. How would your life change if your electricity were shut off for a week or a month?
5. List the foods you had for dinner last night.
6. Where did these foods come from? Do you know how they were made?

Values and a Way of Life

Putting in the Seed

Rebecca Lapp looked at the wide field in front of her. The soil had been plowed and then worked until no clump of dirt was larger than a small stone. One more trip across the field and all the corn would be planted.

Rebecca Lapp was driving a cart, pulled by two large work horses. It was her job to guide the cart up and down the field in a straight line.

In the back of the cart, close to the ground, rode Rebecca's father. Jonas Lapp made sure that the corn kernels were dropped in the right spot. He also made sure they were covered with the right amount of soil.

Plowing the fields with a team of six horses.

These fields are ready for planting.

Many things can ruin a crop. Too much rain, or not enough. Too much sun, or not enough. In just a few days, floods, frosts, or insects can destroy the work of several months. But if nothing bad happened, the care that the Lapps used in planting and growing their corn would pay off. A fine crop would be harvested.

The next morning, Jonas Lapp hitched his horse to the buggy and drove to his neighbor's farm. He put his horse in the barn while his neighbor explained the work for the day. Jonas Lapp then climbed up on a large red tractor. It had a corn planter behind it. The Amish farmer drove to a nearby field and spent the day planting corn. He planted five times as much land as he and his daughter could plant in the same time. He drove the tractor to the farmyard and collected his wages for the day. Then he hitched his horse to the buggy and drove home.

Jonas Lapp will not drive a tractor on his own farm. A tractor is modern and is not necessary. He will help his neighbor for wages, though. But first, his own work has to be finished—and in the Amish way.

At an auction Amish people have a chance to visit with their neighbors.

An Auction

Timothy and Grace Miller stop and read the poster nailed to the fence post. Almost all the Amish in the neighborhood are going to the *auction* at Zee Road Farm. At the auction, used things will be sold. Amish neighbors will also have a chance to tell each other the latest news.

Moses Esh bought the Zee Road Farm from a non-Amish. His son, Elam, was married last month. Elam Esh and his new bride Sarah will live on the new farm.

When the Millers arrive at eight o'clock, the yard is filled with buggies, trucks, and cars. Many non-Amish farmers are there to *bid* on things Elam and Sarah Esh will not keep because they are Amish. There are other items they can keep but don't need. When people bid at an auction, they call out the price they are willing to pay for an item. The item is then sold to the person who is willing to pay the most.

"Sold!" shouts the auctioneer. The first thing to go is a large pile of electrical wiring. Next are the electrical outlets and the fuse boxes from the farmhouse. Only non-Amish farmers bid on the electrical goods.

Two large tractors are sold. Not one Amish bid is made. The Amish do not bid on any of the tractor tools either. The bidding for the livestock is something else. Both Amish and non-Amish make bids. Timothy Miller buys five cows. He pays the auction clerk $1,499 in cash.

Grace Miller buys twelve plain cups and plates when the household products are sold. She will use them at the next worship meeting held at the Miller home. Grace Miller also buys a roll of dark blue cloth. Her husband needs a new suit. His old one is wearing out. Grace Miller will make the new suit. She knows the blue cloth is good. It will last ten years or more.

By the end of the day, everything that was sold is taken off Zee Road Farm. Only a few buggies remain in the yard.

Elam and Sarah Esh move into their new home.

---

1. After reading *Putting in the Seed*, can you name two things the Amish consider important or good?
2. Look again at the story about an Amish auction. Then answer *true* or *false* to the following statements:
   a. The Amish only value new things.
   b. The Amish value saving things.
   c. Amish men and women make their own clothes.
   d. Auctions are a way for Amish people to exchange news.

---

3. Where do you or your family buy most of the things you use?
4. In stores, most products are new. At auctions, most products are used. Would you rather have new or used things? Give reasons for your answer.

Cooperation Among the Amish

A New Barn

The first rays of sunlight are shining on Eli and Rebecca Byler's farm. The large farm buildings smell of fresh paint. On one side of the barnyard, there are piles of new lumber. The Bylers want to build another barn.

Several buggies can be seen coming down the driveway. On the main road and in the distance, there are many others. The Amish are coming from all over. The Lapp family has driven more than five kilometers to get here.

At a barn raising, young women get together to talk.

With so many people working, the barn goes up quickly.

By seven o'clock, nearly two hundred Amish men, women, and children have arrived at the Byler's farm.

Today, there will be a *barn raising*.

Barn raisings are an Amish custom. Many other people in the United States once had this custom, too. At a barn raising, friends and neighbors get together and help someone put up —or raise—a barn or other building.

At the Byler barn raising, the men work on the barn. So do some of the women and children. Other women and children prepare the large noonday meal that everyone will share.

The barn raisers work with handsaws, axes, and hammers. No electric tools are used. Every piece of lumber is carefully measured, cut, and put in place. The floor is put down. Then the walls go up. Finally, the roof goes on.

Joseph Miller is nailing boards on the side of the barn. Then he puts his hammer on the floor and goes for a drink of water. When he returns, he finds his hammer nailed to the floor. Joseph Miller laughs. Someone has played a joke on him.

By late afternoon, the Byler's new barn is finished. They bought all the lumber. Their Amish neighbors have made a gift of their help. The Bylers will return the favor. The next barn raising will be on someone else's farm. Eli and Rebecca will be there to help.

In an Amish community, people often do things together. They feel responsible for one another. Amish people help one

Sometimes Amish women get together at a quilting bee.

another to butcher animals for food. For weddings, worship services, and other large get-togethers, relatives and neighbors help the host family prepare the food. When a family member has an accident or is sick, neighbors come to help at the farm. They may also help care for the children. Amish adults often lend money to young farming couples. When Amish men and women grow old, they stay on the farm and do whatever work they can.

Working together and helping others to achieve a goal is called *cooperation*. The Amish *cooperate,* or work together, to get what they want or need.

TO DO

1. List ways in which the Amish cooperate with one another.
2. List ways in which people in your community cooperate. Some examples are collecting cans for recycling and a car wash.

ON YOUR OWN

3. How do you feel when you cooperate with others?
4. Is it easier to cooperate with people you know, or with strangers? Why?

Making Decisions

Ways of living result from choices people make every day. Your way of living does. So does the Amish way.

You have already looked at some of the choices Amish people make. These choices affect what the Amish wear. They affect how Amish homes look. They affect how the Amish get along with one another. Many of these choices may seem small. But they really are not. They add up to a whole way of life.

The Amish choose not to buy cars or television sets. Many other people in the United States do choose to buy such products. Why is it that different people make different choices or decisions? To answer this question, we must know what goes into making a decision.

Making a decision means choosing between at least two things. Things you choose between are called *alternatives*. Most Amish adults want to know what is happening outside of their communities. Television and newspapers are alternative ways of getting news. Most Amish choose to get their news by reading newspapers and talking with their neighbors about the world. They choose not to watch television. They have made a decision.

Decision making usually starts with a problem. You want something, and there are different ways you may try to get it. One of the alternatives may be better than the other. The problem is to find out which alternative is better.

We can draw a picture of decision making in this way:

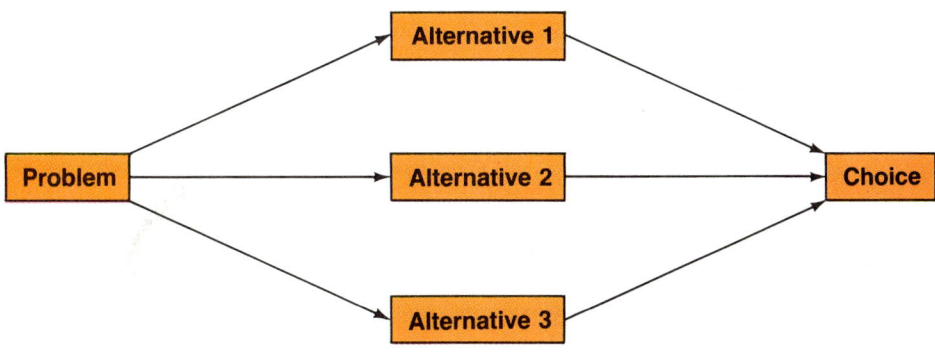

129

There is a problem. There are alternatives. And there is a choice. But other important things are missing from the picture. They are values, knowledge, and results.

The values a person has—what a person believes is important—affect the decision that person will make. People try to pick alternatives based on what they value. Say, for example, that you know a deep dark secret about someone. Your decision to keep it to yourself or tell it to a friend will be affected by what you value. If you believe people have a right to their own secrets, you probably won't repeat it. If your best friend loves secrets, and pleasing your friend is important to you, you will probably tell your friend. Or your decision may be based on whether or not you like the person the secret is about.

Knowledge also is a big part of decision making. What you know about a problem can affect the alternatives you pick. If, for example, you know that doing something can hurt someone, you may not do it. Amish people know that buying a TV will have results that they won't like. They know that other Amish will disapprove.

Knowing more about something often increases the number of alternatives we have. For example, if you only know one way of getting to a friend's house, you have to take that way. But if you also know about a bus that goes there, you have an alternative. And if you know that your older sister can drive you there after school, you have yet another alternative.

The results of a choice are very important in decision making. The results are what happens after you have made your decision. Sometimes, your choice works out the way you planned. Sometimes, it doesn't. The results of one decision help us when we have to make another similar decision.

Most people hope that the decisions they make will have results that are good for them. In making a decision people look at each alternative and choose the one that has the results most to their liking. Sometimes this is not easy. Sometimes people like the results of more than one alternative. Sometimes they do not like the results of any alternative.

Here is a more complete picture of decision making:

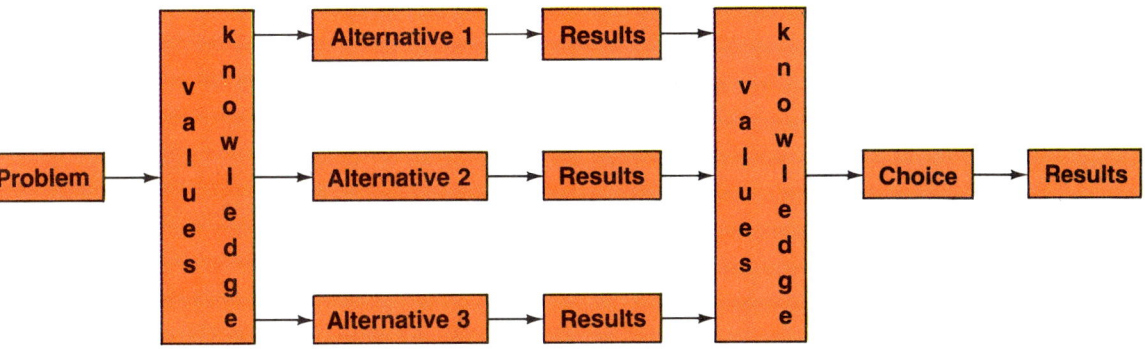

Sometimes, making decisions is very easy. Then, we hardly think about it. But, sometimes, a decision is hard. If you have some money, you might like all the alternatives you can think of for spending it. Your choice would be something you like. But if your teacher says to you, "As punishment you can either stay after school for a week or write a thousand times, 'I will do my homework,'" then you don't like either choice.

---

1. List some choices that Amish people usually make.
2. Match these words to the right meaning:

    choice   (a) things you choose between
    alternatives   (b) what you know about a problem
    value   (c) what you finally decide
    result   (d) what happens after you make a decision
    knowledge   (e) what is important to you.

3. How many alternatives must you have before you can make a decision?

---

4. How does knowledge help us when we are making a decision?

Benefits and Costs of Deciding

Most alternatives offer something that we want or need. This is called a *benefit*. A benefit is anything we hope to gain by choosing one alternative over another.

Suppose you decide to help someone. A benefit might be a "thank you" from that person. Another benefit could be that the person would return the favor later. Feeling good because you're doing what you think is right would also be a benefit.

A *cost* is the opposite of a benefit. A cost is anything we have to pay or give up when we make a decision.

In many decisions, the costs are money costs. Deciding to buy a TV set, for example, means paying or giving up money to get it. And there are other money costs. The TV adds extra money to the electric bill. Later, there will probably be repair costs, too.

These Amish are having a meal at a barn raising. What are the costs and benefits to the people who help at a barn raising?

Amish children do not watch TV. Instead they play many games. What would be the costs and benefits of this choice?

Decisions also include costs that have nothing to do with money. Years ago, some TV sets leaked harmful rays. Sitting too close to such a TV was bad for a person's health. That was a cost. People who watch television all the time miss out on other things. That, too, is a cost.

When we make a decision, we try to make sure that the benefits of our choice are greater than the costs. We try to make sure that we get more than we give up.

Most groups think it is important for their members to value and do certain things. For this reason, they place a high cost on decisions that go against the values and norms of the group.

The Amish believe their old ways are good ways. They do not want other Amish to buy TV sets. If an Amish person does buy a TV, other Amish people stop talking to the person. This is a very big cost to an Amish.

In some cultures, adults in a family punish a child for telling lies. This increases the costs of lying. The bad feelings that come from lying are also a cost. Friends might stop playing with someone who is always starting fights. Having no friends with whom to play is a big cost.

The laws of our government make some choices cost a lot. The cost of stealing or driving too fast can be going to jail or paying a fine. Punishment for breaking a law is a cost.

A group can also give important benefits to members who go along with its values and norms. A group can give friendship, help, or praise. It can make a member feel wanted or important. Can you think of other benefits a group can give?

TO DO

1. Which of the following are costs? Which are benefits?
   a. a thank you
   b. a smile
   c. the price of an item
   d. a punishment
2. List some possible costs and benefits of studying hard for a test.

ON YOUR OWN

3. Think of a group to which you belong. Then think of something you might do that would not be liked by this group.
4. What are the costs of doing this thing?
5. Why do you think the group makes this choice cost a lot?

CHAPTER REVIEW

1. Name several ways in which the Amish are different from many other people in the United States.
2. Write a short paragraph about the Amish, using the word *cooperation*.
3. Draw a picture of decision making. Show how the problem, alternatives, knowledge, values, and results are related.

4
THE AMISH AND CHANGE

What do Amish children learn? What do they want to do when they grow up? Will the Amish change?

Growing Up Amish

Have you ever heard the old saying: "As the twig is bent, so grows the tree"? The twig stands for the child. The tree stands for the adult. This saying means that your childhood is very, very important. What you learn when you are young may stay with you through your whole life.

Let's look at some of the things Amish children learn. As you read, compare these things to what you are learning. Are some of them the same? Are some of them different?

By 6:00 A.M. on weekdays, most Amish children are up and doing their chores. They feed the cows or chickens and bring in wood for the stove.

These children have many chores to do before they leave for school.

Skating to school.

After a big family breakfast, Amish children head for school. The school is usually a mile or more from home. Some children ride on small school buses. A few may go by horse and buggy. The oldest boy in the family usually drives the buggy.

The Amish use one-room schoolhouses built years ago when most people in the United States lived on farms. When necessary, they have built new one-room schoolhouses. These schoolhouses usually have no indoor plumbing.

About thirty children, from six to sixteen years of age, share one classroom. Usually there is one teacher and two teacher's helpers. They are usually Amish. They take turns teaching the various age groups in the class. For example, while the teacher talks to the ten- and eleven-year-olds, the other students read quietly or do other schoolwork. Later, the teacher turns to other age groups. The ten- and eleven-year-olds then do their quiet work.

Amish children at a one-room schoolhouse.

The one-room schoolhouse teaches Amish children that they are all one group. Even though there is a big difference in sizes and ages, they are all Amish.

The subjects most Amish children study are:
>Bible (in German)
>reading (English)
>spelling (English)
>penmanship (English)
>arithmetic
>geography
>Amish history

The schoolbooks they use are written especially for Amish children.

The Amish do not believe that their children need a lot of schooling. Amish children stay in school only as long as the law requires. Children in our country must go to school until they are sixteen. But Amish schools only go to the eighth grade. If Amish students went on to high school, they would have to go to a public school with non-Amish teachers and

Do you study the same subjects in school as these Amish children?

children. The Amish do not want this. High schools do not teach children Amish values only.

Some states have let the Amish set up *vocational* schools to follow the eighth grade. The word *vocational* means "having to do with jobs." In the vocational schools, Amish students prepare for the jobs they will do as adults. They learn more about farming and caring for the home.

TO DO

1. On a sheet of paper, write the headings *Alike* and *Different*. Then, under each heading, list the ways an Amish school day is similar to or different from yours.
2. Name some things an Amish boy or girl might find strange about your school.

ON YOUR OWN

3. Why do you think Amish parents do not want their children to go to non-Amish high schools?
4. Do you think your parents would want you to go to an Amish school? Why or why not?

"When I Grow Up"

Here are some things that Amish girls and boys wrote about their future.
One girl said:

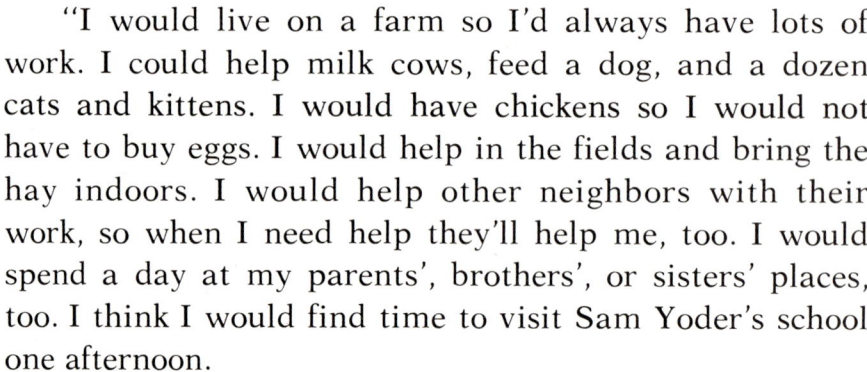

"I would live on a farm so I'd always have lots of work. I could help milk cows, feed a dog, and a dozen cats and kittens. I would have chickens so I would not have to buy eggs. I would help in the fields and bring the hay indoors. I would help other neighbors with their work, so when I need help they'll help me, too. I would spend a day at my parents', brothers', or sisters' places, too. I think I would find time to visit Sam Yoder's school one afternoon.

"The reason why I want to live on a farm and keep house is because there are always so many interesting things to do that I enjoy."

One boy wrote:

"When I grow up I want to be a good farmer. I like to milk the cows and feed the pigs, chickens, horses, cows, and calves. I also bring down the straw and hay that we keep up high in the barn. Father teaches me to farm."

All of these Amish children are telling about what they think is important to them. Do any of them talk about wanting things that their parents do not have?

Another boy said:

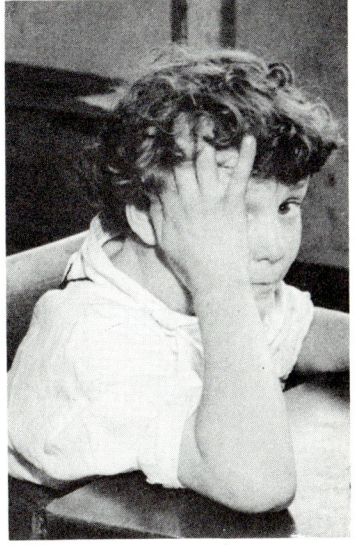

"I like farming because I like to get up early in the morning and do the chores. When I have eaten, I like to go out to the fields and plow or do whatever needs to be done. When I need a tool shed to put my tools in, I will build it because I like to hammer nails. When I would break something, I would go to town and buy a new part, or if I had a welder I would weld it. When it is time to cut and gather grass for hay, I would ask my neighbors to help. And I would bring the hay in after dark when it is nice and cool."

Another girl wrote:

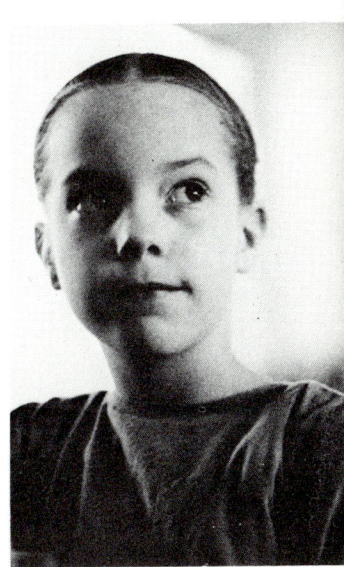

"When I grow up, I want to be a housekeeper, bake, cook, iron, wash, and have a garden. I would have a few flower beds in the lawn so it wouldn't look so bare. I want to have a garden so I wouldn't have to buy vegetables and things. I don't want to live in the city. I don't want to hear all the noise. I want to work to help people."

All of these children talk about wanting to do things the way the Amish have always done them. Unlike many other American children, they did not say they wanted to have things that their parents did not have.

1. What are the main things Amish children want to do as adults?
2. Is there a difference between what the girls want and what the boys want?
3. Can you find places where children mentioned ways of cooperating with others?

4. Try to imagine what your adult life will be like. Write down some of the possibilities. Then, make a list of the things you might have to know.
5. Are you learning any of these things in school? Will you learn some of them later in school? Which ones will you learn outside of school?

Choosing New Things

It was Wednesday. Andy Troyer woke up early. Today was special. There was a horse auction in town, and his whole family was going.

Andy hoped that his friend Calvin Schmidt would be at the auction. Calvin was a year older, and he got to go to town more often. He always had exciting stories to tell. But today Andy wanted to see him for a special reason. Andy was going to trade with him.

Just then he heard his mother calling him. "Hurry up, Andy. It's time to go to town."

Andy Troyer's parents climbed into the buggy. Then Andy, who was twelve, helped his four younger brothers and sisters into the buggy. It would be a long ride. But he didn't mind. They didn't go into town that often.

Clip-clop-clip-clop went the horse. Andy thought to himself, "Calvin has to be at the auction today."

Andy's sister Martha started to hum to the clip-clop sounds of the horse. Soon, the whole family was softly singing.

Amish communities remain much the same over the years.

When they reached the auction, Andy gave the horse some water. He tied it to a post near the other buggies. Then he started walking to the barn where the auction was. He saw Calvin Schmidt and some other boys behind the barn. He quickly ran to them.

"Hi Calvin," he said. "Did you bring it?"

"Yes," said Calvin, "I have it right here. Did you bring your knife?"

Andy handed him the knife. He was sad to trade it. His father had given it to him for his tenth birthday. But he wanted what Calvin had. It was a small transistor radio. It even had an ear plug. Andy could listen to the radio, and his parents would not hear it.

"Andy! Where are you? We are waiting for you." It was his father calling. Andy quickly put the radio under his shirt, and then followed his father into the auction barn. He sat down on the hard wooden bench next to his brothers and sisters.

In town, Amish children sometimes experiment with new things.

It was hard for Andy to sit still. He wanted to go home to look at his new radio. Even more, he wanted to listen to it. But he knew he had to wait until he was alone. He was Amish. His parents did not allow radios in their home.

Finally, it was time to go home. Andy thought the day would never end. The ride home was longer than any he could remember.

After supper, Andy helped wash the dishes. That seemed long, too.

Then he said to his mother, "I'm going to bed. I'm very tired."

His mother looked puzzled. It was only seven o'clock. She watched him closely. "Don't you feel well?" she asked.

"I feel fine. I'm just tired," he said.

Andy's mother watched him run up the stairs. "Something is different about Andy," she thought to herself. "He's been acting funny all afternoon."

Andy was alone at last. He put the radio under his pillow. He took off his clothes quickly and placed them on the wooden bench at the end of his bed. He would wear them again tomorrow.

He jumped into bed. Carefully, he fit the ear plug in his ear. Next, he hid the radio under the quilt. Then he turned the radio on. The music was so different. It was not like the songs he sang at church.

Andy listened to his radio a long time before he fell asleep.

1. What difficult decision did Andy have to make?
2. Look for the number of times Andy does something that separates him from his family. Andy, for example, has to give up something his father gave him. Can you find other examples in the story?

3. Make a list of some of the "modern" things Amish children might be curious about.

The Problem of Change

The Amish live in a country where changes happen often.

In the United States, people often choose new ways of doing things. They buy new models of cars. They take new jobs. They move to new neighborhoods, away from friends and family. By comparison, the Amish way of life has changed very little. Still, it has changed.

Many Amish people today use public telephones. A few may sometimes watch TV at a neighbor's house. Some Amish have even built new homes with electrical wiring. But the wiring is not connected. It is as though they are waiting for a time when it will be all right to use it.

Each year, some of the young people leave their Amish communities. They take jobs as nurses, carpenters, teachers, and factory workers. Others leave to join less strict religious communities. Some Amish who leave their communities become Mennonites (men'e nītz). The Mennonites are a religious group similar to the Amish in many ways. But they use more of the modern conveniences. They also mix with people who are unlike themselves.

This man is decorating chairs in the old Amish way.

Although these Amish children explore new things, most will stay with the Amish way of life.

There are other reasons for change. For example, cars and buggies don't get along very well on the same road. How would you feel if you were riding in a light buggy and a car zoomed past at 88 kilometers (55 miles) an hour? How would you feel if you were in a car and got stuck behind a line of buggies poking along at 8 kilometers (5 miles) an hour?

Also, there aren't too many people who make buggies anymore. Many of these people are old. Almost no young people are going into this business. Someday, there may be no more buggy makers left.

All these things seem to suggest that Amish ways will disappear.

But, will they disappear?

The Amish have more children per family than most other groups in the United States. They are a small subculture. But they are growing faster than most other groups.

Amish parents understand that modern ways can be exciting for their children. They allow the young people a "running around" time. They know that some teenagers sneak into town in make-up and "modern" clothes. Or they buy radios when parents are not looking. But Amish parents also know that when their children become adults, most of them will stay with the Amish way of life. Most of the young people love the way of life they know. Many of the ones who go away return to the community after a few years.

Earlier, you read what some Amish girls and boys wrote about their future. Do you think that these young people will change their way of life very much when they grow up?

The Amish are very sensible, practical people. They know that their way of life has changed since they first arrived in North America. But the Amish are careful to change *very slowly*. In this way, they try to protect their values and ways of doing things.

The Amish are different from other people in the United States in many ways. They live much as they lived hundreds of years ago. The Amish remind us of the right of all people to be different. They help remind us of the freedom many Europeans were looking for when they came to the New World.

1. Name some ways in which the Amish way of life may be changing.
2. Name something that seems to show that the Amish way of life will be around for a long time.

3. Do you think the Amish way of life will disappear? Why or why not?
4. What do you like most about the Amish way of life?

1. List some things Amish children learn at home. Will they use this knowledge and these skills in the future?
2. List some things Amish children learn at school. Will they use this knowledge and these skills in the future?
3. Name some difficult choices Amish young people must face.

UNIT REVIEW

What Do I Know?

1. Match the events on the left with the correct dates on the right.

    Columbus arrives in the New World. (a) 1607
    The Society of Friends settle in   (b) 1620
       Pennsylvania.   (c) 1492
    The Vikings explore the northern coast (d) 1681
       of North America.   (e) 1003
    Jamestown settlement is begun.
    Pilgrims arrive on the Mayflower.

2. In many ways, the Amish way of life is very different from your own. Make a comparison by filling in a chart like this one.

	Amish	My Own
Clothing		
Transportation		
Food		
Family size		
Language		
Chores		
Schools		

3. Match the following people with their achievements:

    Fernando Magellan   (a) explored Florida
    Hernando Cortez   (b) discovered the Mississippi
    Francisco Coronado   River
    Panfilo de Narvaez   (c) conquered the Aztec
    Henry Hudson   (d) discovered New York harbor
    Hernando De Soto   (e) looked for "Cities of Gold"
                           (f) sailed all around the world

4. Fill in the blanks with one of these words: colony, hieroglyphics, cooperation, representative.

    (a) A _____ was chosen to speak before the committee.
    (b) _____ were discovered on the cave walls.

(c) The settling of a _____ required the _____ of all the people.

What Can I Do?

1. Pretend you are an indentured servant. Tell your reasons for leaving your homeland. Explain the conditions of your contract. Describe the place you now live and work.
2. Look at the map on page 73. Describe the world as it was known to the Europeans in 1492.
3. Look at the map on page 89. Make a chart listing the important products of the New England, Middle, and Southern colonies.
4. Read this story. Then answer the questions below.

    John has to write a report about a famous explorer. The report is due on Monday, and here it is Saturday already. He has had lots of time to write the report, but something has always kept him from doing it. He has just begun to read his social studies book when Phil and Maria come by to ask him to go to the movies. There's a new movie in town that John has been wanting to see. John must make a decision.

    (a) List two alternatives John has.
    (b) If he chooses to go to the movies, name one benefit he might receive. Name one cost.
    (c) If he chooses to stay home and do his report name one benefit he might receive. Name one cost.

What Is Important?

1. Look again at the story about John's decision. What decision would you make?
2. Many different occupations are needed in order to start a new colony. Which one do you think is the most important occupation to insure success of the settlement? Which one do you think is the least important? If you were a colonist, what occupation would you like to have? Why?

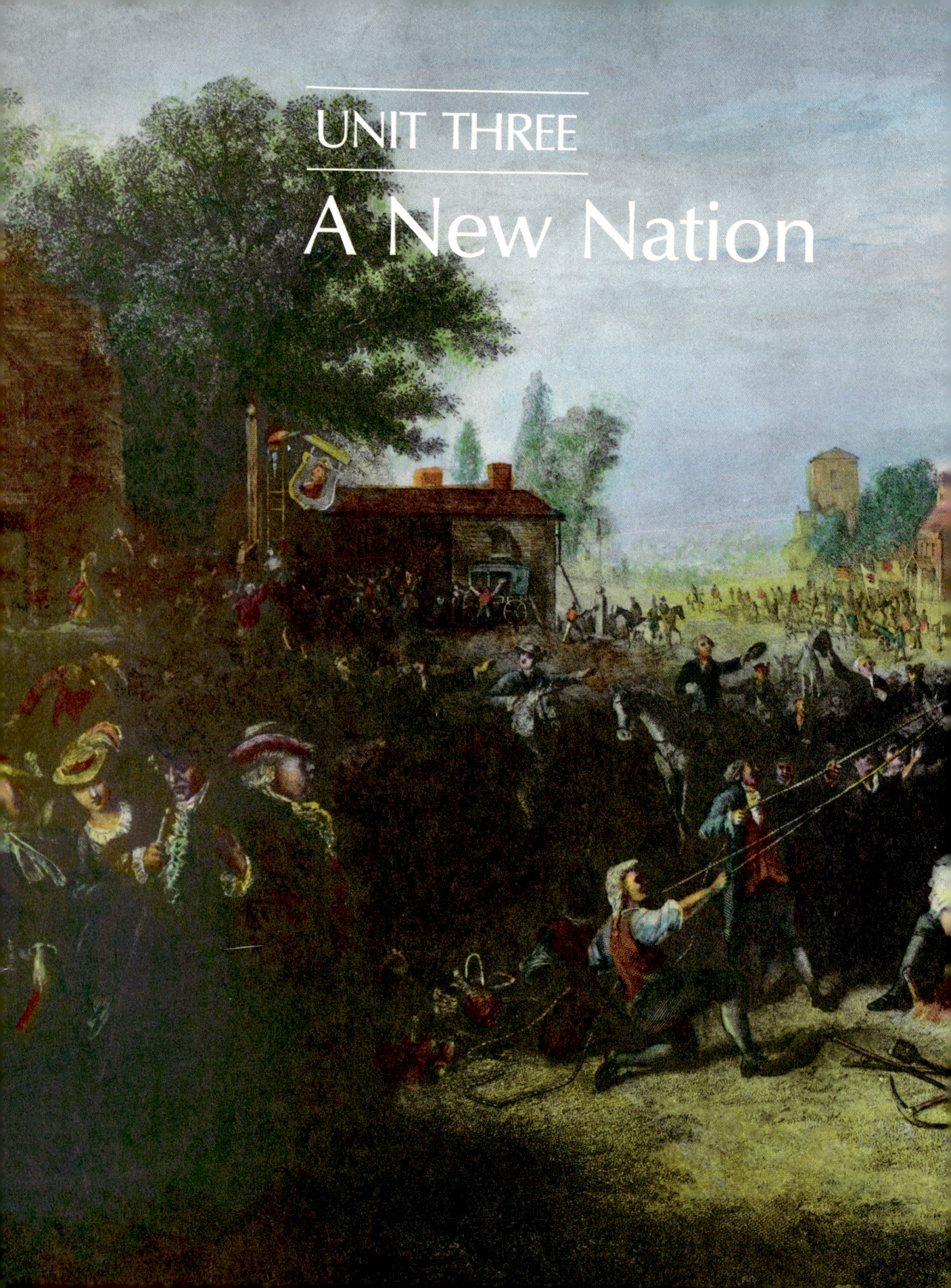

UNIT THREE
A New Nation

1 FREEDOM FROM GREAT BRITAIN

Why did the colonies break away from Great Britain? What great leaders helped guide the Americans during the difficult years of war?

Trouble with Great Britain

In the 1750s, a British traveler wrote these words about the American colonies: "There are so many differences among the Americans! There are big differences in way of life, religion, and wealth. If the Americans are left to themselves, they will be fighting each other from one end of the country to the other."

Twenty-five years later, however, the American colonies put some of their differences aside. They joined together and declared themselves free of British rule. They fought a war against Great Britain and won it. Then, they formed a new nation called the United States of America. The war the colonists fought is called the American Revolution.

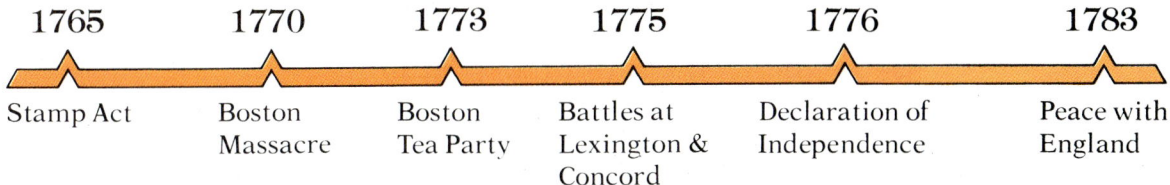

A *revolution* is a war in which the people of a country overthrow the government and start a new government. The American colonists had many differences with Britain. Few Americans wanted war. But they could not find a peaceful way to solve their problems with the British government.

The colonists' main complaint had to do with the *taxes* they had to pay to Britain. These taxes were extra amounts of money added to the price of goods that came into or went out of the colonies. The colonists had not agreed to pay these taxes. All taxes were set by the British *Parliament*, or law-making group. But Parliament had no American representatives in it. The Americans would not accept "taxation without representation." "We have been making our own laws for almost 100 years," said the Americans. "Now Parliament wants to make laws for us."

Britain passed laws taxing sugar, cloth, wine, and other goods. Then, in 1765, Parliament passed the Stamp Act. This law said that the colonists had to buy tax stamps. These stamps had to be pasted on all newspapers, birth certificates, wills,

153

and other important papers. Many Americans became very angry about this tax. They refused to pay it. They warned others not to pay it. Some Americans burned the tax stamps when they arrived at the docks. Others chased the tax collectors out of town. Finally, the colonies joined together and sent a message to Britain. They asked that the stamp tax be stopped.

The British didn't agree. Britain had fought a long war with France. Part of this war was fought in the American colonies. It was called the French and Indian War. It seemed fair to the British that the American colonies should pay for part of it.

In the end, the Stamp Act could not be enforced. Britain did away with it in 1766. But Parliament wanted to show that it had the right to tax the colonies. It placed a tax on tea, glass, and other goods. It also said Americans could only buy tea from Britain. Many Americans stopped drinking tea rather than pay the tax on it. Some continued to bring it in from countries other than Britain. They had to *smuggle* it in, or sneak it past the authorities.

The British king was furious. He tried to force the colonies to obey. British soldiers were sent to the colonies to search for smuggled goods. Feelings among the colonists had been divided. There were still many who did not question Britain's right to pass these tax laws. But few Americans liked having British soldiers searching their homes and stores.

Tax stamps the colonists refused.

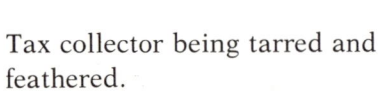

Tax collector being tarred and feathered.

Crispus Attucks, a black, was killed in the Boston Massacre. He was the first to die in the American Revolution.

Small fights broke out between the soldiers and Americans in the cities. In March of 1770, a crowd in Boston began to poke fun at some soldiers. Some of the colonists threw stones. The soldiers became angry and fired their rifles into the crowd. Five Americans were killed. This event came to be known as the Boston Massacre. As a result, feelings became more tense. The colonists would not forget that people had died.

TO DO

1. "Taxation without representation" meant that (a) some Americans did not have to pay taxes, (b) some goods were not taxed, (c) colonists did not have Americans in Parliament to help make tax laws.
2. Britain taxed the colonies (a) to pay for the French and Indian War, (b) to treat Americans as British citizens, (c) to show who was boss.
3. Why did the British send soldiers to the colonies?
4. What was the result of this action?

ON YOUR OWN

5. Name two peaceful ways in which Americans tried to solve their differences with Britain.

Revolution

At the end of 1773, something was to happen in Boston that would have two important results. It would harden the British against the Americans. It would also unite the colonies more than ever before.

In December, British ships entered Boston harbor loaded with tea. The Americans tried to send it back, but this was not allowed. The British tea was cheaper than the Dutch tea the Americans usually smuggled into the colonies. But it had a tax on it. If the Americans bought the British tea, it would mean that they agreed that Britain could tax them. Some of the people of Boston decided to protest against this tax.

On the night of December 16, they dressed in costumes of feathers and war paint like Native Americans. They climbed aboard the ships. Using tomahawks, they broke open the chests of tea. Then they threw the tea into the harbor. This took about three hours. All the while, a crowd watched from the shore. There was no damage to the ships or other trouble. One man wrote, "It was the stillest night that Boston enjoyed for many months."

The Boston Tea Party.

Americans objected to British soldiers being quartered in their homes.

Now the British government decided to punish Massachusetts. It closed the port of Boston to all ships. Parliament passed laws which forced the colonists to make room in their homes for British troops. These things made other colonies worry. If Britain could punish Massachusetts, it could do the same to them.

In September of 1774, representatives from all the colonies met in Philadelphia to talk about the problem. This was the first meeting of the Continental Congress. The members of this congress decided to support the city of Boston. They agreed to *boycott,* or stop buying, British goods. A boycott—a refusal to use or buy something—is a form of peaceful protest. The Continental Congress also agreed to raise a volunteer army. The volunteers were to protect the colonies if Britain used force to break the boycott.

In April of 1775, British soldiers were ordered to take the guns and supplies that the colonists had stored near the towns of Lexington and Concord. On the night of April 18, Paul Revere, William Dawes, and others learned that British soldiers were lined up on the shores of the Charles River. They rode all night to warn the towns.

The American Revolution began at Lexington.

In Lexington, a group of armed Americans waited on the village green. Soon the British soldiers were facing them, only a few yards away. A shot was fired, no one knows by whom. The British then fired at the group. Eight Americans were killed. At Concord, farmers shot back at the British soldiers. The British soldiers had a hard time returning to Boston that night. All along the way, farmers behind rocks and trees fired on them.

The American Revolution had begun.

TO DO

1. Why did the Americans dump the British tea into the water?
2. What two actions of the British helped unite the colonies?
3. A boycott is (a) the name of the First Continental Congress, (b) a kind of peaceful protest, (c) a decision to go to war.

ON YOUR OWN

4. Name some of the actions taken by the British up to the time of the Battle of Lexington.
5. In your opinion, what could the British have done that might have prevented a revolution?

Fighting for Independence

A second Continental Congress met in Philadelphia in May of 1775. Among the representatives were Samuel and John Adams of Massachusetts, Benjamin Franklin of Philadelphia, and Thomas Jefferson of Virginia. The colonists had not yet decided to break away from Britain. But they realized they needed a regular army to defend themselves against the British soldiers. They also needed a leader to raise and train such an army. George Washington had served as colonel in the French and Indian War. The members of the congress respected his military experience. They chose him as commander in chief of the new Continental Army.

Before Washington could take command of the army, he heard the news of the first major battle. It took place in June of 1775. The battle began when British ships arrived with more troops in Boston harbor. Three thousand American volunteers came to the defense of Boston.

The Americans took up positions near a place called Bunker Hill. From there, they could watch the ships in the harbor. The night before the battle, the Americans dug trenches and set up barricades. They also hid behind bushes and trees to stop the British from going around behind the barricades.

The next day, three British generals led 2,000 soldiers against the Americans. The British soldiers marched shoulder to shoulder. Their best fighters, called *grenadiers* (gren′ə dirz′), were in the lead. The British thought that if they attacked in

The Battle of Bunker Hill proved that Americans could stand up to the British.

large numbers, the Americans would be afraid and would give up. The fighting began and went on all day. The Americans did not give up. When they ran out of ammunition, they loaded their guns with scraps of metal, glass, and rocks. Many soldiers on both sides were killed and wounded. The white socks of the British soldiers were made red by the blood that covered the grass.

Still, the British had better guns and more ammunition. At day's end, they won the Battle of Bunker Hill. But the Americans won the glory. This battle made it clear to everyone that the Americans would not be easy to beat.

One of the Americans who fought at Bunker Hill was a black man named Salem Poor. Poor was later praised for his bravery by several of his officers. About 5,000 black Americans served in the American army during the Revolutionary War.

Women also fought in the Revolution. Deborah Sampson joined the army disguised as Robert Shurtleff. She fought in several battles and was wounded in a battle near Tarrytown, New York. Her identity was discovered when she was put in a hospital in Philadelphia. Margaret Corbin fought beside her husband in a battle at Harlem Heights in 1776. When her husband was killed, Margaret took up his gun and fought with great bravery until she was wounded three times. Other women also helped the army.

Left: Molly Pitcher at the Battle of Monmouth.

Right: Deborah Sampson joins the army in disguise.

By the middle of 1776, it seemed clear that Britain would never give the colonies the rights they wanted. Members of the Second Continental Congress decided that a declaration of independence should be written. This declaration would announce to the world that the colonies meant to become a free and *independent* nation. It would give the reasons why the colonies would no longer be a part of Britain. On July 4, 1776, after much discussion, the Declaration of Independence was signed by representatives from all the colonies.

Throughout 1775 and 1776, George Washington and his army had many problems. There were not enough supplies. Tired and hungry Americans were fighting fresh and well-equipped British troops. The Continental Army lost several battles. George Washington was desperate. He wrote to Congress: "Ten more days will put an end to the existence of our army." By the middle of December, the Revolution seemed lost.

Then, on Christmas night, Washington led a surprise attack. He and his soldiers crossed the freezing Delaware River while the enemy were celebrating the holiday. The plan worked. The Americans defeated the enemy soldiers at Trenton and Princeton. Washington marched his prisoners through the streets of Philadelphia. At last, the Americans had a reason to be happy.

1. Name two important decisions made by the Second Continental Congress.
2. On what date was the Declaration of Independence signed?
3. Number the following events in the order in which they happened:
    Washington crosses the Delaware on Christmas night.
    The Declaration of Independence is signed.
    George Washington is made commander in chief of the Continental Army.
    The British send more troops into Boston Harbor.

4. Why did the colonists decide to write the Declaration of Independence?

The War Ends

In 1777, the Americans had one of their biggest victories. General Burgoyne, a British officer, tried to capture the Hudson Valley of New York. His plan was to cut off New England from the rest of the colonies. Then Britain could win the war easily. Burgoyne marched his army south from Canada. He was to be joined by British troops from New York City, led by General Howe. Burgoyne's army was large and slow. He had trouble moving his heavy equipment along the winding, hilly roads in the wilderness. The Americans, led by Benedict Arnold and others, made the going harder. They chopped down trees to block the roads. They destroyed bridges. The colonists fought in the style of Native Americans. They attacked in small groups. They fired at the British from hiding places in the forest. The British were not used to fighting this way. They were angry and confused. When the British reached Saratoga, they were surrounded by Americans, most of whom they could not see. After fierce fighting, Burgoyne surrendered in October, 1777. Howe's army never arrived to help. On his own, General Howe had decided to capture Philadelphia, instead.

The victory at Saratoga was a turning point for the Americans. As a result, the French, who had a strong navy, agreed to join the war against Britain.

Part of the American Revolution was fought at sea.

THE REVOLUTIONARY WAR

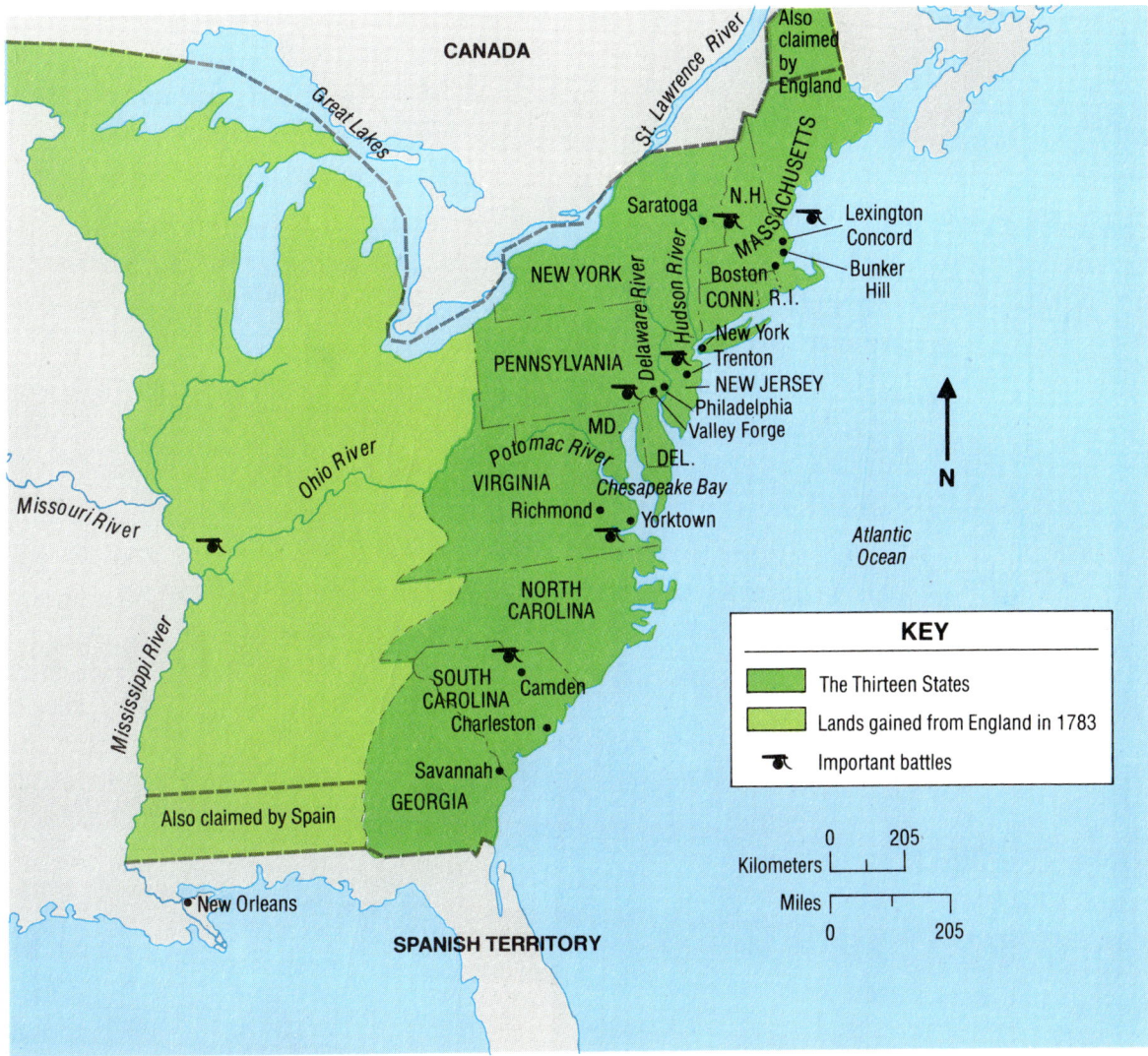

Howe's troops spent the winter of 1777–1778 in Philadelphia. They were warm and well fed. Washington and his soldiers did not have such an easy winter. Only 20 miles away, in Valley Forge, they suffered terrible cold and hunger. The men did not have enough warm clothes. Many were barefoot. Over 3,000 died that winter from cold and disease. The women who traveled with the army tried to find food for the soldiers. They nursed the sick. They sewed and washed clothes. They buried the dead. During this "winter of despair," many soldiers lost heart and went home. But Washington did not give up. He continued to drill the soldiers who were left. When spring came, the worst had passed.

In 1778, the tide turned in favor of the Americans. The French navy captured British ships on their way to North America. This made it hard for the British to get fresh troops and supplies. In the meantime, George Rogers Clark led a frontier army to victory against the British in the Ohio Valley.

Now the British sent their largest army into the South. In 1779 and 1780, General Cornwallis and 7,000 British troops invaded several Southern colonies.

In the summer of 1781, Cornwallis moved his army to Yorktown, Virginia. This was a costly mistake. Yorktown was surrounded by water on three sides. The French navy defeated the British fleet that was guarding the coast. The British could not obtain supplies or escape by sea. American troops moved in. Cornwallis was trapped. His soldiers were exhausted. On October 19, 1781, Cornwallis surrendered his army to George Washington at Yorktown.

A British fort surrenders to George Rogers Clark.

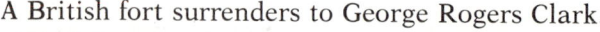

General Rochambeau, from France, was present at the seige of Yorktown.

This was a final defeat for Britain. The war in America had lasted six years. The British were tired of it. King George III and Parliament decided to bring the soldiers home.

Two years after the surrender at Yorktown, the British and the Americans made a formal peace. They signed a treaty in Paris, France, in 1783. The United States of America had won independence.

1. Choose the best answer. Saratoga was an important American victory because (a) the British generals did not agree, (b) the French agreed to help the Americans, (c) it proved Americans could fight like Native Americans.
2. Number the following events in the order in which they happened:
    victory in the Ohio Valley
    the "winter of despair"
    victory at Saratoga
    victory at Yorktown
3. In what year was the War for Independence over? In what year was a treaty signed?
4. Which answer is not true? The British decided to stop fighting because (a) they were tired of war, (b) the war was long and expensive, (c) the British army was destroyed, (d) the British troops were exhausted.

Leaders: Helping People Decide

The Revolution for American independence was not fought only on the battlefield. Before the war and during it, Americans needed leaders. These leaders and their ideas helped shape what people thought and did about problems the British were causing. The leaders helped people make up their minds about new ideas such as independence.

Samuel Adams of Boston was one of these leaders. Samuel Adams wanted to unite the colonists against the British. He wrote articles and made speeches. He did everything he could to make the colonists act. Adams started a *Committee of Correspondence* in Massachusetts. This committee wrote to committees in other colonies. The committees shared news about the British and told each other of their own plans. Adams was also the head of a group of Americans called the Sons of Liberty.

Samuel Adams.

In this picture, the Americans raise a liberty pole.

The Sons of Liberty did many things to protest British laws and taxes. One such protest was the Boston Tea Party. They also held parades. They sang songs and danced around the Liberty Tree, a big elm near Boston. Sometimes they would tar and feather a British official. Not everyone agreed with Samuel Adams. Many people thought he went too far.

Women, too, worked against British rule. They formed boycott groups against merchants who supported Britain. They formed anti-tea leagues. These leagues tried to get people to use drinks made from other plants as substitutes for tea. A group called the Daughters of Liberty was formed. The Daughters of Liberty joined the Sons of Liberty in street marches and meetings. They read newspapers out loud to people who could not read. Groups of women would spin yarn and weave cloth. Then they would make these into uniforms and bandages for soldiers.

Mercy Warren was a poet and playwright (plā′ rīt) who used her pen against the British. She made fun of them in her plays. She criticized the British in letters to her friend Abigail Adams. Then she had the letters printed in the newspapers for all to read. Once she wrote: "Be it known unto Britain even American daughters are politicians and patriots. They will aid the good work with their efforts."

Mercy Warren. Thomas Paine.

Another person who used his pen against the British was Thomas Paine. In January, 1776, he wrote a small book called *Common Sense.* In it, he listed reasons why the colonies should be independent. He wrote that Britain could no longer rule the colonies. Britain was too far away. North America was too big to be ruled by a little island. Paine said that other countries would always trade with the colonies as long as "eating is the custom in Europe." Because *Common Sense* was well written, many people read it. It helped thousands of people decide that the colonies must be independent.

TO DO

1. Name three ways in which leaders of the revolution helped other Americans decide for independence.
2. According to Thomas Paine, which of the following were good reasons to want independence: (a) other nations would always trade with the colonies, (b) Britain was too small to rule a large continent, (c) Britain was too far away, (d) all of the above?

ON YOUR OWN

3. Think of some leaders in your school or nation. In what ways do they try to help others decide?

Leaders: Lending Faith and Courage

Some leaders have special talents. They can write well or make good speeches. Others stand out because they have certain personal qualities. Among these might be the will to hold firmly to a task. Other qualities could be courage and a sense of fairness.

John Adams, a cousin of Samuel Adams, was a good speaker and writer. He also stood out because he worked hard and long for what he believed in. John Adams had often spoken out against the British. As a young lawyer in Boston, he wrote newspaper stories and petitions against British laws and taxes. After the Stamp Act, he decided that independence was the only way to solve the problems of the colonies. Together with Benjamin Franklin, he proved to Congress that a declaration of independence should be written.

John Adams.

Abigail Adams.

Abigail Adams was married to John Adams. When she heard that the Continental Congress might declare independence, she wrote the following letter to her husband.

"I long to hear that you have declared independence. And by the way, in the new code of laws . . . I wish you would remember the ladies, and be more generous . . . to them than your ancestors. Do not put such unlimited power in the hands of husbands. Remember, all men would be tyrants if they could. If particular care and attention is not paid to the ladies, we are determined to stir up a rebellion and will not regard ourselves as bound by any laws in which we had no voice or representation."

The person who wrote the Declaration of Independence was Thomas Jefferson. A lawyer and planter from Virginia, Jefferson was also a fine writer. He believed that people could govern themselves and that they had a right to do so. The declaration said "all men are created equal" and have certain rights, given by God, which no one can take away. Among these rights are "life, liberty, and the pursuit (pər süt′) of happiness." The Declaration went on to say that governments draw their powers from the people. When a government is no longer fair and just, the people have a right to change it. The Declaration of

Thomas Jefferson.

Independence gave people faith that independence was fair and right. They needed that faith during the years of war.

Once the fighting had started, Americans had no greater leader than George Washington from Virginia. Congress chose him to lead the army because he had more military experience than most Americans. He could also help bring the American people together.

Everywhere, people admired Washington's courage and steadiness. These qualities were worth a great deal to a people at war. Washington's job was difficult. He had to make an army out of groups of rebellious shopkeepers and farmers. There was very little time or money to do this. As a general, Washington did make mistakes. The Americans lost more battles than they won. But Washington saw that his job was more than winning. It was to keep on fighting, no matter how badly the war was going. Even after the worst defeats, with the army hungry and in rags, Washington would not surrender. This set an example for other Americans. It raised their spirits. It gave them courage to keep on fighting.

Every age had its leaders. They are people who believe in something. They are the men and women who help people to make their beliefs come true.

George Washington.

TO DO

1. Match the names John Adams, Thomas Jefferson, and George Washington with the things they did: (a) kept on fighting, (b) helped convince Congress that a declaration of independence should be written, (c) wrote that when a government is not just, people have a right to change it.
2. Now match Adams, Jefferson, and Washington with the qualities they showed as leaders: (a) courage and faith that the Americans would win, (b) the ability to inspire the nation through beliefs, (c) the will to work hard for what he believed in.
3. Who was Abigail Adams? What did she say in her letter to John Adams?

ON YOUR OWN

4. In the Declaration of Independence, Jefferson wrote that governments draw their power from the people. Write a paragraph telling what you think this means. Use complete sentences.

Why the Americans Won

Few people thought the Americans could win the Revolutionary War. In 1776, the British had the world's strongest navy. They had more money and soldiers than the Americans did. The British had factories that could produce guns, ammunition, and clothing for war.

The Americans seemed easy to defeat. They had no army or navy. They showed no signs that they could work together. Some Americans wanted to keep their ties with Britain and fought against the colonial army. Some escaped to Canada. Many other Americans did not care who won the war. They sold supplies to both sides.

Yet, six years after the fighting began, the colonies had won their independence. How had this come about?

The British actually had many disadvantages. The war was not popular in Britain. Many British people agreed with the goals of the colonists. Also, Britain had been at war with France, Spain, and Austria before the American Revolution broke out. It had been fighting wars in its colonies all over the world. Wars were expensive. The British people did not want to continue paying for them with high taxes.

The British navy had too few sailors and ships for all the jobs the government wanted done. The army could not get enough men to join. The British had to hire soldiers from other nations to help them fight. This, too, cost money. Britain also had to worry about enemies close at hand. France and Spain might invade Britain.

Britain had another main disadvantage. The American war was fought 4,800 kilometers (3,000 miles) away. Supplies and orders took a long time to arrive in North America. European soldiers were not used to the hot summers and cold winters of the Northern colonies. They did not like marching where there were no roads.

The Americans had some important advantages. The war was fought in their homeland. People will fight very hard to protect their own families, homes, and land. The colonists were

A portrait of George Washington, the Marquis de Lafayette, and Tench Tilghman. Tench Tilghman carried the news of Cornwallis's surrender from Washington to the Continental Congress.

Baron Von Steuben.

used to the land and the climate. They had learned how to fight in the wilderness from the Native Americans.

The Americans had a fine leader in George Washington. They also had many friends in Europe. Some of these friends came to the colonies to fight. Americans needed the skills of these European leaders. The Marquis de Lafayette (Mär kē′ də Laf′ē et′) and the Comte de Rochambeau (Komt də Rō shäm bō′) came from France to lead divisions of Washington's army. Thaddeus Kosciusko (Tha dē′us Kos′ē us′kō) from Poland and the German Baron von Steuben came to help train Washington's soldiers. These foreign friends admired what the Americans were trying to do.

The turning point in the war came in 1778. It was then that the French agreed to send soldiers and ships to help the Americans. Without French help, the Americans might not have won.

Maybe the greatest advantage the Americans had was their desire to be free and independent of Britain. People like Thomas Jefferson and Thomas Paine had written of this desire in exciting words. Patrick Henry, a great speaker from Virginia, had given the Americans a *slogan*, or inspiring phrase. In the Virginia Convention, he gave a speech that became famous. It ended with the words, "Give me liberty, or give me death."

Thaddeus Kosciusko.

TO DO

1. Name some of Britain's advantages and disadvantages during the Revolutionary War.
2. Name some advantages and disadvantages of the American colonists.

ON YOUR OWN

3. In your opinion, what was the *most* important advantage the Americans had? Explain your choice.

CHAPTER REVIEW

1. List several reasons why the colonies decided to break away from Britain.
2. Who was an important leader during the American Revolution? Why was she or he important?
3. List four or more things that helped Americans win the war.

2 A NATION IS BORN

How was the Unites States governed after the Revolution? What new kind of government did the Constitution set up? What freedoms are guaranteed to all United States citizens?

Early Government

During the Revolutionary War, the thirteen American colonies were all working for the same goal. They had to win the war. When the fighting was over, the differences between the colonies became important again. The colonies were now states in one nation. Some states earned money from farming. Others were centers for manufacturing and trade. Some states had slaves, while others did not. Some states claimed large areas of land to the west. Others had no western territory. In the years after the war, each state wanted to take care of its own interests.

There was, however, a central government. It was created in 1781. At that time, all the states accepted an agreement called the *Articles of Confederation*. The central government was made up of a single congress, much like the Continental Congress. Each state had one vote.

The Articles of Confederation gave Congress certain powers. Congress could set up post offices, charge postage, and coin or print money. Congress could trade with Native American groups to the west. It also had the power to raise an army and make peace treaties.

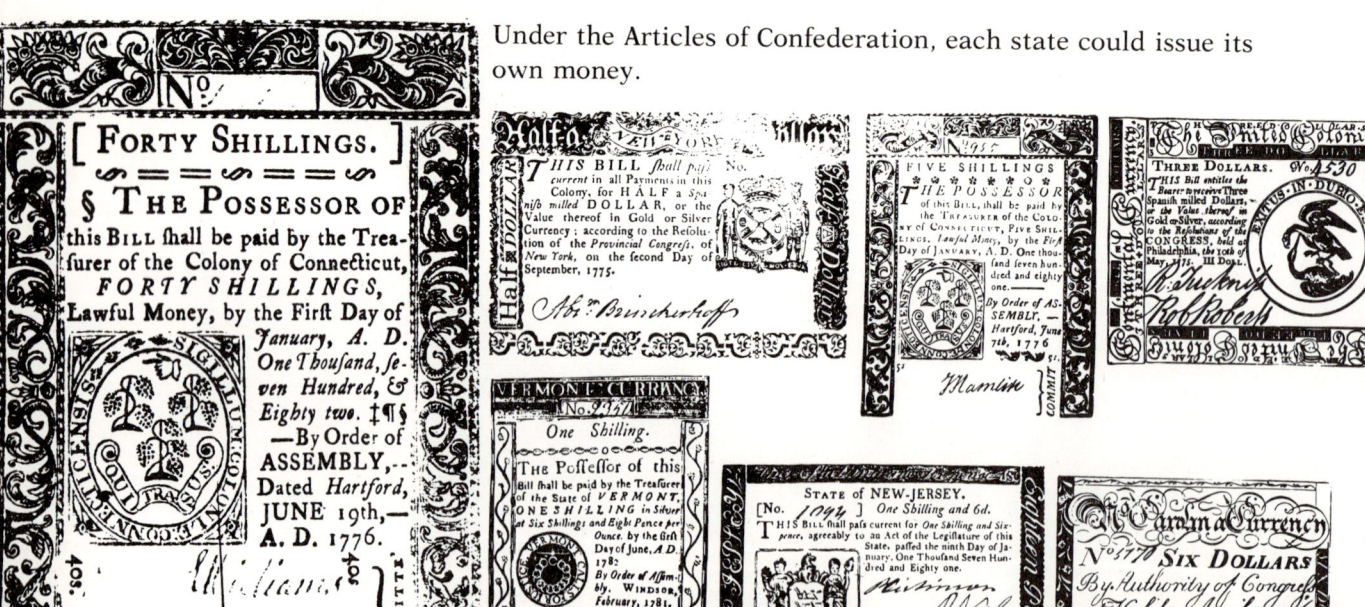

Under the Articles of Confederation, each state could issue its own money.

Under the Articles of Confederation, the states agreed to work together. But each state also had its own government. The states wanted their own governments to be stronger than the central government. So, the Articles of Confederation did not give Congress some important powers. Congress could not make trade agreements that would go against any state laws. More important, Congress did not have the power to tax the states. It could only *ask* the states to pay their share of expenses. The state governments collected the money. Then they turned it over to Congress, if they chose to. Many states did not choose to pay. Congress had no way to pay the war debts and other expenses.

An even bigger problem existed with the Articles of Confederation. Congress could not change any part of the Articles unless *every* state agreed. Since the states had different interests, they could not all agree on any changes. So Congress remained weak.

Many people thought that such a weak government could not hold the United States together. The states might all go their own ways. They would not be able to defend themselves against foreign nations.

Some citizens were afraid that there would be another revolution. After the war, times were very hard. Trade had not completely started up again. There was very little money to rebuild factories and businesses. Farmers could not sell their crops. Citizens in all states were having trouble paying their taxes. The worst problem was in Massachusetts. The farmers in that state were very poor. The Massachusetts government often took away a farmer's land as payment for taxes.

The farmers tried to stop this by legal means. This did not work. Then, in January of 1787, Daniel Shays took stronger action. He led a group of farmers to attack a government building where weapons were stored. But the state militia fired on the farmers. Daniel Shays and the farmers did not have weapons with which to defend themselves. They gave up the attack and fled. The windows of John Adam's house were broken during this uprising. But he understood the feelings of the farmers. Adams wrote to Thomas Jefferson that Shays' Rebellion was the action of a desperate people.

The farmers attacked the tax collectors during Shays' Rebellion.

Many people were worried. They were afraid such things might happen again if they didn't have a fair and strong government. Everything the colonies had fought for might be lost.

1. Name three differences among the states that became important after the Revolutionary War.
2. What was the name of the agreement that set up the first central government in the United States in 1781?
3. List four powers that the Articles of Confederation gave to Congress.
4. What powers did the Articles keep from Congress?

The Constitutional Convention

In May, 1787, fifty-five representatives chosen by their states met in Philadelphia. They came to discuss the problems of the Articles of Confederation. They soon decided that they would have to rewrite the Articles. For four months, they talked and argued about what the government of the United States should be like. When they were through, they had written the *Constitution of the United States*.

The representatives at the Constitutional Convention faced one main problem. They had to give the new government enough power to do the necessary jobs. But they did not want to give it too much power. If the government had too much power, it might take away the people's freedom. The members of the Convention did not want the new government ever to behave as Britain had behaved before the Revolution.

George Washington presided at the Constitutional Convention.

The representatives tried to solve this problem in several ways. One way was to carefully divide the powers of government between the state governments and the *federal,* or national, government. Some powers belong only to the federal government. Among these are the powers to print money and make treaties. The federal government can also collect taxes directly from the people for certain things. Other powers belong only to the states. State governments can pass laws about education, traffic, cities, and other things inside their boundaries. They can also collect taxes to pay for services the states provide.

The representatives also had to make many *compromises.* A compromise is reached when people on both sides of an argument agree to give in a little. Then each side can get part of what it wants. For example, the large states wanted the number of votes in Congress to be based on population. The more people a state had, the more votes it should have. The small states did not agree. They wanted all states to have the same number of votes. Otherwise, the large states would have too much power over the small ones. The representatives decided that there would be two parts to Congress. One part of Congress would be based on population. In the other part of Congress, each state would have two votes.

There were other compromises. One solved a problem for the states that had slaves. These states wanted slaves to count as part of their population. In this way, they could have more votes

Benjamin Franklin published this cartoon. The sections of the snake are the states.

182

in Congress. Yet they did not want to count slaves if there was to be a tax based on population. The compromise was to count only three out of every five slaves.

The Constitution was finally finished. Now it was up to the states to approve it. If nine states accepted it, it would become the law. Everywhere, people were talking about it. The people who were against the Constitution were called *antifederalists*. They were afraid of a strong central government. They didn't think enough powers were left to the states. Many people wanted the Constitution to spell out the people's rights. Still others did not like the Constitution because it did not do away with slavery.

The *federalists*, those who were for the Constitution, believed that a strong central government was necessary. Then other nations would respect and trust the United States. This would be good for trade and business. Also, the United States would be better able to defend itself. Federalists agreed that if the Constitution were accepted, they would support changes to protect the rights of the people.

The federalists won. By June of 1788, nine states had accepted the Constitution. The Constitution would become the basic law of the land. Between 1788 and 1791, the remaining four states joined the union.

TO DO

1. Which of these powers belong to the states: (a) laws about education inside state borders, (b) power to print money, (c) power to collect taxes, (d) power to make treaties with other nations?
2. Choose the correct answer. A compromise is made when (a) one group convinces another to do what it wants, (b) people agree to forget the whole thing, (c) each group agrees to give in a little.

ON YOUR OWN

3. Why were the representatives careful not to give the federal government too much power?
4. Would you have been a federalist or an antifederalist? Give an argument for one side or the other. (Remember what the government was like under the Articles of Confederation.)

Rules for a New Government

The writers of the Constitution divided the powers of government between the states and the federal government. They also divided the powers of the federal government, itself. The Constitution set up a government with three separate branches, or parts.

One branch makes the laws. This is the *legislative* (lej′ə slā′ tiv), or lawmaking, branch. It is called *Congress*.

The second branch carries out the laws. This is the *executive* (eg zek′yə tiv) branch.

The third branch settles questions about what the laws mean. This is the *judicial* (jü dish′əl) branch, or the courts.

Each branch has some—but not all—of the power needed to run the country. Each branch has some power to check, or limit, the other two. This keeps any one branch of the government from becoming too strong.

OUR NATIONAL GOVERNMENT

LEGISLATIVE
THE CONGRESS

1. Suggests and passes the laws
2. Approves judges and heads of department chosen by the President
3. May accuse executive or judicial officials of wrongdoing
4. Approves treaties
5. Has the right to declare war

EXECUTIVE
THE PRESIDENT

1. Makes the laws of Congress work
2. Suggests new laws and may veto laws
3. Chooses judges and heads of government departments
4. Makes treaties with other nations
5. Is Commander in Chief of the Armed Forces

JUDICIAL
THE SUPREME COURT AND LOWER COURTS

1. Settles questions about the laws
2. May rule that the President or other official has acted illegally
3. Settles questions about treaties

You know that Congress is made up of two parts. The *House of Representatives* is the part that is closest to the people. The number of representatives a state has depends on its population. States with more people have more representatives than those with fewer people. Representatives are elected every two years by the people of their state. The other part of Congress is the *Senate*. There are two senators from each state. They are elected every six years.

Representatives and senators discuss proposals for new laws. These are called *bills*. For a bill to become law, both parts of Congress must agree on it. The President must sign it.

Through the laws it can make, Congress controls trade between states and with other countries. It has the right to print money. It decides how much money people must pay in taxes to the federal government. Congress also has the right to declare wars. These are important activities in any government.

The executive branch is headed by the President, who is the leader of the country. The President is elected by the people every four years. When the United States Constitution was written, no other country elected its leader. Most countries didn't think their people were wise enough to choose a good leader.

The President directs the people who carry out the laws of the nation. Some of these people collect taxes. Some of them make deals and settle problems with other nations. Others have duties such as giving licenses to radio and TV stations. The President is also the Commander in Chief of the Armed Forces.

The President may recommend new bills. But Congress must approve them before they become law. The President also has the power to *veto,* or stop, a bill passed by Congress. Presidents can veto bills they think are not good for the country. Congress can try to pass a bill again. But it takes two-thirds of the members of Congress to pass a bill after the President has vetoed it.

The judicial branch has courts in all parts of the country. The highest court is called the Supreme Court. The Supreme Court has nine members. They are not elected. The President chooses them. The Senate must approve the President's choice. Supreme Court members may serve for as long as they live.

The Supreme Court in session in 1935.

The Supreme Court can decide whether or not a law passed by Congress or by a state is *unconstitutional*. A law is unconstitutional if it does not fit in with the ideas and purpose of the Constitution. No one has to obey a law that the Supreme Court has called unconstitutional. The Supreme Court can also decide if an action by the President is unconstitutional.

TO DO

1. Match the three branches of the Federal Government to the jobs they do:

    executive branch   carries out the laws
    judicial branch   makes laws
    legislative branch   settles questions about what the laws mean

2. Which of these statements is *not* true: (a) there are two senators from each state in Congress, (b) the President is chosen by the Supreme Court, (c) the right to declare war belongs to Congress, (d) the President can propose new laws?

ON YOUR OWN

3. Name one way in which each branch of the government can check or limit another branch.
4. What kinds of things could happen if the President or the Congress had all the powers of government?

The Bill of Rights

Built into the Constitution is a way of changing it. Such change is called an *amendment*. Amendments are hard to make. Three out of every four states have to agree to an amendment before it can become a part of the Constitution.

When the federalists were trying to have the Constitution accepted, they promised that some changes would be made. These changes would describe people's rights. In 1791, three years after the Constitution was accepted, the first ten amendments were added. These amendments make up the United States *Bill of Rights*. Since 1791, the Bill of Rights has been very important in United States history.

Here are some of the main points of the Bill of Rights. Read them carefully. You can see in them what early citizens meant by the word *freedom*.

Amendment 1: Congress will make no law that (a) sets up a religion, helps one religion over another, or takes away a person's right to believe in a religion; (b) takes away the freedom of newspapers to print the news; (c) takes away a person's right to say what he or she thinks; (d) tries to stop people from getting together in a peaceful crowd to complain about the government.

Amendment 2: The people's right to bear arms cannot be taken away.

Amendment 3: In peacetime, no soldiers can be sent to live in someone's house without the agreement of the owner. In wartime, laws must be passed if this is to be allowed.

Amendment 4: The government can't search people's homes and property without a good reason. The courts must give permission to search.

Amendment 5: People cannot be made to say anything against themselves in court. People cannot have their lives, freedom, or property taken away except according to the laws.

The government cannot take away the right of newspapers to print the news.

The government cannot take away the people's right to peaceful protest.

Amendment 6: People in court because they have been accused of committing a crime have the right to a *trial,* in public. They have the right to have a fair *jury* listen to the case. They have the right to know why they are being tried. They have the right to a lawyer to defend them.

People accused of a crime have the right to a trial by jury.

Amendment 7: People in court because of a disagreement about money have the right to a jury if the amount in question is over twenty dollars.

Amendment 8: Punishments for crimes cannot be cruel or strange. In case of fines, punishments should not be greater than the crime deserves.

Amendments 9 and 10: If a right is not mentioned in the Constitution, that doesn't mean the people don't have the right. Any rights not given to the United States in the Constitution belong to the states or the people.

Many more amendments have been added to the Constitution since the Bill of Rights. These amendments have made it possible for the Constitution to meet the needs of a changing nation.

TO DO

1. Look up the word *amend* in a dictionary. What does it mean?
2. Which amendment protects people from having their homes searched illegally?
3. Which amendment tells about freedom of religion?
4. Which amendment would you look up if you wanted to discuss the death penalty?

ON YOUR OWN

5. Which two amendments do you think are most important? Explain your choices.

CHAPTER REVIEW

1. Name two reasons why Congress could not govern the nation under the Articles of Confederation.
2. What is a compromise? Why was it important that the states compromise?
3. Choose the best answer: the Constitution is (a) an amendment, (b) part of the federal government, (c) the basic law of the United States, (d) the agreement that helped govern the nation right after the Revolution.
4. What is the United States Bill of Rights?

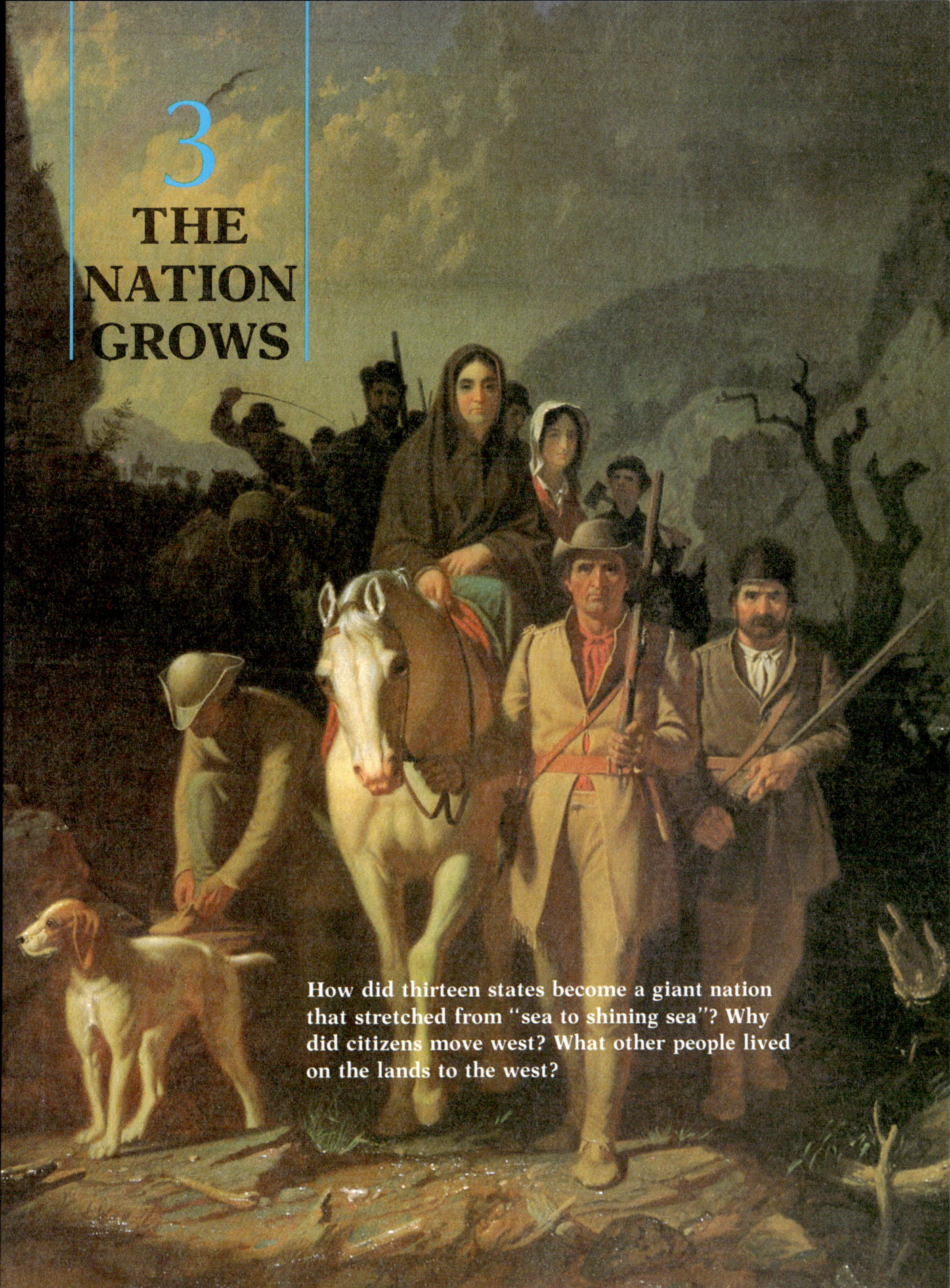

3
THE NATION GROWS

How did thirteen states become a giant nation that stretched from "sea to shining sea"? Why did citizens move west? What other people lived on the lands to the west?

Moving West

"The West" has meant different things to different people. It depends on when you lived.

To the early European explorers in North America, the West was the Atlantic coast. As settlements grew, the West became the area where settlements ended and the woods began.

For about one hundred years, only a few Europeans crossed the Appalachian Mountains. These mountains formed a natural boundary. They were very difficult to cross. At the time of the American Revolution, the Appalachians were the gate to the western *frontier.* A frontier is an unexplored or unsettled region.

Daniel Boone, hunter, explorer, and ex-soldier, was the first white person to lead a group of settlers through the Appalachians. In the South, near Tennessee, there was a path through the mountains. It was called the Cumberland Gap. Native Americans had used it for hundreds of years and had opened up trails around it. In 1775, Daniel Boone and about thirty woodcutters began clearing a road west through the Cumberland Gap. They joined trails. They cut down trees and bushes and rolled rocks out of the way. The road came to be known as "Wilderness Road." It was 480 kilometers (300 miles) long. Farmers, hunters, and trappers in large numbers began moving west.

By the end of the Revolutionary War, the territory of the United States stretched from the Atlantic Coast to the Mississippi River. The territory did not include Florida, which belonged to Spain.

In 1785, the government decided to make it easier for people to settle the Old Northwest. This was the frontier region between the Mississippi and the Ohio rivers. Find the Old Northwest on your map on page 191.

The government divided the land and offered it at very low prices. It passed laws about the rights of settlers. When a part of this territory had 60,000 people, it could become a state. The pioneers would then govern themselves.

Some of the first Americans to move to the Old Northwest were *land speculators.* They came to buy land cheaply so they

WESTWARD GROWTH

could sell it later for a profit. But most of the early settlers came to stay. Most were poor farmers who wanted land on which to build a home and a farm. These early pioneers faced a long hard trip over poor roads, through rivers, and across lakes. They faced dangers from the Miami, Sauk, and Fox peoples. These Native American groups fought to keep the settlers away from their hunting lands. They knew life would be hard. But they believed that better times would come. Soon they would have neighbors. Towns would grow. There would be churches and schools. In time, they would sell their crops. Then they could buy some of the things they had gone without.

By 1820, the United States had about 10 million people. Two-and-a-half million lived between the Appalachians and the Mississippi River. New states had joined the union. Kentucky joined in 1792 and Tennessee in 1796. Mississippi, Alabama, Ohio, Indiana, and Illinois had become states by 1819. The western frontier was moving farther west.

Many people traveled west in covered wagons.

TO DO

Choose the best answer:
1. After the Revolutionary War, "the West" meant (a) the Atlantic Ocean, (b) the Pacific coast, (c) the Cumberland Gap, (d) the land beyond the Appalachian Mountains.
2. A frontier is (a) land to the west, (b) all the things we do not know, (c) an unexplored or unsettled area.
3. The early western pioneers were willing to suffer hardships because (a) they knew better times would come, (b) they wanted to build a home and a farm, (c) they wanted cheap land, (d) all of the above.

ON YOUR OWN

4. Look at your map of the United States on page 193. What states today make up the territory once called the Old Northwest?

Life on the Frontier

The workload on the frontier was shared by all. The men and women, and even the children, cleared the forest and turned it into farmland. They planted food, raised livestock, and hunted wild animals.

The frontier cabin was a sort of factory. There, raw materials were made into things that could be used. Wood from the forest was made into tools. Cotton, flax, or wool was woven into cloth. The cloth was then made into blankets, shirts, and other clothes. Hogs and cattle were butchered at home. The meat that was not eaten was salted and saved. Grain and corn became breads, puddings, or souplike porridges. Cream was churned into butter. Animal fat was made into soap and candles.

Often the early settlers built homes of logs.

A woman who lived in the Old Northwest in the early 1800s remembers what it was like:

We did most of our work in the summer kitchen. That was where we had the big brick oven. We used to fire it twice a week and do a sight o' baking all at once. We'd make a hot fire in the oven. Then, when the bricks were heated through, we'd scrape out all the coals with a big iron scraper. We would dump the coals into the fireplace. Then we'd shove in the roast and fowls, the pies, and bread. At other times, we'd use the open fireplace.

It was so easy, since we had no screens, to let the flies spoil everything. My mother just wouldn't have it so. We weren't allowed to bring apples into the house in summer.

The home was a factory. This woman is making candles.

Apples attracted flies. If any of us dropped a speck of butter or cream on the floor, my mother would run for a cloth to wipe it up. At mealtime, someone stood and fanned to keep the flies away while the others ate.

In warm weather, we washed outdoors. We used our well water. We'd draw a barrel of water and put one shovel of ashes into it. It would just suds up like soft water, so white and clean. Our starch was of two kinds. It was made from a dough worked round and round until it was smooth. Or it was made from grated potato cooked to the right consistency.

My mother used to spin. She made beautiful fine thread. I used to love to watch her at the spinning wheel. I can just close my eyes and see Ma standing over there spinning a thread as far as from here to the bed—say, twelve feet long.

When I was eight years old, she wove me a plaid dress of which I was very proud. I remember the pattern. There were eight threads of brown, then one of red, one of blue, one of red, then brown again. It made the prettiest flannel. That dress lasted me for years.

Like the Amish and the earliest settlers in the 1600s and 1700s, the western pioneers had to depend on their neighbors. Life on the frontier could be rough as well as lonely. Cooperation was important for difficult jobs. Visiting and sharing was important to people who often lived 5 or 6 kilometers (3 or 4 miles) from one another. A man from Ohio described the cooperation of pioneers in this way:

Houses and barns were raised by the collection of many neighbors together on one day. Men rolled up the logs in a clearing. They grubbed out the underbrush. Then they cut the logs for a house or barn. When such a gathering of men took place, the women also shared a job. There was quilting, sewing, or spinning of thread for some poor neighbor. This would bring together a mixed party. Usually, after supper there would be a dance or at least plays. These filled a good part of the night. The evening wound up with the young fellows seeing the girls home in the short hours or, if they went home early, sitting with them by the fire.

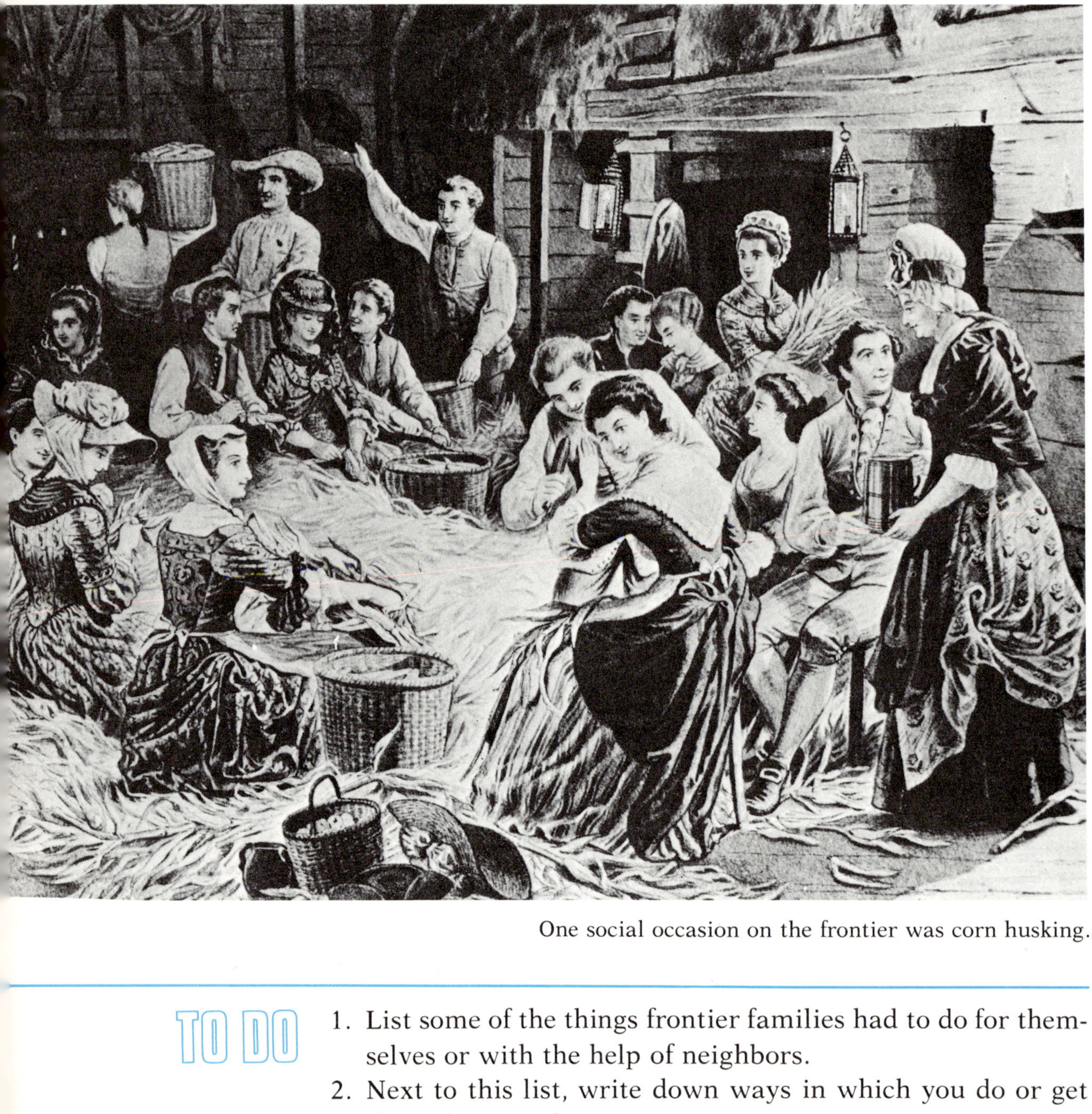

One social occasion on the frontier was corn husking.

TO DO

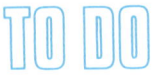

1. List some of the things frontier families had to do for themselves or with the help of neighbors.
2. Next to this list, write down ways in which you do or get these things today.

ON YOUR OWN

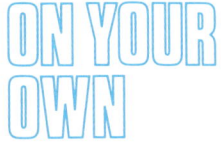

3. Would you like to have lived in the Old Northwest in the early 1800s? Give reasons for your answer.

Beyond the Mississippi

Thomas Jefferson was elected the third President of the United States in 1800. He served two terms. Probably his greatest contribution as President was the Louisiana Purchase.

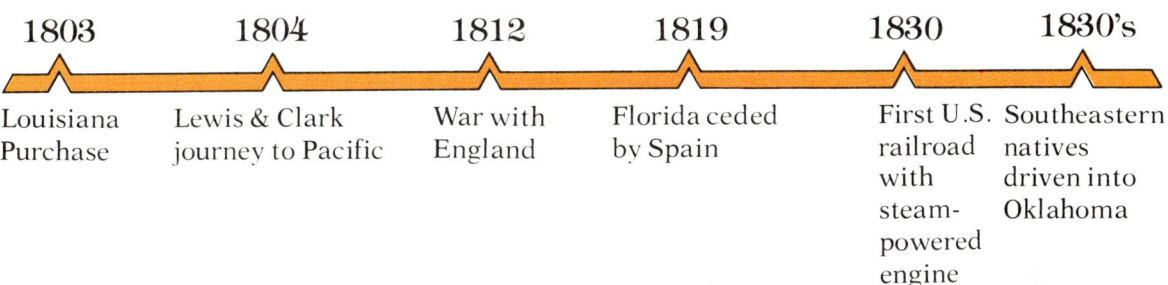

1803 — Louisiana Purchase
1804 — Lewis & Clark journey to Pacific
1812 — War with England
1819 — Florida ceded by Spain
1830 — First U.S. railroad with steam-powered engine
1830's — Southeastern natives driven into Oklahoma

When Jefferson became President, France owned much of the land west of the Mississippi River. It also owned the port city of New Orleans. New Orleans was very important to American farmers settling west of the Appalachians. They wanted to send their goods down the Mississippi and ship them from New Orleans. This was easier than sending them over the mountain roads.

In 1803, Jefferson sent two representatives to France to try to buy New Orleans. To his surprise, the French ruler offered to sell the whole Louisiana Territory. For $15 million, Thomas Jefferson bought a territory that doubled the size of the United States. Look at the map on page 193. The Louisiana Territory stretched from the Mississippi River to the Rocky Mountains.

The following year, President Jefferson sent a band of forty-two people to explore Louisiana. They were led by Meriwether Lewis and William Clark. Lewis and Clark were to learn all about the land, climate, animals, and plants of the new territory. They were to study the languages and customs of the Native Americans of the area. They were also told to map the rivers and to go beyond Louisiana to the Pacific Ocean.

One-and-a-half long years later, the daring explorers reached the Pacific. A brave young Shoshone (Shə'shōn ē) woman named Sacajawea (Sak'a gä wē ä) had guided them

Lewis and Clark met many Native Americans on their explorations.

much of the way. Lewis and Clark made careful notes of all they saw and learned. They opened the way for millions of settlers who would follow.

In 1812, a war broke out between Britain and the United States. There were several reasons for this war. One reason was that the British were causing trouble in American lands west of the Appalachians. During the War of 1812, the Americans tried to invade Canada. It was a short war. Neither side won or lost. But in treaties signed after the war, the boundary between Canada and the United States was set all the way to the Pacific Ocean. The United States and Britain also agreed to share the Oregon Territory. A few years later, in 1819, the United States bought Florida from Spain.

As more and more citizens moved into the new territories, they came into contact with the people who had lived there for thousands of years. There were fierce battles as Native Americans tried to keep the settlers away. These battles were usually followed by treaties. In these treaties, the native peoples would agree to trade some of their lands. In return, the government promised to protect their rights to their remaining lands.

Sacajawea helped Lewis and Clark.

East of the Mississippi, the South was becoming an important cotton-growing area. Thousands of settlers crossed the Appalachians looking for good cotton lands. Several Native American groups lived in the Southeast. Most of them were farmers. Some, like the Cherokees (Cher′ə kēz), had become used to European ways. They owned cotton land and cattle. They had developed their own written language. They also had schools and a newspaper. These things didn't make any difference to the settlers who wanted their lands. In 1830, Congress passed a law ordering all Native Americans to move west of the Mississippi. Congress promised them that the lands of the Great Plains would be theirs forever.

Cherokee written language.

201

These Native Americans have been forced to leave their land.

So the native peoples of the United States were moved from their homes. Many were sent to dry, treeless places very different from the woodlands they knew. President Andrew Jackson sent the army to force out those who would not leave. During their long march west in the middle of winter, one fourth of the Cherokee population died of hunger, cold, and sickness. This march is known today as the "Trail of Tears."

TO DO

1. How far west did the United States go in 1803, after the Louisiana Purchase?
2. Which of the following was a result of the War of 1812: (a) the United States bought Florida from Spain, (b) the United States won control of the Oregon Territory, (c) the boundary with Canada was set all the way to the Pacific?

ON YOUR OWN

3. Why did settlers and Native Americans fight so often, as settlers moved west?
4. Look at your map of the United States on page 191. What states today make up what used to be the Louisiana Territory?

Oregon and the Southwest

While the Far West was still a frontier, a group of hardy explorers was crisscrossing its deserts, mountains, and rivers. These were the fur trappers.

Trappers often lived and worked along with Native Americans. Many of them caught beaver by the streams and rivers of the Oregon Territory. They sold the fur from beaver and other animals to trading companies. These companies then sent the furs to the East and to Europe. Jim Beckwourth, a black, was a famous mountaineer and trapper. He also became a chief of the Crow tribe.

By the 1830s and 1840s, the trappers' system of trails was being used by traders, missionaries, and farmers. News of Oregon's rich soil, forests, and rivers was bringing a new wave of settlers to the West.

These new pioneers traveled in large covered wagons called *Conestogas* (Kon'ə stō'gez). The wagons traveled in groups of about sixty led by a captain, or wagonmaster.

Jim Beckwourth

These settlers have stopped to cook a meal.

Wagon trains usually left from Independence, Missouri. The trip west took about six months. There were many dangers. Sometimes, there were attacks by the native people of the Plains. But the everyday dangers were worse. The summer sun blazed down. The ovenlike heat dried out the wooden parts of the wagons. The spokes in the wheels would often break or fall out. Animals and people sometimes drowned crossing steams. Bad drinking water and spoiled food weakened people. As a result, deadly diseases sometimes swept through wagon trains.

By the middle 1840s, Americans in the Oregon Territory asked to join the United States. In 1846, Britain agreed to give up its claims on this land. It was decided that Oregon was part of the United States because United States pioneers had traveled there and had built their homes there.

South of the Oregon Territory, other United States citizens

Thousands of people used the Oregon Trail to the West.

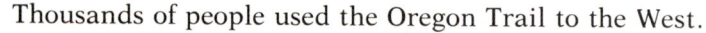

were settling a large stretch of land that belonged to Mexico. This is the area we now call the American Southwest. Look at the map on page 193. Draw an imaginary line from San Antonio, Texas, through Santa Fe, New Mexico, to San Francisco, California. Along this line, and south of it, Spanish-speaking missionaries, soldiers, ranchers, and farmers had explored and settled the land.

In 1821, the people of Mexico won their independence from Spain. And they welcomed United States trade and settlement in their northern lands. The Santa Fe trail became an important trade route. Long trains of pack mules carried goods back and forth between Santa Fe and Independence, Missouri. New England shipowners sent ships around South America to trade for cattle hides in California.

Many citizens came to Texas. Some became ranchers. They copied the houses and ways of the Mexican ranchers. They rounded up the wild cattle and horses that roamed on the prairies. Others became owners of large cotton plantations.

By 1834, the United States citizens outnumbered the Mexican people in Texas. They felt they could no longer live under Mexican laws. In 1836, the Texans declared their independence from Mexico. For nine years, Texas was an independent country. It had its own constitution and president, Sam Houston. It was called the Lone Star Republic. Then, in 1845, Texas joined the United States as the twenty-eighth state.

The border between Texas and Mexico had not been settled, however. In 1846, Mexican and United States soldiers shot at each other in the disputed area. At the same time, many United States citizens were interested in gaining California and other lands in the Southwest. In 1846, the United States declared war on Mexico.

The war with Mexico lasted two years. After many battles, United States soldiers captured Mexico City. In 1848, Mexico and the United States signed an agreement. The Rio Grande became the border between Texas and Mexico. What are now the states of California, New Mexico, and Arizona became part of the United States. The United States mainland as we know it today was almost complete.

Longhorn cattle were grazed on the plain.

TO DO

1. United States pioneers made the dangerous trip to Oregon because: (a) they wanted to become ranchers, (b) they heard about the rich farming and forest lands of Oregon, (c) Mexicans had invited them to settle there.
2. Many citizens moved to the Southwest (a) for the rich cotton and ranching lands, (b) to trade for beaver fur, (c) to sell cattle hides to the Mexicans.
3. Look at your map on page 193. Name the territories that became part of the United States between 1845 and 1848.
4. What states today used to be a part of Mexico?

ON YOUR OWN

5. Give two reasons why the United States went to war with Mexico in 1845.

The Gold Rush

It was a clear, cold morning in January. I shall never forget that morning. As I was taking my usual walk, my eye was caught by a glimpse of something shining in the bottom of a ditch. There was about a foot of running water there. I reached my hand down and picked it up. It made my heart thump, for I felt certain it was gold. The piece was about half the size and the shape of a pea. Then I saw another piece in the water. . . .

The exact date was January 24, 1848. The place was a ditch near the Sacramento River in California. James Marshall, a Scottish carpenter, had made an exciting discovery.

News of the gold spread quickly to all parts of the country and the world. A new wave of pioneers was to rush to the Far West.

Newspapers in the East were filled with stories about the rich gold deposits in California. Guidebooks told people what to take. They listed the following supplies: a shotgun, horseshoes, pots and pans, a water barrel, a lantern, bars of lye soap, a rubber knapsack, a harmonica, a pick, and a pan.

Farmers left their fields. Ships lay deserted in San Francisco Bay as sailors ran into the hills to hunt for gold. Other people came overland. They traveled from the East, first by railroad, then by steamboat. Then they crossed the Plains in wagons and on mules. Others, including some foreigners, came by sea.

In 1849, more than 80,000 hopeful newcomers arrived in California. They were called the *forty-niners*. They crowded into mining camps with names like Red Dog, Poker Flat, and Grub Gulch.

Life for the forty-niners was very different from the wonderful stories they had heard. A Philadelphia schoolteacher described it in this way:

We made $3.00 each today. This life has affected my health. Our diet consists of hard tack [a hard biscuit made of flour and water], flour we eat half cooked, and salt pork. Sometimes, we have some salmon which we buy from the

Indians. Vegetables are not to be found. Our feet are wet all day while a hot sun shines down upon our heads. The very air parches the skin like the hot air of an oven.

After our day of labor, we lie down in our clothes. We rob our feet of their boots to make a pillow out of them. Near morning, there is always a change in the temperature, and several blankets become necessary. The feet and hands of a newcomer become blistered and lame. Besides all these causes of sickness, the worries of so many men who leave their families to come to this land of gold, all work to the same result.

We are quickly beginning to realize that our chances of making a fortune are about the same as those of drawing a prize in a lottery.

By the middle of the 1850s, many forty-niners had left. Most left poor. Some traded a bag of gold dust for a ticket home by ship. Some stayed as laborers with big mining companies. These businesses had heavy equipment that could blast rocks where gold had been found. Some stayed to farm the rich valleys of the area. Others stayed as artisans and saloonkeepers in the towns that had sprung up all over California.

These people are mining gold in California.

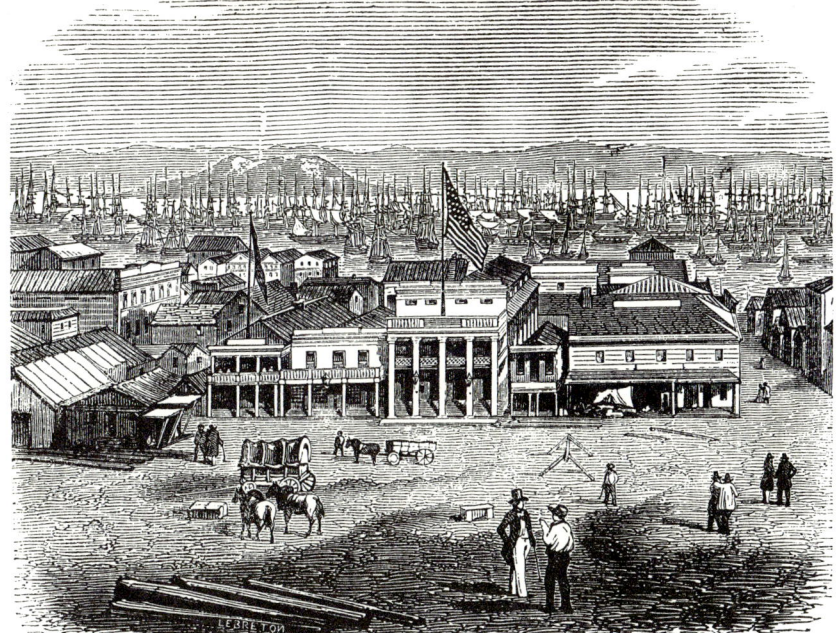

San Francisco was clogged with ships during the gold rush.

San Francisco had become an important center of trade almost overnight. Thousands of people had come to the town during the gold rush. These people needed food, shelter, and supplies. More and more ships arrived bringing goods to town. The newcomers needed lawyers to arrange the sale of property. The needed banks. Soon, homes, churches, and schools were being built.

The gold rush was over. But it opened up yet another part of the American West.

Choose the best answer:
1. The main idea of this lesson is: (a) the gold rush brought thousands of people to the West, (b) most forty-niners left poor, (c) James Marshall made an important discovery.
2. Look again at the description of life in a mining camp on page 207. The main idea in the schoolteacher's story is: (a) none of the forty-niners made a fortune, (b) good food was hard to find, (c) life in the camps was very difficult.

TO DO

3. How were the forty-niners like many of the Spaniards who came to the New World 300 years before?

ON YOUR OWN

Mexican Americans in the Southwest

There were about 80,000 Mexican Americans living in California and the Southwest in the 1850s. These Spanish-speaking people were the pioneers of what had been the frontier lands of northern Mexico. They founded and settled many of the cities that have Spanish names today. Most of these people were mestizo. They had Indian, Spanish, and sometimes black ancestors.

The 1848 treaty which ended the war with Mexico promised them "all the rights of citizens of the United States." What happened to these people, living now under a new government?

The Mexican Americans soon became a minority. Before the gold rush, most of the people in California were Spanish-speaking. By 1850, the population of California had grown to 380,000 people. Now only 15 out of every 100 were Spanish-speaking. The same thing happened in Texas and Arizona. As more English-speaking people moved into these lands, the proportion of Mexican Americans became smaller. This meant that Mexican Americans now had less power. It was harder for them to protect their rights.

Mexican Americans had problems in the mining camps of California. Life was especially hard for those with darker skins. Most Mexican Americans were still seen as "foreigners" by other Americans. The other Americans didn't want "these foreigners" taking any gold. Many were thrown out of the camps.

The *American Flag*, a Texas newspaper of the time, explained that there was a *double standard* of justice. This meant that United States justice did not treat Spanish- and English-speaking people in the same way. Here is what the newspaper said:

> Americans have at times committed offenses which have been overlooked. If committed by Mexicans, they would have been punished harshly. But, when election time comes, it is wonderful to see the friendship there is for the Mexican voters and the protection they are given. Promises of all kinds are made to them. And, as they are made, the promises are broken.

Throughout these years, Mexican Americans continued to press for their rights. A few were elected to positions in government. Many joined organizations to discuss problems they shared as Mexican Americans. The Spanish-language newspapers encouraged people to vote. They told them to have pride in their language and to learn English, as well.

San Antonio was an important city when Texas joined the United States. Today, more than half the people in San Antonio are Mexican Americans.

After 1910, there were political problems in Mexico and few jobs. Many jobs were open in the United States at that time. Many more Mexicans now moved into the United States Southwest. This new group reminded the older Mexican Americans of their cultural ties with Mexico. It also gave them the strength of numbers to work together for a better future.

Cesar Chavez leads a demonstration.

TO DO

1. In which of these ways were Mexican Americans different from other people settling in the Southwest: (a) they spoke another language, (b) they were newcomers to the area, (c) they came to make a better living?
2. Name some of the problems faced by Mexican Americans in the mid-1800s.

ON YOUR OWN

3. Choose the correct meaning. A double standard of justice means: (a) that two groups are not treated in the same way under the law, (b) that Mexican Americans were punished harshly for things they didn't do.

CHAPTER REVIEW

1. What was the western boundary of the United States after the Revolutionary War?
2. What was its western boundary in 1848?
3. In which of these ways did the United States get its new lands: (a) it fought wars, (b) it made treaties, (c) it bought land, (d) all of the above?
4. Make a list of the hardships faced by western pioneers. Write down as many as you can think of.
5. What groups of people lost much of their lands as Americans moved west?

4
SPANISH-SPEAKING AMERICANS

Who are Spanish-speaking Americans today? Where do they live? What are some values and traditions of Hispanic Americans?

Se habla español

Have you ever seen this sign before? It is found in many stores and public places in the United States. Do you know what the sign means in English?

In English, *se habla español* (se äb′lə es′pän yōl′) means "Spanish is spoken here." This sign tells Spanish-speaking customers that someone there can speak their language. Why do you suppose such signs are needed?

Today, there are about 11 million Spanish-speaking people in the United States. That is five out of every hundred people here. Another word for Spanish-speaking is *Hispanic*.

Hispanic Americans share the Spanish language. They also share other parts of Spanish culture. But they are not all the same, just as other United States citizens are not all the same. Hispanic Americans have different backgrounds and ways of living.

Most Hispanic people in the United States have come from countries settled by Spain 400 years ago.

As you know, Mexican American families have been living in the Southwest for hundreds of years. Many more Mexicans have arrived since the early days. Mexican Americans today are the largest Hispanic group in the United States.

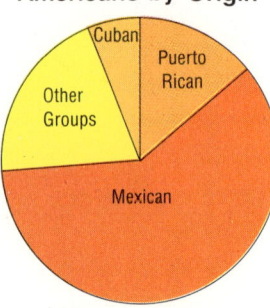

Spanish Speaking Americans by Origin

LARGEST HISPANIC GROUPS IN THE UNITED STATES

1970 TOTAL POPULATION					
Mexican Origin		**Puerto Rican Origin**		**Cuban Origin**	
6,455,000				689,000	
STATES WITH LARGEST POPULATION					
California	1,857,267	New York	916,608	Florida	250,406
Texas	1,619,064	New Jersey	138,896	New York	89,596
Arizona	239,811	Illinois	87,477	New Jersey	68,048
Illinois	160,419	California	50,929	California	47,560
New Mexico	119,049	Pennsylvania	44,263	Illinois	20,796
Colorado	103,584				

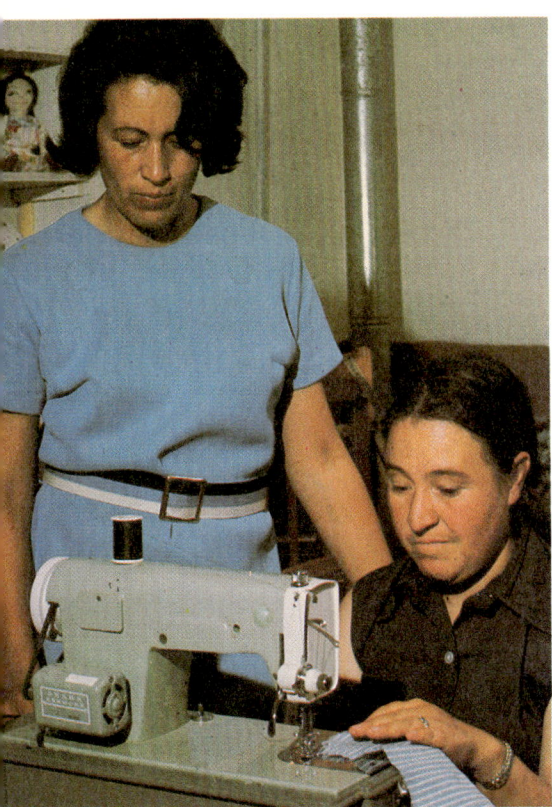

Hispanic Americans are active in all walks of American life.

Puerto Rican Americans are the second largest Spanish-speaking group. Puerto Rico is an island southwest of Florida. All Puerto Ricans are United States citizens. Americans can travel between the mainland United States and Puerto Rico as easily as they can go from New York to California.

Cubans came to the United States in large numbers in the 1960s. They left Cuba after the Cuban government became Communist in 1959. Many Cubans settled in Florida. Most of them have become United States citizens.

Look at the population for persons of Mexican, Puerto Rican, and Cuban origin living in the United States. Then look at the map of the United States on page 30. Find the states where most Spanish-speaking people live.

Most other Spanish-speaking people here have come from Spanish-speaking countries in Central and South America. Below is a list of them. Do you know anyone from these countries?

Argentina	Ecuador	Paraguay
Bolivia	El Salvador	Peru
Chile	Guatemala	Puerto Rico (United States)
Colombia	Honduras	Uruguay
Costa Rica	Mexico	Venezuela
Cuba	Nicaragua	
Dominican Republic	Panama	

This part of your book is mainly about Mexican Americans. You will learn something about Mexican Americans as you come to know the Morelos family. The Moreloses live in San Antonio, Texas. Anita Morelos, the eldest child, is about your age.

1. About how many Hispanic Americans are there?
2. What are the three main Hispanic groups?

3. In what states do most Hispanic Americans live? Can you think of some reasons why these groups live where they do?
4. Look at the pictures of Hispanic Americans on page 215. What kind of jobs are they doing?
5. In what other ways do you think these people are different from one another?

Mexican Traditions and the Roman Catholic Church

Most Hispanic Americans are members of the Roman Catholic church. The Catholic church played an important role in the history of all Hispanic countries, including Mexico. Many of the cities in the American Southwest are named after Catholic saints. San Francisco, Santa Barbara, and San Antonio are examples.

Today, going to church and to religious festivals helps create a feeling of *cultural identity* among many Mexican Americans. Cultural identity is a feeling of belonging, or togetherness, among members of a cultural group. Shared beliefs and a common history help create this feeling of togetherness. *Traditions*, things that people do year after year, are also important to cultural identity.

Among Mexican Americans, Christmas, or *La Navidad* (Lä Nä′vi däd′), is one of the happiest religious holidays. From

Mexican Americans on a *Las Posadas* procession.

December 6 to December 24, one may see people singing Christmas carols and asking for shelter. They are acting out the story of Mary and Joseph. They search for a place to stay overnight as Mary and Joseph did in Bethlehem. This tradition among Mexican Americans is called *Las Posadas* (Läs Pō sä′däz). *Posada* means "inn" or "shelter."

Las Posadas is like a traveling play. The whole neighborhood is the stage. At the first two stops, "Mary" and "Joseph" are turned away. At the third house, they receive *posada*, or shelter. They usually come into the house and are served cake or cookies. Each night, the procession gets closer and closer to the church. Finally, on Christmas Eve, the actors arrive at the neighborhood church. There they receive the last posada. Then, at midnight, Christmas Mass is held at the church.

In Mexico and some areas of Southwestern United States, part of the Christmas celebration is held on the night of January 5. In the Christmas story, this is the date when the three wise men bring gifts to the infant Jesus. In towns close to the Mexican border, Mexican American children leave their shoes on the doorstep overnight. On the following morning, January 6, they find their Christmas presents near their shoes. This day is called *El Dia de los Reyes* (El Dē′ə dā lōs Rā′es), or day of the kings.

The *piñata* (pin yä′tə) is another Christmas tradition among Mexican Americans. A *piñata* is a clay pot decorated with paint and paper. It is made to look like a clown or like a rooster, peacock, or other animal. It is filled with wrapped candies, gum, small toys of all kinds, and balloons. A young child is blindfolded and given a long stick. The child is then turned round and round and told to swing at the *piñata*.

Sometimes the *piñata* is hung from a rope over a beam or a tree. As the child swings at it, the *piñata* can be jerked out of reach. In this way, each child gets a turn before the *piñata* breaks. Finally, it is broken, and the goodies fly out in all directions.

Other American families also have religious celebrations in December, such as Christmas or Hanukkah. The Eastern Orthodox religion celebrates Christmas on January 7. Many families do special things during these holidays. Some burn a big Yule log in the fireplace. Other families make hot, spicy punches. Some

Children enjoying a piñata party.

families open Christmas presents on Christmas Eve rather than Christmas Day. Others light candles or sing by a piano. These family traditions have something to do with cultural background.

TO DO

1. Which of the following things help create a feeling of cultural identity in a group: (a) a common language, (b) a common friend, (c) shared beliefs, (d) a common history, (e) traditions?
2. What are traditions? Define the word in one or two complete sentences.

ON YOUR OWN

3. If your family celebrates Christmas or Hanukkah or another special religious holiday, do you also do special things? What things?
4. Will you do these things when you are grown up?

The Morelos Family

Manuel Morelos and Rosa Delgado were born and raised on small farms near Allende (ä yān′dā), a town in northern Mexico. Both came from large families. They went to the same school in Allende.

Manuel Morelos quit school when he was in the eighth grade. He went to work packing oranges to help his family. Rosa Delgado finished the ninth grade. Then she, too, had to go to work in the orange groves. Later, Manuel Morelos studied mechanics in the nearby city of Monterrey. He loves this kind of work, but there were no jobs for mechanics in Allende.

After Manuel and Rosa were married, they moved to San Antonio. It was very hard at first. But finally, Manuel Morelos was able to find a job as a mechanic. Rosa Morelos is very good at sewing. At times, she works at a curtain factory.

The Morelos family and neighbors.

Anita Morelos, their daughter, was born in San Antonio. Then, over the years, the other Morelos children were born—Elena, Pepe, and Manuelín. The Morelos children are *first-generation Americans.* This means that they were born in the United States, but their parents were not.

Fruit market near the Morelos home.

The Moreloses live in a *barrio* (bär′yō). *Barrio* is the Spanish word for "neighborhood." This word, like many other Spanish words, has also become part of English. In English, *barrio* means a neighborhood of Spanish-speaking people. There are several barrios in San Antonio.

Barrios are important in preserving Mexican American culture. Mexican families just arriving in the United States find Spanish-speaking people in the barrios. Shopkeepers speak Spanish. Supermarkets carry Mexican foods and spices. Old people and young children can talk to each other in the language they know best and love.

In places with large numbers of Hispanic Americans, signs are in Spanish and English.

People in the barrio also help one another a great deal. Neighbors or relatives take care of the children when a parent has to go to work, go shopping, or go to the doctor.

In the barrios, the family is very important. Like the Moreloses, many Mexican Americans came from small farming communities. In small farming communities, parents, children, grandparents, uncles, aunts, and cousins are very close. They see each other often. They depend on each other in good times and bad. Older members of the family are greatly respected. Relatives usually live near one another. This kind of large family with many relatives is called an *extended family*. One hundred years ago most families were extended families.

Many American families are *nuclear* (nü′klē ər) *families*. This means that family life centers mainly on parents and children. Grandparents, uncles, aunts, and cousins usually don't live near one another. They don't see one another very often. Many American families move often.

Extended families remain important to Mexican Americans. Most Mexican Americans write, telephone, and visit relatives when they can. They keep up with family news. They usually help one another in many ways.

Sometimes, it is hard to keep up these family relationships. A young couple may move to another neighborhood or city. This separates them from other relatives. But others, especially Mexican Americans living close to the Mexican border, are able to keep in touch with members of their extended families. Family relationships are an important part of Hispanic American culture.

TO DO

1. Name two things that are typical of life in a barrio.
2. Do you have an extended family or a nuclear family?
3. List some advantages and disadvantages for both kinds of families.

ON YOUR OWN

4. Were you born in a foreign country? Or are you a first-, second-, third-, or fourth-generation American?
5. Make a chart of your family. Include as many aunts, uncles, cousins, and other relatives as you can think of. Some of these relatives may live in foreign countries. You might use different colors to show relatives you have never met and relatives you see only once a year, once a month, or once a week. Ask your parents to help you with this chart.

At Home

These three conversations take place in the Morelos home. At home, the Morelos family almost always uses Spanish. Remember, then, that these conversations would be in Spanish.

Read the conversations carefully. See what you can learn about the Morelos family and Mexican American culture.

CONVERSATION 1

Rosa Morelos: Anita, finish your food. We have ice cream tonight. Your father and I have something to tell you.

Pepe: What is the matter, *mamá*?

Rosa Morelos: Your father has a new job, Pepe. Now we can afford to move to a bigger house.

Elena: Move, *mamá*?

Anita: I don't want to move, *mamá*. I like my house and my friends.

The Morelos family at home.

Manuel Morelos: Anita, you have said many times that you wish you had your own bedroom.

Anita: Sí, papá. But I like to walk to school with Angela. Maria moved and now she has to ride a bus, and children call her names sometimes. Also, the church is very far from her house. *Mamá* likes our church and Father Esteban. Don't you, *mamá?*

Rosa Morelos: Sí, Anita, but moving to a bigger house will give us many advantages. Your father and I will decide.

Manuel Morelos: Don't worry about it, children. *Mamá* and I will think about it for a while. Maybe friends are more important than a new house—yes?

CONVERSATION 2

Rosa Morelos: Manuel, I want to speak with you about an important matter. Can you come into the kitchen? Please close the door.

Manuel Morelos: Is something wrong, Rosita?

Rosa Morelos: Nothing is wrong, but I've been thinking about Allende and our relatives. They can't come to San Antonio for a visit. We should go there . . . perhaps in July. You and the children can go then. The children should get to know their cousins. And I would like to see my sister again.

Manuel Morelos: It's a good idea. I think we have enough money saved up. I will make plans at work, and we will tell the children. You and Anita can write a letter to Allende.

CONVERSATION 3

Manuel Morelos: Anita, leave the TV alone.

Anita: But *papá*, I want to see Disneyland.

Manuel Morelos: Anita, you know that I always watch *Señor* Ortega's (Ôr tā'ga) news program.

Anita: But why, *papá?*

Manuel Morelos: I want you and Elena to listen to Spanish being spoken. You speak mostly English at school, and I speak English more and more at work. *Mamá* and I want you always to know Spanish.

Anita: We speak Spanish at home, in church, in the stores, and with our friends. How can I ever forget it? Even the

Watching television.

newspaper is in Spanish. Oh, *papá*, would it be all right for Pam to give me her English newspaper once in a while? We sometimes have to bring articles from the newspaper to school.

Manuel Morelos: That's fine. You have permission to read Pam's newspaper. But we will continue to listen to Spanish programs on television. Besides, it will help you when you meet your cousin Raul (Rä ül´).

TO DO

1. What is the main idea in Conversation 1?
   a. Anita wants her own bedroom.
   b. Anita's friend Maria moved away.
   c. Rosa Morelos wants to know how the children feel about moving.
2. Why does Rosa Morelos want her children to know their cousins better?
3. Why is it important for the Morelos children to know Spanish?

ON YOUR OWN

4. Name two of Anita's responsibilities in the Morelos family.
5. Can you find examples of things that are important to the Morelos family?
6. Are these talks different from conversations that might take place in your family? If so, how? Are they similar? If so, in what ways?

Learning in Two Languages

Do you remember your very first day in school? Do you remember your feelings on that day? Were you excited? Were you nervous?

Probably you could understand what your teacher and classmates were saying. But suppose the first thing your teacher said was in Polish, or German, or Japanese? How would you have felt? What would you have done?

For many Hispanic American children, Spanish is the only language spoken at home. When the children reach school age, they speak and understand only Spanish. But the language in their schools is English.

Today, especially in the Southwest, this is changing. More and more lessons are taught in both Spanish and English. This means that children can learn in their first language. In this way, they won't fall behind in their lessons. Then, little by little, they can learn English as their second language. When this happens, they will become *bilingual* (bī ling′gwel). If you are bilingual, you can speak, read, and write in two languages.

Hispanic American children today are learning in two languages in school.

These children are using their Spanish texts.

Anita Morelos is enrolled in a bilingual program at school. In the fifth grade, she is studying reading, science, math, and social studies in both English and Spanish. Her classroom has books in both languages. Ms. Ricardo (Ri kär′dō), her teacher, is bilingual.

Anita speaks both English and Spanish perfectly now. In a way, this means that she has two cultures instead of only one. And she is growing up proud of both.

TO DO

1. Look up the word *bilingual* in a dictionary. What does the prefix *bi-* mean? What does *lingua* mean?
2. What would you call someone who spoke many *(multi)* languages?

ON YOUR OWN

3. Name two reasons why it might be good to teach subjects in English and one other language.
4. List as many jobs as you can think of in which it would be important to know two languages.

CHAPTER REVIEW

1. What are the three largest groups of Hispanic Americans?
2. Where do most Mexican Americans live? Why do most of them live in this area?
3. Describe one Hispanic tradition.
4. Name at least three things that are valued in Mexican American culture.

228

5
PLANNING A TRIP

What decisions have to be made when planning a trip? How do you use a road map? What kinds of changes happen when you go from one country to another?

Planning the Trip to Allende

ANITA'S CLOSET

Shoes
Sandals
Rainboots
Winter coat
Spring coat
Raincoat
Jeans
Sweater
Blouses
Cotton dresses
Wool dresses
Mittens
Cowboy hat
Bathing suit

Have you ever taken a long trip? What are some of the things you might have to think about before you start on a trip? What are some decisions you might have to make?

Anita and her family are going to the town of Allende. Allende is located in northeastern Mexico in the state of Nuevo León (Nü ā′vo Lə ōn′). Anita's mother and father were born in Allende. Many of their relatives still live there. Anita has never visited Allende before.

Among other things, Anita has to decide what clothes to take. She wonders what the weather will be like in Allende. The charts on this page tell how warm Allende is and how much it rains during the month of July, when Anita will be visiting.

On this page is a list of some things Anita has in her closet. Which items would you take if you were going to Allende in July?

Of course, there are other things to think about. The Moreloses are going to stay on a farm. But they will also be driving through cities and towns. They may decide to spend several days visiting the city of Monterrey (mänt′e′rā). How would these things influence your choice of clothes if you were Anita? If you were Anita's brother?

Anita's father has asked her to choose a route for the trip. To do this Anita needs a road map. She also needs other information.

Her parents have told her they will leave San Antonio at noon. They do not want to drive at night. The family will spend

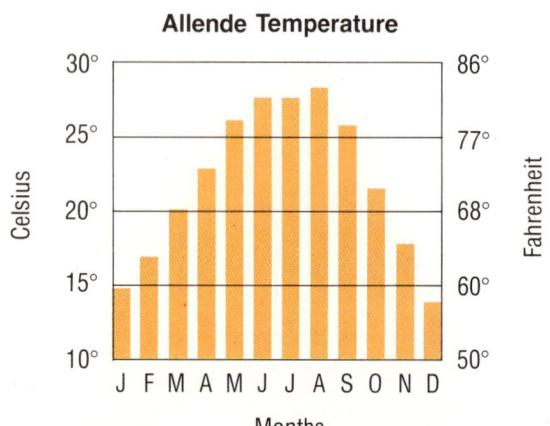

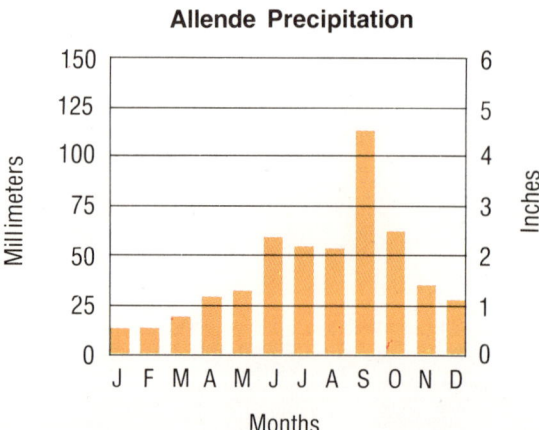

the night at a place chosen by Anita. The next day they will drive the rest of the way. They want to arrive at the farm in the afternoon.

Anita talked about her plans for the trip with a friend. Her friend had been to Mexico only a few months before.

Here are some other things Anita's parents told her. Many of the roads in Texas are fairly wide, straight, and new. You drive at a speed of 80 kilometers (50 miles) per hour on them. Of course, you go much slower driving through a city. The roads in Mexico are narrower and more winding. It is best to figure on driving at about 60 kilometers (38 miles) an hour on these roads.

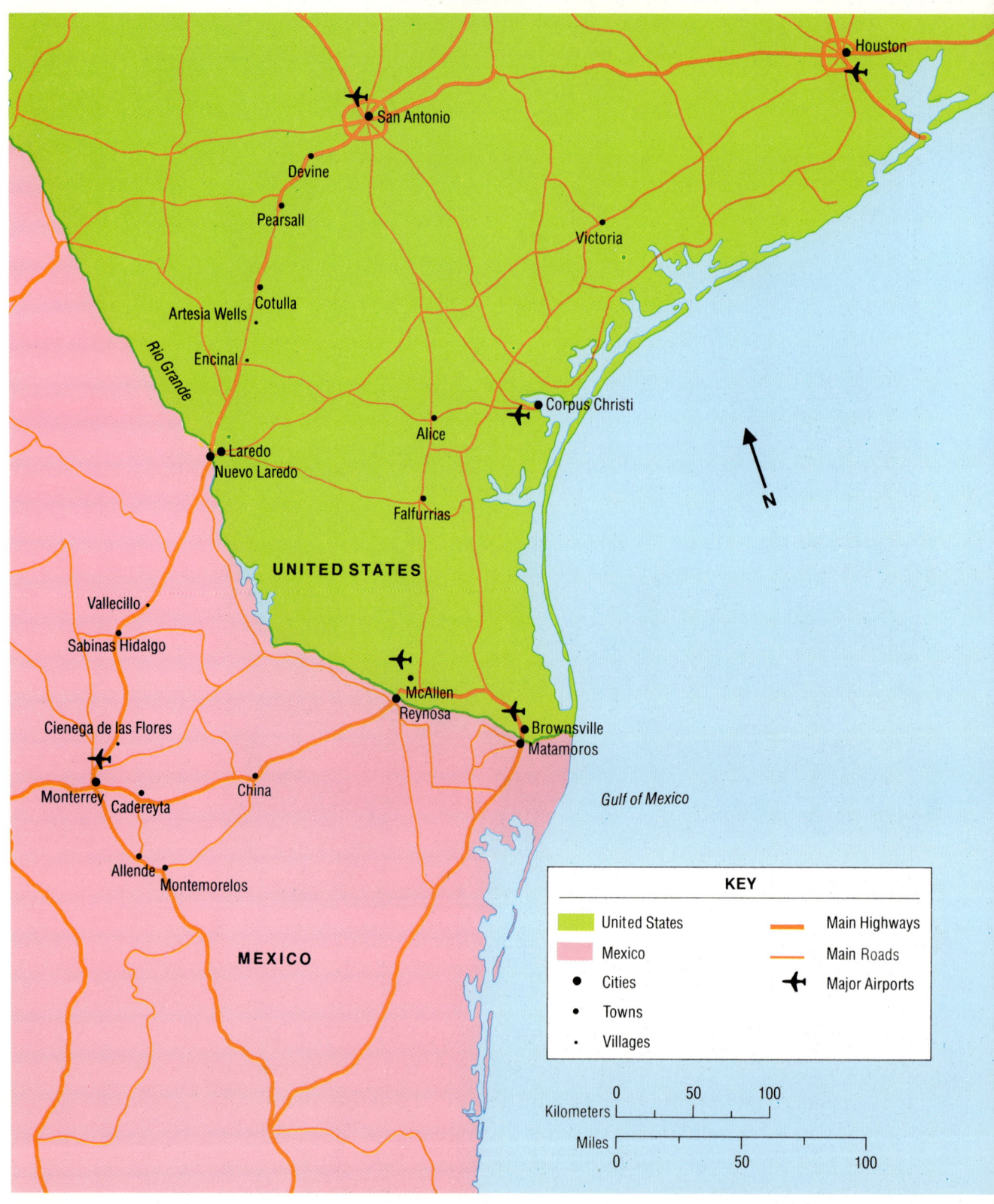

When she picks places to stop for meals and to stay overnight, Anita has to remember something else. Small towns may not have good restaurants. Motels in small Mexican towns probably will not be as comfortable as motels in larger towns. For example, they may not have hot running water for showers. Still, it might be more interesting to eat or stay in places that aren't all new and shiny and just like many other places.

The chart on this page lists some of the communities along the route. It also gives the population of these communities. It can help you decide with Anita where to stop for the night.

COMMUNITIES ALONG THE ROUTE

	POPULATION		POPULATION
San Antonio	654,153	Nuevo Laredo	150,922
Devine	3,311	Vallecillo	2,135
Pearsall	5,545	Sabinas Hidalgo	19,223
Cotulla	3,415	Cienega de las Flores	906
Artesia Wells	671	Monterrey	1,112,050
Encinal	738	Allende	14,908
Laredo	69,024		

1. Study Anita's road map on page 232. The map key describes three kinds of roads. Which do you think is the quickest route from San Antonio to Allende? Why?
2. Using the distance scale, figure out how many kilometers Allende is from San Antonio along this route.

3. How many hours will it take the Moreloses to drive from San Antonio to Allende without stopping? To figure this out, you divide the distance (total number of kilometers) by the speed (average kilometers per hour) at which the Moreloses will be traveling.
4. Where do you think the Morelos family should stay overnight? Why would this be a good place to stay?

Scenes along the Way

Here are pictures of some of the things Anita will see on her trip from San Antonio to Allende.

1. What is the land like along the route to Allende?
2. List the different ways of making a living shown in the pictures.

3. Can you tell which pictures were taken in the United States?
4. Which were taken in Mexico?
5. Try to find two or three of these places on the route map on page 232.

235

Crossing Borders

When the Moreloses drive into Mexico, they will be crossing a national boundary. Sometimes, national boundaries follow rivers. Sometimes, they are marked by a high wall. Boundaries between nations are also called *borders*.

At the Mexican border, signs are in English and Spanish.

On the map on page 193, find the national boundary between Mexico and the United States. Start at the Pacific Ocean and move east toward the Gulf of Mexico.

The governments of Mexico and the United States are friendly toward each other. Citizens of both countries are usually allowed to cross the border without waiting a long time. It is also easy to travel between Canada and the United States or Mexico.

Still, each country has its own laws and rules. Each country tries to protect its citizens and its businesses. Neither Mexico nor the United States wants to let in plants or animals that might carry harmful insects or diseases. Mexico wants to make sure that cars, cameras, or other items will not be brought in by tourists and sold without taxes to Mexican citizens. The United States does not want its citizens to buy too many things that cost less in Mexico. It wants its citizens to buy mostly United States products. In this way, the United States tries to protect its businesses and industries.

The Moreloses are United States citizens. When crossing the border either way, they need proof that they are citizens. This proof can be a *passport,* a small book with your picture in it. United States citizens can get passports from the United States government. Mexico will also accept other proof of citizenship. This proof can be a birth certificate or a card showing that you are a voter. If you were born outside the United States, it can be a letter from the government saying that you have become a United States citizen.

The United States accepts the same proof from its citizens who are coming back from Mexico.

People who plan to stay more than seventy-two hours in Mexico must also get a tourist card from the Mexican government. The Moreloses need one. This card allows tourists to visit Mexico for up to six months. But it does not let tourists work in Mexico or do any business there.

The Moreloses are driving into Mexico. They have to think about car insurance. Most United States insurance doesn't cover travel in other countries. So the Moreloses should buy Mexican insurance at the border. If they have an accident and they don't have Mexican insurance, the Moreloses can be kept in jail until they pay for any damage they may have caused.

The Moreloses can bring only six gifts for their relatives in Mexico. If the cost of the gifts is more than $80, they will have to pay Mexico a tax. This is called a *duty.* If they bring more than one camera, they also have to pay a duty. And they have to bring back the cameras when they return. Otherwise, the Mexicans will say they sold it.

The Morelos family will get insurance here.

On each side of the border there are *custom officials.* These officials look at tourists' papers and baggage. They can take anything that is not allowed into or out of their countries. They can make visitors pay a duty on certain things.

When the Moreloses leave the United States, the U.S. Customs officials will probably not stop them. On the way back, these officials will probably search the Moreloses' car and suitcases carefully. They will look at the Moreloses' papers.

As the Moreloses come into Mexico, the Mexican customs official will carefully check their car and suitcases. On the way out, these officials will do the same thing all over again.

Customs officials often search cars and luggage to make sure people bring only legal amounts of goods across borders.

1. Match the following:
   a. border   checks tourist's papers and baggage
   b. passport   a boundary between two countries
   c. duty   something needed to cross a border
   d. customs official   a tax on imports
2. Name two kinds of rules countries usually have at border crossings.
3. Explain the reasons for these rules.

4. Have you ever crossed a national boundary? If so, which one? Do you remember any special things that were needed?
5. Do you think people should be able to go from country to country without passports and without being searched by customs officials? Why, or why not?

Into Mexico

When you cross a national boundary and go into another country, many things change.

The money changes. In Mexico, the basic unit of money is the *peso* (pā′sō). Here are some pictures of Mexican money. The chart will help you to change United States dollars into Mexican pesos and back again.

Mexican money is based on the **peso.** The peso contains 100 **centavos.** The dollar sign ($) is also used for pesos. There are 22.50 pesos to every American dollar. Here is an exchange table for 1977:

U.S. dollars		Mex. pesos		Mex. pesos		U.S. dollars
$1.00	=	$ 22.50		$1.00	=	$0.045
5.00	=	112.50		5.00	=	0.225
10.00	=	225.00		10.00	=	0.45
20.00	=	450.00		20.00	=	0.90
50.00	=	1,125.00		50.00	=	2.25

Very often, the prices of things change a lot from country to country. In Mexico, for example, many things cost less than in the United States. Foods such as onions, tomatoes, and meat cost less. The prices at movies and restaurants are usually lower. But some things, such as cars, cameras, and other machines, are more expensive.

Road signs often change. Many countries have what is called the International System. This system is the same in many different countries, so that foreign visitors can easily understand road signs. The United States is slowly changing to the International System.

Driving laws and speed limits also change. In Mexico, the speed limit is 100 kilometers per hour (kph), or 62 mph. In the United States, it is usually 88 kph, or 55 mph.

Weights and measures sometimes change. The United States is just beginning to use the metric system. In Mexico, the Moreloses have to use kilometers, grams, and liters, instead of miles, ounces, or quarts. Manuel and Rosa Morelos grew up using the metric system. It will not be hard for them to switch.

Languages often change across borders. In Mexico, the official language is Spanish. What is the official language in the United States?

At Laredo, people often walk across the border to shop in Mexico.

Behavior patterns also change. In parts of Mexico, people have their big meal in the early afternoon. This is usually between 1:30 and 3:30 P.M. Then they have a light dinner at about 8:00 or 9:00 P.M. Sometimes, shops and other businesses will close during the afternoon meal time.

Food and the way foods are prepared also change. In Mexico, most typical main meals will include *frijoles* (frē hō′lās), *tortillas* (tôr tē′yes), *salsa* (sal′sə), and *plátanos* (plä′te nōs′).

This woman is making tacos.

Frijoles is the word for many different kinds of beans. Tortillas are flat, thin pancakes made of either corn or wheat flour. Salsa is a tomato sauce usually prepared with hot peppers and garlic. Plátanos are a kind of banana, usually fried.

Some changes take place as soon as a border is crossed. But changes in behavior patterns and language happen more slowly. The area for many miles on each side of a border usually contains many of the cultural elements of both countries. Such an area can be called a *bicultural* zone. In a bicultural zone, two different cultures are mixed together.

Suppose the Moreloses cross into Mexico through the border towns of Laredo and Nuevo Laredo. Laredo is on the United States' side. Nuevo Laredo is on the Mexican side. Although there are differences between the two towns, there is little difference in the use of language. One can get along very easily in Spanish in Laredo and in English in Nuevo Laredo.

Other parts of a culture, such as building styles and foods, also don't change quickly across national boundaries. In San Antonio, Texas, parts of the city look like any Mexican city. Los Angeles, California, has many Mexican restaurants. And Monterrey, Mexico, has Kentucky Fried Chicken and Coca-Cola stands. All these places lie in a bicultural zone. Bicultural zones are usually exciting, complicated places.

TO DO

1. Look at the road signs on page 241. What do you think they mean?
2. Why can people in different countries understand the International System of road signs?
3. What is a bicultural zone? Answer using complete sentences.
4. Look carefully at the pictures on pages 222 through 238. Find and list three examples of cultures being mixed.

ON YOUR OWN

5. Have you ever visited a foreign country? If so, what things about that country seemed different to you?

Allende, at Last!

Anita stared out the car window. The land looked peaceful in the quiet afternoon. The sign on the mountain road ten minutes ago had read "Allende." They had to be very close.

Along the way, Anita had seen much farming land. Most of it was used to grow oranges. She knew her relatives in Allende had a small orchard with about 400 orange trees. Later, Anita learned that oranges are the most important crop of the area.

Orange groves near Allende.

The municipal building in Allende.

Before reaching town, Anita also saw several chicken ranches. On some of them, the chickens are raised and sold for meat. On others, chickens are raised for their eggs. Anita's mother explained that Allende's oranges, eggs, and chickens are sold in other Mexican towns and cities.

Finally, Anita could see the outline of the *pueblo*, or town, of Allende. The Moreloses had to drive through the pueblo before reaching their relatives: Allende is like many other Mexican pueblos. The important buildings surround a public square. On one side is the municipal building. This building holds the mayor's offices, the post office, and a small hospital. On the opposite side of the square is the church. On the other two sides are the bank and several stores.

Here are other buildings Anita saw, not counting houses:

four elementary schools	one plumbing store
one high school	one hardware store
three vocational schools	five drugstores
two lumber yards	four dry-goods stores
two gas stations	several general stores
three auto-repair shops	several taverns
two large auto-parts stores	two poolrooms
two warehouses	three restaurants
two tailor shops	one movie theatre
one radio- and TV-repair shop	

The bus station in Allende.

Anita waves to her relatives as she arrives.

Then, just outside of town, Manuel Morelos turned the station wagon onto an unpaved road. In the distance, the Moreloses could see several people in front of a small blue house. They were waving wildly at the car. "Hey," thought Anita, "those must be our relatives." *"Mamá! Papá!"* she yelled, "We have arrived!"

The relatives are happy the Morelos family has arrived.

1. What are the important products of Allende? Where are they sold?
2. Can you list at least ten kinds of jobs found in Allende?
3. Which ones are similar to jobs in your community?

1. Name some decisions you might have to make when planning a trip by car.
2. Name at least three kinds of information that can be found in a road map.
3. List five things that might change when one goes from one country to another.
4. Make a list of the ways in which the pueblo of Allende seems different from your own home town.

UNIT REVIEW

What Do I Know?

1. *Salem Poor, Thomas Jefferson, Samuel Adams, Mercy Warren,* and the *Marquis de Lafayette* all contributed to the struggle for independence. Match one of these names to each of the statements below:
   - (a) Wrote the Declaration of Independence.
   - (b) Came to the colonies to help lead the American army.
   - (c) A poet and playwright who wrote against the English.
   - (d) A leader of the group that organized the Boston Tea Party.
   - (e) Fought bravely in the Battle of Bunker Hill.

2. Match the words on the left to their correct meaning on the right:

amendment	(a) a way of changing the Constitution
bill	(b) a part of Congress
independent	(c) free from control of others
federal government	(d) money paid by people to support a government
tax	(e) a proposal for a new law
House of Representatives	(f) the national government

3. Number the following territories in the order in which they became a part of the United States:
   - the American Southwest
   - the Old Northwest
   - the Thirteen Colonies
   - the Oregon Territory
   - Louisiana

4. What are the missing words in the following statements:
   - (a) Another word for Spanish speaking is _____.

(b) Breaking a *piñata* is an example of a cultural _____ _____ among Mexican Americans.

(c) People born in the United States whose parents were born in another country are called _____.

(d) An important value of many Mexican Americans is a closely-knit _____.

(e) In a border area, cultures are usually _____ together.

What Can I Do?

1. Below is a *bar graph* showing the average monthly temperature in the city of New Orleans. Look at the graph. Then answer the questions that follow:

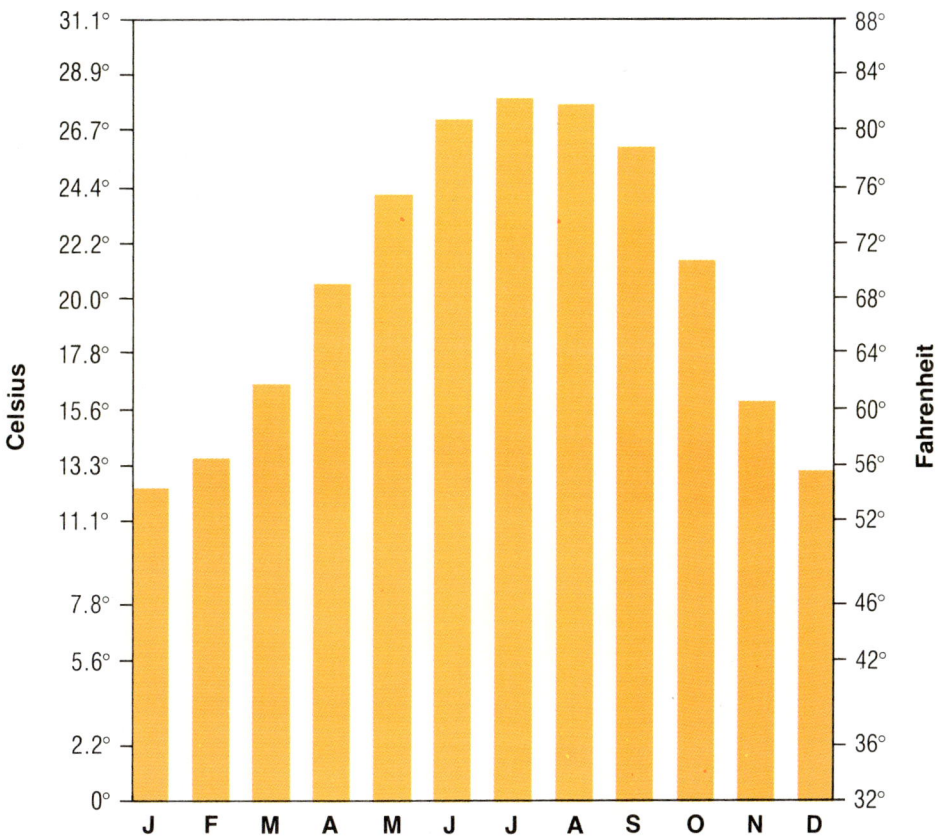

(a) Which is the warmest month in New Orleans?
(b) How many degrees Celsius does it get in the month of December?
(c) How many degrees Fahrenheit does it get in December?

2. Here is a simple road map of an imaginary place. Examine the key. Then answer the questions that follow:

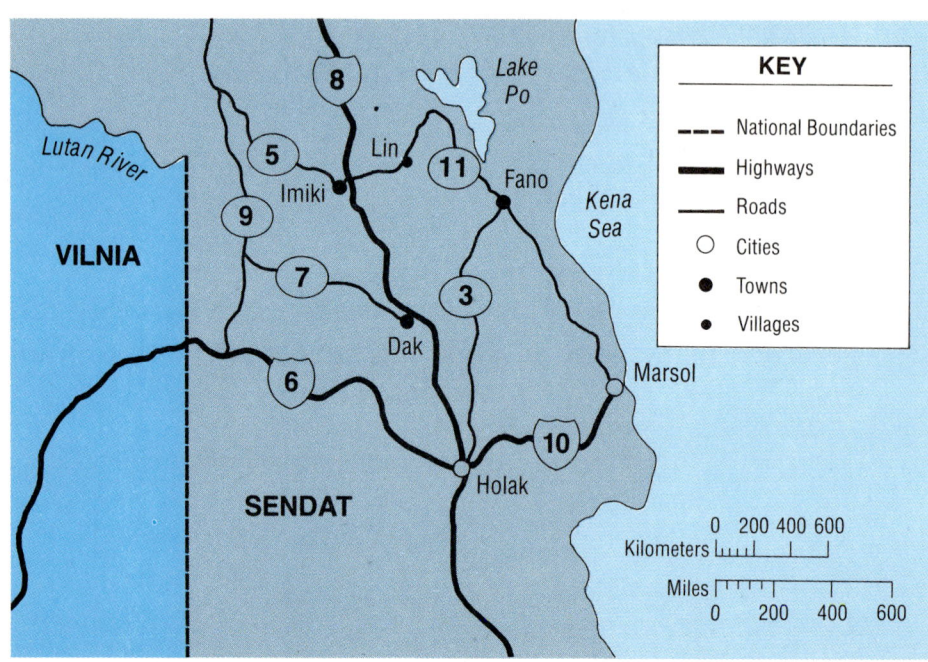

(a) What river serves as an international border between the nations of Vilnia and Sendat?
(b) Name a port city and a village in Sendat.
(c) What is the distance in kilometers between the towns of Imiki and Dak along Highway #8?
(d) Imagine that you live in Holak and are visiting relatives in the village of Fano. What roads would you travel on? Give reasons for your choices.

3. A pioneer woman describes her family's move into the Old Northwest. Read the account. Then answer the questions that follow.

   Our journey lasted fourteen days, and it rained every day. We cut down bushes on which to lay our beds. Our clothes would be wet upon our backs the next morning. Then our wagon broke down. I got on the horse, with my babe in my lap. I was on the horse from sunrise until dark, with a child in my arms two years old.

Finally, we reached a small settlement where we stayed with friends. Here I had our first baby girl. Two days later we moved on to build our own home.

The weather was very cold. The snow was about a foot deep. I crawled under the wall and lit a fire while the men sawed out a door. The snow was up to the top of our shoes inside the cabin. We threw some boards on the snow, and put our beds on them. The next morning the mud was as deep in our cabin as the snow had been. The weather stayed cold. We almost froze.

We were nearly three miles from our nearest neighbor. We thought we had brought enough corn flour with us. But it gave out. I had to pound corn in an iron pot, with an iron wedge driven into the end of a piece of wood. I sifted it through a basket lid. We used the finest flour for breakfast, the coarser for dinner and supper.

I was taken sick in July, and both our children. I shook forty days with the fever. Then we got some medicine. I never saw another woman, except once, for three months.

a. At what time of year do you think this family traveled to the Old Northwest?
b. What were some of the responsibilities of the woman?
c. What were some of her husband's responsibilities?
d. List ten modern comforts the pioneer family did not have.

What Is Important?

1. Which of these events do *you* think was most important to the future of the new American nation? Give reasons for your answer.
    the signing of the Declaration of Independence
    the Battles of Lexington and Concord
    George Washington made commander in chief of the army
2. Name three personal qualities you would look for in a government leader. Then explain your choices.

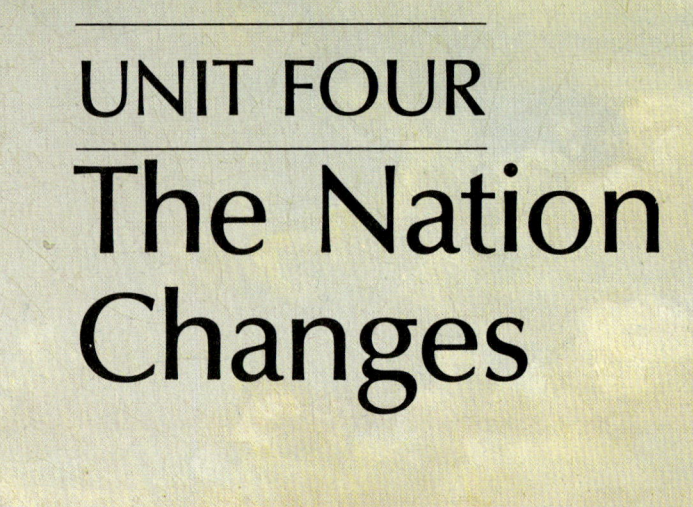

UNIT FOUR
The Nation Changes

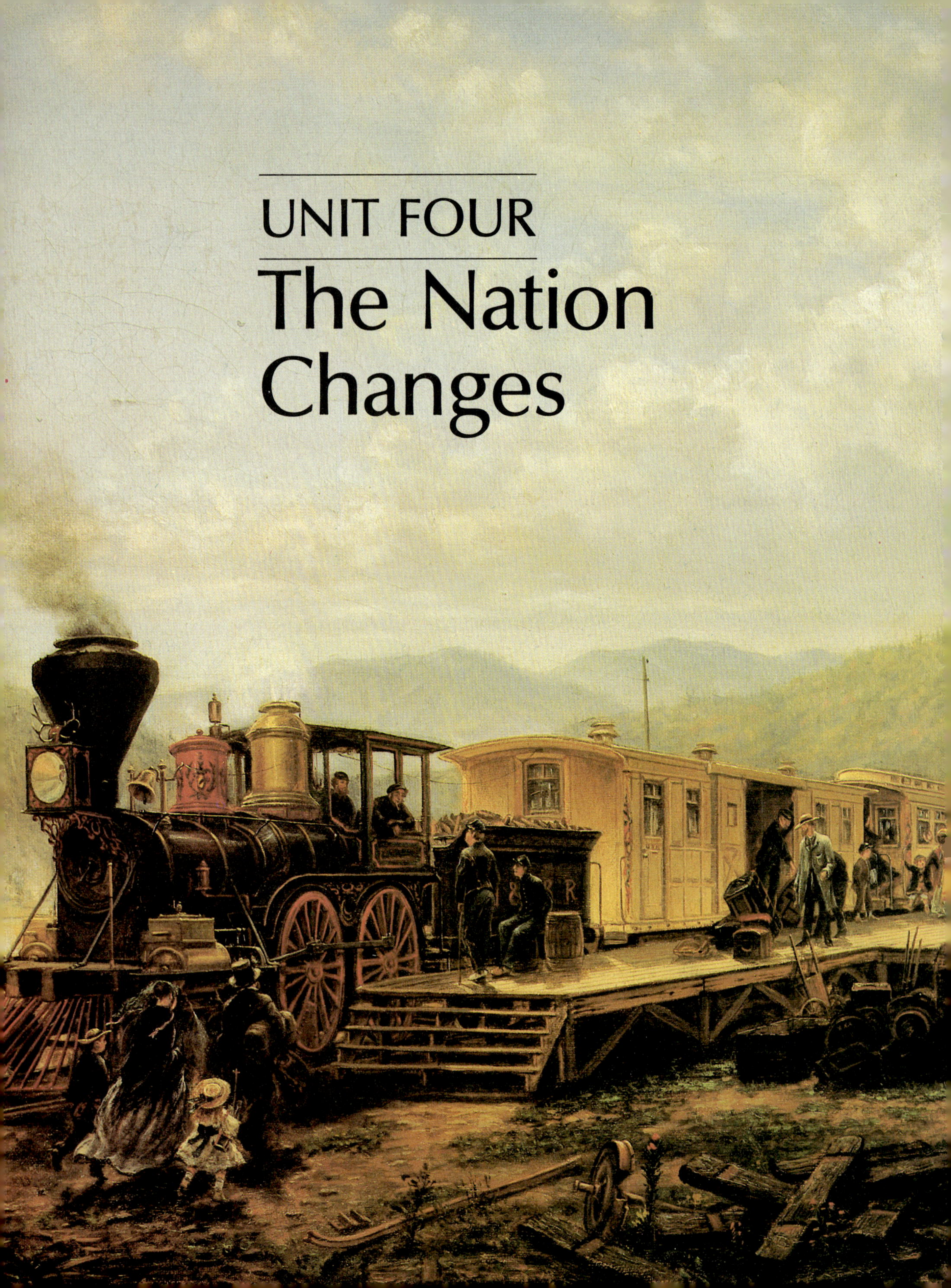

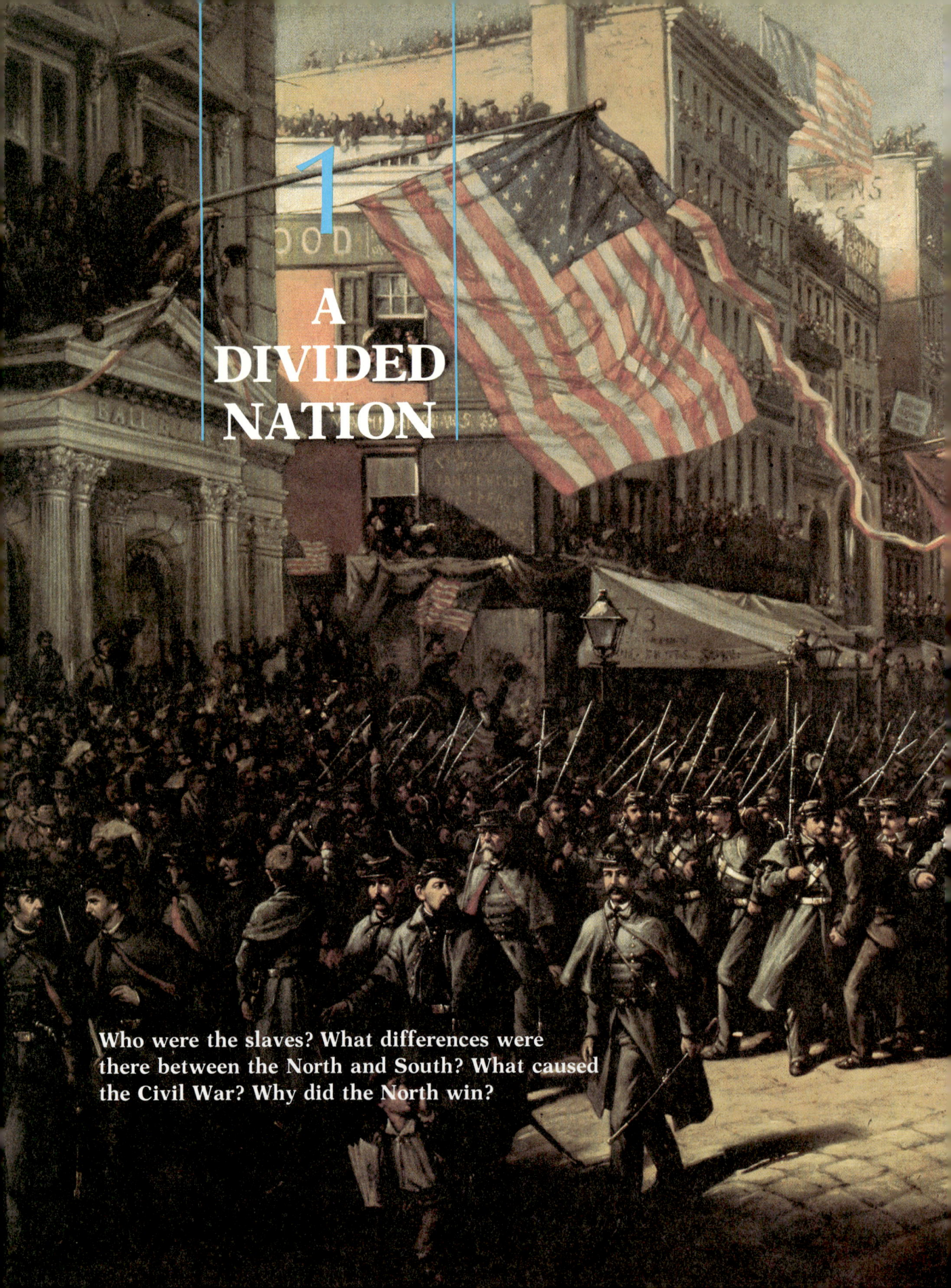

1 A DIVIDED NATION

Who were the slaves? What differences were there between the North and South? What caused the Civil War? Why did the North win?

Slavery

In the years following 1619, the first blacks were brought to the Southern colonies as indentured servants. They had to work for only about seven years to earn their freedom. As time passed, the colonists passed laws about blacks. Blacks soon were brought to the colonies as slaves.

Slaves could not earn their freedom by their work. They could be set free only by their master. Slaves usually had to work their whole lives without any pay. Only a very few slaves

Slaves enjoy a rare moment of free time near their quarters. Often they had to use such free time to do their own chores. Families had little chance to rest or to be together.

were allowed to buy their freedom. They earned the money from work their masters allowed them to do for other people.

The blacks sold in the colonies were captured in Africa. After their capture, they were packed into the holds of ships. On the voyage, many became sick and died. Others leapt overboard and drowned in the sea rather than be slaves. But most were chained down and could not escape.

In most parts of the United States in the early 1800s, blacks had no rights at all. They did not have the right to vote. It was against the law for them to go to school with whites. In some states, it was even against the law for them to learn to read and write. Free people had the right to come and go as they pleased. Slaves did not. They had to have a pass, or paper, from their master in order to leave the master's land. Slaves were often separated from their families

Blacks are sold at an auction to the highest bidder.

This old picture shows runaway slaves going down the road in a large group. Do you think the picture is accurate?

when they were sold. They were not paid. They had to work very long hours. If they did not do as they were told, they could be whipped. If they tried to escape, they were hunted down with dogs. When caught, they could be tortured or even killed.

Until about 1800, there were slaves in almost every state in the United States. But slaves were not a big part of the Northern way of life. Northern factories hired workers. They did not use slaves. By 1850, all Northern states had made slavery illegal.

In the Southern states, however, most of the field workers were slaves. One out of every four families owned slaves. But out of the 5 million whites living in the South, only about 10,000 families owned most of the slaves. These people were often rich and had large plantations.

Here is a description of slavery on a Virginia plantation in 1778. It was written by an English soldier.

"The slaves are called up at daybreak. They barely have time to swallow a mouthful of hominy or hoe cake. They immediately go out to the fields, where they do hard labor without stopping until noon. Then they get barely

After cotton was picked, it had to be cleaned. Here, slaves use a cotton gin to remove the seeds.

an hour to eat hominy and salt pork. If their master is very kind, he may give them a little milk or rusty bacon twice a week. Or he may give his slaves an acre of ground, where they can grow their own food on Saturday afternoons. After their noon dinner, the slaves return to work in the fields until dark.

"At dark, their work is still not over. They must then strip tobacco or husk corn until late evening. They eat their last meager meal and then lie down to rest. They sleep on benches or on the ground in crowded miserable shacks.

"These poor creatures must submit to all manner of insult and injury without resisting. If they dare to defend themselves, the law directs the Negro's arm to be cut off."

The only power that the blacks had came from their strength as individual men and women. They had to be smart and strong to stay alive. Being "smart," in this case, often meant playing dumb. They could pretend sickness or clumsiness. They would "accidentally" break tools. Some of them fought back and suffered the results.

But even in the early 1800s, many people wanted to do away with slavery—to *abolish* it. These people were called abolitionists. At first, some Southerners were among them.

---

1. The first blacks were brought to the colonies as indentured servants. True or false?
2. Were there ever slaves in the Northern states?
3. Why were slaves used on Southern plantations? What did they do?
4. Name three differences between slaves and free people in the United States.

TO DO

---

5. Do you think slavery was unfair? Why, or why not?

Blacks against Slavery

Many blacks in the United States were slaves. But there were also free black men and women in both the North and the South. All black people in America had to fight against one main idea. This idea was that black people somehow didn't have the same skills or talents as whites. It was mostly free blacks, mainly in the North, who had a chance to prove that this idea was false. Many of them were explorers, preachers, writers, artists, scientists, and inventors.

Several free blacks became wealthy businesspeople during the 1700s and 1800s. Paul Cuffe of Massachusetts owned a fleet of ships and much land in New England. James Forten of Philadelphia became a sail manufacturer. He had fifty people working for him. John Jones was a rich Chicago businessperson. In Texas, one of the largest cattle ranches was owned by a free black.

Black inventors made many contributions. Norbert Rillieux invented a new way of refining sugar in the 1840s. Also in the 1840s, Lewis Temple invented a new whaling harpoon that became the standard one for this important industry.

In the 1840s, several blacks returned to the United States from Europe. There, they had received their medical degrees. They set up practices in New York and Massachusetts and became well known. Dr. James McCune Smith was one such doctor.

From among the small group of free, educated, successful black people in the United States came some of the first attacks against slavery. Benjamin Banneker wrote to Thomas Jefferson in the 1700s. He asked Jefferson how he could have written the Declaration of Independence and still be a slave-owner. In 1827, the Reverend Samuel E. Cornish and John Russwarm set up the first black-owned, black-run newspaper. It was called *Freedom's Journal*.

Many escaped slaves also spoke and acted against slavery. Three of the most famous of these were Frederick Douglass, Harriet Tubman, and Sojourner Truth.

Frederick Douglass

Escaped slaves arrive at a "station" on the Underground Railroad. These were often the homes of farmers along the route.

Frederick Douglass became one of the most powerful abolitionist speakers of his time. In 1847, he set up his own newspaper, *The North Star*. During the Civil War, he urged blacks to join the Union Army. Many did. After the Civil War, Douglass never stopped fighting. He continued to try to win equal rights for his people and for all people in the United States. In 1895, on the day he died, he spoke to a meeting in favor of women's right to vote.

Harriet Tubman escaped from a slave farm in Maryland. She then went back into the South to lead other escaping slaves to the North and to Canada. In nineteen trips, she risked her life to rescue three hundred people from slavery all over the South. And she never lost a "passenger" on the Underground Railroad. The Underground Railroad was made up of routes that escaped slaves followed to go north. "Stations" on the railroad were places for escaped slaves to hide during the day.

Harriet Tubman

Harriet Tubman carried a pistol. Sometimes, she had to tell slaves who became frightened or tired, "You go on, or you die." During the Civil War, she served as a spy for the Union Army.

Sojourner Truth was a very important speaker against slavery and for women's rights. She often compared the situation of slaves to the situation of women. She saw many similarities and called attention to them.

At one women's rights meeting, men in the audience were shouting and making fun of the women who were speaking. At first, Sojourner Truth sat quietly. One male speaker after another got up and spoke against women's rights. It was becoming more and more difficult to continue the meeting. Then, Sojourner Truth stood up. She attacked the male speakers with powerful words. Here is part of what she said:

"That man over there says that women need to be helped into carriages, and lifted over ditches, and to have

Sojourner Truth

the best place everywhere. Nobody ever helps me into carriages, or over mud puddles, or gives me any best place!"

She raised herself to her full height of 6 feet and spoke in a voice like rolling thunder.

"And ain't I a woman? Look at me, look at my arm! I have ploughed, and planted, and gathered into barns, and no man could head me! And ain't I a woman? I could work as much and eat as much as a man—when I could get it—and bear the lash as well! And ain't I a woman?

"I have borne thirteen children, and seen most of them sold off to slavery. When I cried out with my mother's grief, none but Jesus heard me. And ain't I a woman?"

1. What was the one main idea all blacks in the United States had to fight against?
2. Match the names in the left column with the activites in the right column.
   - a. Harriet Tubman
   - b. James Forten
   - c. Sojourner Truth
   - d. Lewis Temple
   - e. Frederick Douglass

   (1) invented a new harpoon
   (2) founded *The North Star*
   (3) spoke out forcefully against slavery
   (4) helped 300 people escape slavery
   (5) manufactured sails

3. Why do you think Sojourner Truth compared the condition of women to the condition of slaves?

Who Shall Rule?

During the first half of the 1800s, the Northern and Southern parts of the United States grew in different ways. In the North, cities became centers of wealth and manufacturing. There were many workers with different skills. In the South, there was little manufacturing. Most of the people were farmers. The wealth of the South came largely from plantation crops, such as tobacco, cotton, rice, and sugar cane. Slaves did much of the work on the plantations.

Meanwhile, the West was growing fast. Plains farmers grew grain and corn and raised cattle and hogs. Western cities, such as Chicago and Cincinnati, grew rapidly as centers where Western products were sold and shipped to the

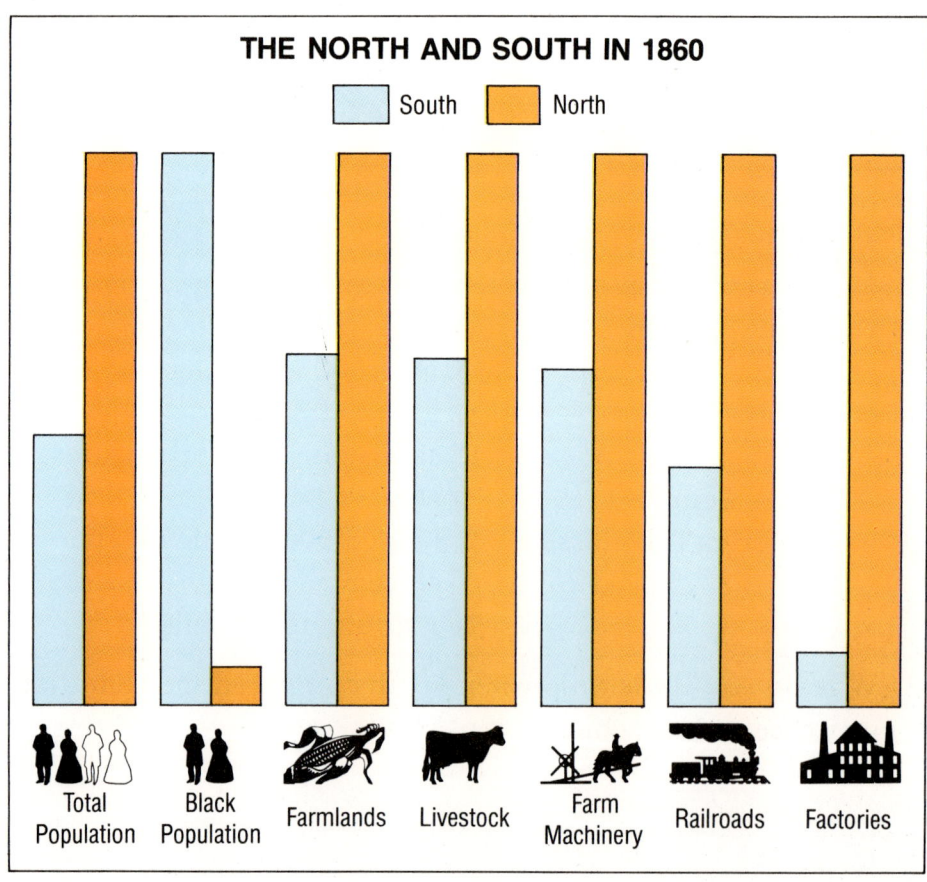

East. Many of the Western territories became new states.

As these changes took place, one question became more and more important. Who would control the federal government in Washington? Would Congress make laws mainly for the benefit of the North, with its banks, factories, and crowded cities? Or would it make laws in favor of the South, with its plantations, slaves, and smaller population? As new states joined the Union, it became very important whether they would vote with the North or with the South in Congress.

Look at the chart on page 264. It shows some of the big differences between the North and the South in 1860.

The map shows which states were "free" and which were "slave." Free states did not allow slavery. Slave states did.

SLAVE AND FREE STATES IN 1861

265

The map also shows territories that could be either slave or free, depending on what the people in them wanted. Slavery was one main factor dividing the North and the South. New territories that joined the Union as free states voted with the North. Those which joined as slave states voted with the South. Whoever had the most votes in Congress would control the federal government.

Another big problem was the *tariff,* or tax, placed on goods brought into the United States from Europe. Northern factory owners did not want to have to compete with goods made in European factories. The North wanted Congress to pass a high tariff. This would force people in the United States to buy goods made in the states, which would then be cheaper than European goods.

The South did not want a high tariff. Southerners didn't manufacture much, so they had to buy manufactured goods. Without the tariff, European goods were cheaper than Northern goods. Also, Europeans paid a higher price than the North for Southern cotton, tobacco, and other crops. The main source of wealth in the South was trade with Europe. The question of the tariff was a main cause of conflict between the North and the South.

Slavery was yet another cause of conflict between the two halves of the nation. In the late 1700s, some cotton was grown in the South. But the seeds had to be picked from the cotton fiber by hand. This could not be done quickly enough for planters to make a real profit. At that point, slavery was becoming less important to the Southern economy. Then, in 1793, Eli Whitney invented the cotton gin. The machine cleaned cotton fibers ten times faster than a human worker could. Cotton then became a great source of wealth. The number of slaves in the South increased from less than 1 million in 1800 to over 3 million by 1850. Slaves were needed to raise the cotton.

But in the North and elsewhere in the world, feelings about slavery had changed. Slavery was looked upon as wrong. It was seen as an injustice to those who were slaves. England freed slaves in its territories in 1833. In the United States, the movement to abolish slavery became very strong in the North. But the stronger the *abolition* (ab'lish'ən) movement grew in the North, the stronger the South defended slavery.

An 1860 abolitionist meeting is broken up.

Many important citizens and lawmakers in the North spoke out against slavery. William Lloyd Garrison founded a newspaper, *The Liberator,* in Boston. In it, he wrote articles attacking Congress for being so slow to take action against slavery. In 1852, Harriet Beecher Stowe wrote a book about slavery in the South. It was called *Uncle Tom's Cabin.* It made many Northerners aware of the horrible things that happened to slaves. Many people who read the book became angry.

The Presidential election of 1860 became the time of decisive action. Abraham Lincoln, a member of Congress from Illinois, was nominated for President by the Republican Party. The Republicans were against slavery. The Democrats of the South were for it. Because the Democrats were divided, it was almost certain that the Republicans would win the election.

TIMELINE: 1860 — 1866

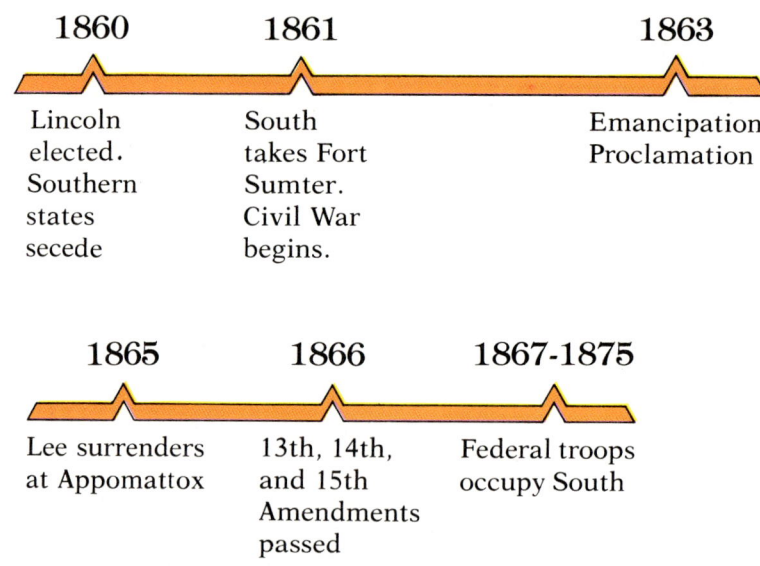

1860 Lincoln elected. Southern states secede

1861 South takes Fort Sumter. Civil War begins.

1863 Emancipation Proclamation

1865 Lee surrenders at Appomattox

1866 13th, 14th, and 15th Amendments passed

1867-1875 Federal troops occupy South

Abraham Lincoln was elected President of the United States in 1860.

Jefferson Davis, President of the Confederate States.

Southerners began to talk about *secession* (si sesh'ən). Secession meant seceding, or withdrawing, from the United States. Southerners said that the United States was created when the states agreed to come together to form a new nation. Just as they had agreed to join the Union, some Southerners believed that they had the right to leave it.

On December 20, 1860, after Lincoln was elected President, South Carolina seceded. Within four months, five other states seceded. They were Georgia, Florida, Alabama, Mississippi, and Louisiana. Later, Texas, Virginia, Arkansas, North Carolina, and Tennessee joined the Confederacy. These states formed a new country, called the Confederate States of America. They elected Jefferson Davis their president.

Lincoln took office in March, 1861. In his first speech, he said he wouldn't break the laws that protected slavery. But he also made it clear that he didn't think the Confederate States had the right to leave the Union. He said that the South had no legal right to destroy the government. But, he said, the President had a legal obligation to "preserve, protect, and defend" the government.

Lincoln said that he would keep control of all federal property in the South, especially forts. The Confederacy wanted Union soldiers to leave the forts. In Charleston, South Carolina, there was a federal fort called Fort Sumter. The Confederacy ordered the soldiers there to leave. The commander of the fort refused, and the Confederates then fired cannons at the fort. This happened on April 12, 1861. It was the beginning of the Civil War.

The Confederate flag flies over Fort Sumter.

1. What is a tariff?
2. Why was the tariff a problem between the North and South before the Civil War?
3. Why did the invention of the cotton gin make slavery more important to Southern planters?
4. Look at the map on page 265. How many slave states were there? How many free states?

5. Why did the Southern states leave the union? What do you think they hoped to gain? What were they afraid of losing?

Civil War

The Civil War lasted from 1861 to 1865. It was the bloodiest war people in the United States had ever fought. On one side, the South, or the Confederacy, fought to protect states' rights and the Southern way of life. On the other side, the North, or the Union, fought to preserve the federal union.

The North had many advantages. Three-fourths of the nation's wealth was produced in the North. Northern factories made everything the Union Army needed. There were 22 million people in the North, and only 8 million in the South. The North had most of the nation's ships, banks, factories, and railroads.

The South did have some advantages. Most of the war would be fought on Southern territory. Confederate soldiers would fight bravely to defend their homes. Union soldiers would have to fight in unfriendly and unfamiliar territory. Many of the nation's high-ranking army officers were from the South. That meant that the Confederate Army would have better generals. The South also had cotton. Many European countries wanted that cotton to make cloth. Those countries might help the South in order to get cotton.

Soldiers leave for war. Most thought it would soon be over.

Lincoln realized how important European trade was to the South. So the first war action he took was to order the Union Navy to blockade Southern ports. From the beginning of the war, the South had great difficulty getting supplies through the Union blockade.

On July 21, 1861, the first major battle took place between the Union and Confederate Armies. The Union Army had hoped to capture Richmond, Virginia, the capital of the Confederacy. They thought they could win the war quickly. But the Confederate Army met them at Bull Run, a small creek between Washington and Richmond. The Union Army was defeated. The North began to realize that it would be a long war. The South called this battle First Manassas.

For two years after the Battle of Bull Run, things went badly for the Union Army in the East. The Union soldiers were led by General George McClellan. He knew how to organize and train troops, but he was slow to attack. The South, under General Robert E. Lee and General Thomas "Stonewall" Jackson, won many battles. In the West, the Union Army did somewhat better under General Ulysses S. Grant.

Robert E. Lee was a brilliant general.

In the North and in the South, many soldiers were volunteers. The South also had a draft law. The North did not start to draft soldiers until 1863. But under the Northern draft law, anyone who did not want to fight could avoid the draft by paying $300 to the federal government. This was unfair to poor people, who could not afford to pay that money. Many riots broke out in New York and other large cities in the North over this issue.

The abolitionists hoped that the war would free the slaves. And they thought that free blacks should be armed to fight with the North against the South. Blacks had fought in the Revolution and in the War of 1812. But some white people did not know this. They thought that blacks would not fight. Finally, Lincoln allowed the blacks to be armed. They proved to be brave soldiers. There were 186,000 blacks who fought in the Union Army.

Lincoln believed that if he freed the slaves, many more black soldiers would fight for the Union cause. Also, Lincoln did not want Europe to support the South. If he freed the slaves, Europe would sympathize with the North. So Lincoln issued the *Emancipation Proclamation* (i man′sə pā′shən prok′lə mā′shən), which freed some slaves throughout the nation on January 1, 1863.

Freed slaves leave the plantations as troops pass by.

By July, 1863, Union forces, under General Grant, controlled the Mississippi River. Texas, Arkansas, and most of Louisiana were now separated from the rest of the Confederacy. In the East, the Union Army met General Lee's at Gettysburg, Pennsylvania on July 1, 1863. There was a long, hard battle. Each side lost about 25,000 soldiers. But the

Desperate fighting went on for three days at Gettysburg.

Union Army commanded by General Meade had won. From that point on, the tide turned against the South. In 1864, Lincoln made General Grant head of all the Union armies.

In November, 1863, Lincoln made a famous speech at the Gettysburg battlefield. It is called the Gettysburg Address. In it, Lincoln said that the soldiers buried there had given their lives so that "government of the people, by the people, for the people shall not perish from the earth."

Ulysses S. Grant, Commander of the Union Army.

The war continued for almost two more years. But the South was steadily losing ground. Finally, the two armies met at Petersburg. They fought from trenches for several months. Then, on April 2, 1865, General Lee retreated. On April 9, 1865, Lee and Grant signed a treaty at Appomattox (Ap′ə mat′əks), Virginia. The war was over.

The American Civil War was the first "modern" war. In the past, most wars had been fought by small, specially trained armies. *Civilians*, those people not in the army, did not have much to do with those wars. In the past, generals tried to defeat each other's armies in the field. They did not try to destroy cities. But in the Civil War, the civilian population suffered more than ever before. It was the first war in which great armies with heavy cannons and equipment moved over vast areas of land and through cities. Over 600,000 people died, and 400,000 were wounded.

TO DO

1. List the advantages of the North at the beginning of the Civil War.
2. List the advantages of the South.
3. Tell why Lincoln issued the Emancipation Proclamation.

ON YOUR OWN

4. Tell what you think the following phrase means: "government of the people, by the people, for the people . . ."

After the War

At the end of the Civil War, the North was prosperous. But the South was largely ruined. Factories in the North had grown rich making and selling supplies to the Union Army and Navy. Farmers in the West had grown rich providing the Army with food.

In the South, factories and farms lay in ruins. There was little food. A very large number of young Southern men had been killed or badly wounded. Confederate money was worth nothing.

Slaves were now free. But freedom was something new to them. Because they were no longer slaves, they had to find ways to support themselves. There were few jobs in the South. This meant that blacks and poor whites now competed for the same jobs. For this reason, many poor whites resented the blacks. Also, few blacks had money to buy their own land. Some had to stay on plantations and other farms, working for people who had been slave masters. Most blacks,

Columbia, South Carolina, lies in ruins. By the end of the war, such sights were common all over the South.

who had nothing under slavery, remained desperately poor as free people.

A black scholar, W. E. B. DuBois, described the situation of blacks after the war in this way:

W.E.B. DuBois. In 1909, he would help to found the National Association for the Advancement of Colored People (NAACP).

"To white Americans, everything black seemed ugly. Everything Negroes did was thought wrong. If they fought for freedom, they were beasts. If they did not fight, they were cowards and born to be slaves. If they stayed on the plantations, they loved slavery. If they ran away, they were lazy loafers. If they sang, they were silly. If they frowned or complained, they were trouble-makers.

"All hatred that the Northern and Southern whites had for each other during the war gradually focused on the blacks after the war. Blacks were looked on as the cause of the war. But they were really its victims.

"It was said that blacks were not smart enough to be educated. And it was said that free, educated black citizens and voters were an even worse problem. Equal education and job opportunities for blacks would lead to social equality. It was said that this would lead to a mixing of the white and black races. And this, it was said, would be the ruin of civilization."

Abraham Lincoln felt sympathy for the South. He planned to provide money, food, and supplies to help *reconstruct*, or rebuild, the South. But five days after the signing of the treaty at Appomattox, Lincoln was killed. He was shot by an angry Southern white who blamed him for destroying the South. Andrew Johnson became President. Johnson wanted to carry out Lincoln's Reconstruction plan, but Congress had its own plans.

In 1865, the federal government set up the *Freedman's Bureau.* This agency was to help former slaves learn a new way of life. The Bureau gave out goods and clothing. It set up schools in which black men, women, and children could learn to read and write.

Black women learn to be seamstresses at a Freedman's school.

Black children attend class in a separate school.

Meanwhile, several Southern states passed laws called *Black Codes*. These laws prevented blacks from voting, serving on juries, and carrying guns. In some states, blacks were allowed to work only as house servants or farmhands.

Congress did not like what was happening in the South. In 1867, federal troops were sent to run parts of the South. State elections were held in which black men voted for the first time. People who had been Confederate leaders during the war were not allowed to vote.

New state governments were elected. They were made up of blacks and of white Southerners who had not taken part in the war. Some Northerners, who had come south after the war, also took part in the new state government. The white Southerners who could not vote resented these officeholders. They called the Northerners *carpetbaggers*. A carpetbag was an old-fashioned suitcase made of carpet cloth. The former

Confederates had a name for the white Southern officeholders, too. They were called *scalawags* (skal'ə wagz).

Black officeholders had never had a position in the government before. Often, the carpetbaggers and the scalawags took advantage of them because they had little experience.

During Reconstruction, the Congress sent to the states three important new amendments to the Constitution. These were the Thirteenth, Fourteenth, and Fifteenth Amendments. All were approved by the states.

The Thirteenth Amendment abolished slavery.

The Fourteenth Amendment said that all citizens must be treated equally by the law.

The Fifteenth Amendment said that no citizens could be stopped from voting because of their race or color.

In 1875, the federal troops left the South. And, in spite of the new amendments, black Southerners were put down again. New laws were passed that *segregated*, or separated, Southern life into two parts. For example, whites and blacks were to use separate schools. But the schools for blacks were not as good as the schools for whites. Blacks had to pass special tests in order to vote.

In the North and the South, educated blacks tried to stop segregation. They did this in many different ways.

Booker T. Washington believed that blacks should try to gain skills and become good workers. He thought that

Booker T. Washington

when blacks had money, businesses, and skills, equal rights would follow. Booker T. Washington was able to win support for his ideas from wealthy people. He set up the Tuskegee Institute in Alabama. At first, the institute trained people for practical jobs, such as bricklaying, shoemaking, and dairy farming.

Another black leader, W. E. B. DuBois, disagreed with Booker T. Washington. He said that blacks must learn to do more than lay bricks, make shoes, and raise cows. He believed that blacks had to stand up against laws that made segregation possible. These laws said that blacks could not enjoy the same rights as other citizens. So these laws had to be changed.

TO DO

1. What difference was there between the North and the South as a result of the Civil War?
2. What did the Freedman's Bureau do?
3. What amendment abolished slavery?

ON YOUR OWN

4. Would Black Codes be allowed under the Fourteenth Amendment? Why or why not?
5. Do you think segregation was fair? Why or why not? Do you think segregation exists today?

CHAPTER REVIEW

1. Give two reasons why slavery was important to the South.
2. List three famous blacks, and tell what they did to fight slavery before the Civil War.
3. Write a definition of the following words, and use each word in a sentence.
    a. tariff
    b. secession
    c. abolition
    d. Underground Railroad
    e. civilians
    f. reconstruction
4. On a sheet of paper, list in separate columns the advantages enjoyed by the North and the South in the Civil War.
5. What were the Black Codes? How did they limit what blacks could do?

2
THE INDUSTRIAL REVOLUTION

What new machines were invented in the 1800s? How did ways of making goods begin to change? Who were the immigrants? What problems did they have? How did business and industry grow in the United States?

The Beginning of a Modern Nation

For thousands of years, throughout the world, most work was done with human or animal muscle. A few other sources of power were also used. The force of both wind and water helped move boats down rivers and streams. Windmills were used to grind grain into flour. They were also used to pump water from wells.

People made goods at home or in small shops. One person, or a few, would manufacture a wool garment, doing all the work by hand, with the help of a few simple tools. The

In this textile mill, big machines card cotton. This is one step in preparing the cotton for spinning into thread.

Workers put cash registers together from parts made by other workers.

same person might cut the wool, wash it, dye it, spin it into thread, weave it into cloth, and then make a garment.

Then, in a span of about 100 years, this way of life changed, especially in the United States. During the 1800s, new sources of power were developed. Many new machines were also invented. These machines did the work of many people. They helped people produce more food and more goods faster. They also helped people send these goods across longer distances more quickly. With the new machines, many people began to work together in factories, each making only one part of a product. Now, for example, different people would do each step in making a wool garment. The cut wool would be brought to the factory by the people who cut it. Different people would wash it. Others would dye it. People working at machines would then spin it into thread. Others, working at different machines, would weave it into cloth.

Factories were built in cities. Many people in the United States left the farms for work in cities. Thus, cities in the United States began to grow. From 1800 to 1860, the population of the United States grew from 5½ million to 31 million people. Still, in these years, most people were farmers.

Eli Whitney, the inventor of the cotton gin, had another important idea. He wanted to make the parts of guns in such a way that parts from one gun could be used in other guns made in the same factory. Instead of skilled workers making one part at a time, less skilled workers would produce many parts that were exactly the same. These would be called *interchangeable parts*. Although Eli Whitney's gun factory failed, his idea spread. Today, assembly lines and the spare parts for all machines are a result of Whitney's idea.

In 1831, Cyrus McCormick offered a horse-drawn *reaper* to Midwestern farmers. This machine, operated by one worker, could cut fifty times more wheat than many workers cutting the wheat by hand. A few years later, another machine, called a *thresher*, was invented. The thresher separated the wheat grains from the rest of the plant. The mechanical reaper and thresher caused wheat production to boom. They were soon followed by corn planters, huskers, and other machines. The Central Plains became the new breadbasket of the nation. A *breadbasket* is a region where large supplies of grain are grown.

Also in the early 1800s, the steam engine was improved. Many of the new machines, such as the thresher, began to be powered by steam. In the North, steam engines were used to spin thread and weave cloth in New England factories. By the 1830s and 1840s, high-powered steamboats were carrying goods on all the big rivers and lakes in the eastern half of the United States.

The first railroad car powered by a steam engine in the United States was built in 1830. The railroad was only 21 kilometers (13 miles) long. Soon, thousands of kilometers of railroad tracks were being built.

Steamboats and railroads carried raw materials to factories in the North. There, for example, meat was processed, cotton was turned into cloth, and sugar was refined. These and other processed goods were then sent to all parts of the country. Some goods were sent across the Atlantic to Europe.

This picture represents progress in travel and communication. How many examples can you find?

In 1844, Samuel Morse perfected the telegraph. By way of electric signals over a wire, messages could be sent many miles. A newspaper reporter in Washington described the tremendous impact of this new invention. During a Democratic National Convention in Baltimore, he wrote:

"Never before was anyone aware of what was happening in a distant city 40, 100, or 500 miles away. For example, it is now exactly 11 o'clock. The telegraph announces as follows: '11 o'clock—Senator Walker is *now* answering Mr. Butler on the adoption of the two-thirds rule.' It takes quite a mental effort to realize that this is a fact that *now is* and not one that *has been*. The telegraph is a most wonderful achievement."

By 1860, there were 80,000 kilometers (50,000 miles) of telegraph wires joining together different parts of the nation.

There were many inventions in the first half of the 1800s. New ways of making steel were being developed. Ways to mold rubber into firm shapes were invented. So were the tricycle and the safety pin. A new kind of printing press was developed. Thousands of newspapers and books could now be printed in an hour. Many of the things and ways of working that we take for granted today had their beginnings during this time.

TO DO

1. Name three ways in which the United States changed in the first half of the 1800s.
2. Match each term on the left with the effect it had, on the right:

   a. telegraph   1. caused wheat production to boom
   b. steamboats   2. helped raw materials and finished goods move faster
   c. reaper and thresher 3. made it possible for more goods to be made faster
   d. factory system   4. improved communication throughout the nation

---

ON YOUR OWN

3. Which of these inventions do you think was most important to the development of the United States: the steam engine, the telegraph, or the reaper? Explain your choice.
4. What machines today tell us what "now is," much as the telegraph did in the early 1800s?

Immigration

Between 1815 and 1915, more than 30 million *immigrants* arrived in the United States. These were people from other countries who came to make the United States their home.

Immigrants came for many reasons. Some were *driven* away from home by hardships such as hunger, poverty, overpopulation, or political and religious troubles. Some were attracted to the United States by the promise of a better life. They had heard stories about cheap land, high wages, and even about streets paved with gold. Some came because of the promise of greater freedom in this new nation.

In the mid-1800s, the United States needed workers almost everywhere. Workers were needed to build railroads and bridges. They were needed in the slaughterhouses of Chicago and in the iron and coal mines of Ohio and Pennsylvania. They were needed in factories and on farms. They

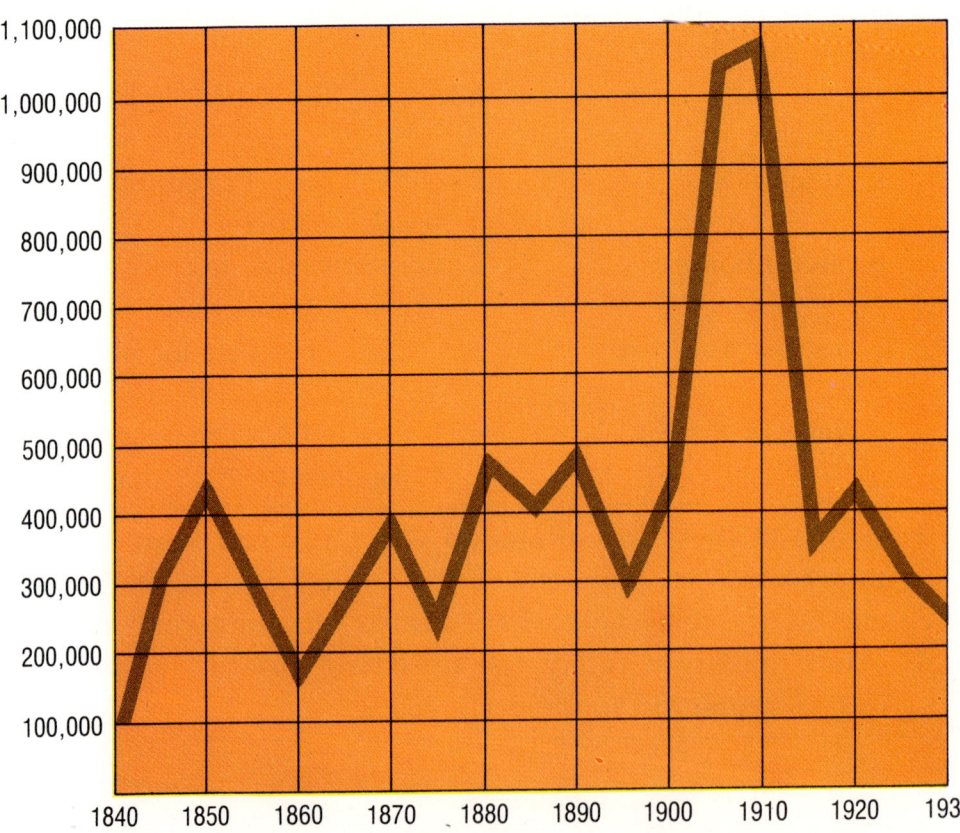

IMMIGRATION 1840 to 1930

Irish immigrants bound for America in 1874.

Around the year 1900, immigrants wait to be admitted to New York.

were needed to build homes and buildings in the growing cities. American companies advertised in Europe for people to come to the United States.

There were two periods when immigrants came in greater numbers than usual. Between 1815 and 1860, large numbers of people came from northern Europe. The largest groups were Irish and Germans. Some Asians, mostly Chinese, also came during this time.

In 1815, Ireland was the most crowded country in Europe. Most people had no land and little food or money. Families would send their younger members to the United States. The young people, in turn, would find jobs and send money home. Then the whole family would move to the United States. In the 1840s, the potato crops failed in Ireland. Everywhere people died of starvation and fever. Within ten years, 1½ million Irish people left for the United States.

Most Irish immigrants landed in Northern port cities such as Boston, New York, and Philadelphia. They did not have enough money to buy farms. Most settled in the poorest areas of these cities. Irish people got the worst jobs and lowest pay. The men dug canals, built roads and railroads, and worked in textile factories. The women worked in factories or as household servants.

In this painting, a family of German immigrants are comfortable on their farm in the Midwest.

Most German immigrants could afford to move on from the Eastern port cities. Many bought farms in the Midwest or started businesses in the newer Western cities of Detroit, Milwaukee, and Chicago.

The gold rush of 1849 brought many Chinese to California. Floods, typhoons, and hunger had forced many Chinese to leave their homes. From United States merchant ships reaching China, they heard about high wages and gold. In 1850 alone, 25,000 young Chinese arrived in California. The Chinese worked in the gold mines. They helped build the first railroad to cross the nation, which was finished in 1869. Later, they worked in lumbering, fishing, and canning companies, and on farms in California.

The second great wave of immigrants came mostly from eastern and southern Europe between 1890 and 1910. Giant factories and businesses in the United States needed more and more workers. After 1900, as many as 15,000 people would arrive in one day.

Many of these immigrants were Jews from different parts of Europe seeking religious freedom. Southern Italians also came in large numbers. They were driven away from Italy by a very difficult life. Some Sicilian workers made only 8 cents a day. People had to live in straw houses and sometimes in tombs and caves.

Greeks, Hungarians, Russians, and Poles also came to the United States during this time. Mexicans traveled north to cities and farms throughout the United States Southwest. Japanese people arrived on the West Coast. There they took jobs as farm workers and servants. Many eventually bought their own land.

Life in the United States was very difficult for almost all the new immigrants. And yet, many found some of their dreams coming true.

1. Match each immigrant group below to the main reasons why that group came to the United States:
   a. Chinese   1. starvation at home and the attraction of the gold mines of California
   b. Irish   2. religious freedom
   c. Jews   3. failure of potato crops
   d. Germans   4. farmland in the Midwest
2. Why was the United States able to receive so many people?
3. What answer is incorrect? An immigrant is a person who (a) wants a better job, (b) comes from another country to live in the United States, (c) comes from another country as a tourist, (d) leaves the United States for another country.

4. Find out when your family came to the United States. From where did they come? What problems did your family have upon arrival in the United States?

Problems of Immigrants

Arrival in the United States did not mean easier lives for most immigrants. The streets, they quickly discovered, were not paved with gold.

Most of the immigrants were poor. When they first arrived, many could not speak English. They did not often know where to go, where to stay, or how to find jobs. Swindlers cheated many immigrants. They promised to find them jobs

Immigrants always hoped for better lives. This old cartoon shows an Irishman planning to go to New York. In a few years, he is rich enough to go back to visit Ireland.

This picture of an immigrant Chinese family is unusual. In the beginning, few Chinese women came to the United States. There was little family life in Chinese communities.

and places in which to live. Then, after taking the immigrants' savings, they would disappear.

Most immigrants worked at hard, dangerous, and low-paying jobs. Immigrants from the second giant wave stayed mostly in the city slums of New York and Chicago. These immigrants lived in overcrowded apartment buildings called *tenements*. Whole families had to share one small, dark room. The living conditions were so bad that sicknesses spread, and many children died.

The immigrants whose race, culture, language, or religion was most different from those of other people in the United States often had the hardest time. The Irish were mostly Catholic. People in the United States at that time were mostly Protestant and suspicious of Catholics. Many businesses would not hire the Irish. They put up signs that read, "No Irish need apply."

The Chinese looked different. The men wore pigtails hanging down their backs. The people's words and ways were strange in the United States. The Chinese read their books from back to front. They read their sentences from right to left. As early as 1854, a judge ruled that Chinese people could not become United States citizens. Chinese families often were allowed to live only in certain neighborhoods. In 1882, Congress passed a law that for many years stopped any more Chinese people from coming into the country.

The Japanese suffered many of the same kinds of problems as the Chinese. Japanese children were made to go to separate schools. Later, there were laws to stop Japanese from buying property.

When people in the United States needed workers, they welcomed the immigrants. When there were fewer jobs, they became angry that so many immigrants had come. They said that immigrants had no skills and worked for less money. They worried that the immigrants would take away the jobs of the people of the United States. Others thought that the immigrants were making the United States different. They didn't want all these people of different races, religions, and languages. In 1921 and 1924, Congress passed new immigration laws. Few people from southern and eastern Europe and from Asia were now allowed to come in.

Life in the United States was very difficult for almost all the new immigrants. Most worked hard, hoping that their children would be better off someday. And their lives did improve.

1. List three or four of the problems faced by many of the immigrants who came to the United States.
2. Name two reasons why other people in the United States were hard on the immigrants.

3. Do you know of any other group that has suffered the hardships faced by immigrants of the nineteenth and early twentieth centuries? Name such a group and some of the problems the group has faced.
4. Why do you think people in the United States feared and distrusted the immigrants they thought were different from themselves?

Big Business and Industry

After the Civil War ended in 1865, the ways people lived in the United States changed rapidly.

The United States was becoming an industrial nation. Giant steel, oil, banking, railroad, and other companies were being developed. Factories were being built everywhere. Machines were doing more and more work, and more goods and services were being produced. People used machines in other ways, as well. People now traveled by railroad instead of on horseback. As a result, transportation was faster than it had ever been before. Energy was no longer supplied only by surface sources, such as wind and water. Fuels, such as

Steel helped the railroads grow. With steel, elevated tracks and long railroad bridges could be built.

295

Workers stare as a "gusher" comes in. Every new oil well added to the growing oil-refining industry. This man, John D. Rockefeller, owned most of that industry.

oil and coal, were taken from the ground. Oil also had to be processed. Cities began to grow, as more and more people moved from farms. Chicago is a good example of this movement. In 1860, Chicago had 106,000 people. Only fifty years later, in 1910, it had twenty times that number.

By 1900, the United States had become the largest industrial country in the world. There were many reasons for this. One was the growth of railroads. They brought distant parts of the country closer together. In 1860, the United States had only 56,000 kilometers (35,000 miles) of track. By 1900, almost six times that many kilometers had been built—more than in all of Europe and Russia, together.

Several very famous people made great fortunes during this period. They also built huge industries. Cornelius Vanderbilt, Jay Gould, and Collis P. Huntington were some of those who became rich and powerful railroad owners. John D. Rockefeller began as a young boy working for $3.50 a week as a clerk in a grocery store. He started his own oil refining company when he was in his twenties. And by the time he died, he had become the richest person in the United States. His company controlled most of the oil-refining business in the United States.

Steel became important for building railroads and cities. Because it was much stronger and sturdier than wood, it was used to replace wooden bridges. Railroad tracks could then be built over wide rivers and valleys. Taller buildings, called *skyscrapers*, could now be built because of the strength of steel. As more steel was needed, steel mills grew. They gave jobs to more men and women. Andrew Carnegie, who had come from Scotland as a young boy, became the world's richest steel manufacturer. His first job had been tending the furnace in a cotton factory for only $1.20 per week. Carnegie's steel company later was worth 500 million dollars.

In 1870, Alexander Graham Bell patented the telephone. This made it possible to communicate by voice over great distances. Thomas Alva Edison invented a practical, long-lasting light bulb. He developed a new system that brought

New York's Flatiron Building was finished in 1902. It had twenty stories. People were astonished that a building could be so tall.

electricity into homes and businesses. He was also responsible for the record player and the movie projector.

Elevators were invented, which led to the construction of even taller buildings. With the growth of factories, manufacturing, transportation, and communications, cities became larger, as well. New services were introduced. More schools and hospitals were built. Small homes were often replaced by large apartment houses. Some little shops became department stores.

As the size of factories grew, large companies could buy more raw materials for less money. These companies could then sell their products at a lower cost. Since the products could be bought cheaply, more people were able to buy them. As more people bought products, more transportation was needed to ship those products around the country. All these developments helped the United States become the industrial giant we know today.

1. Name three things that contributed to the growth of industry in the United States in the late 1800s.
2. Name three people who made large fortunes during this period.
3. Name two advantages large companies have over small companies.

4. How did transportation change during the 1860s? What other changes did that bring about?
5. What, in your opinion, was the most important development leading to industrialization? Explain why you think so.

1. Name four important inventions that changed the way people lived and worked during the 1800s.
2. Who were three big immigrant groups that came to the United States? Where did they come from? Why did they leave their homes?
3. What problems did the new immigrants have when they arrived in the United States?

3

THE PASSING FRONTIERS

How were the Great Plains settled? How did the Native Americans of the plains live? How was their culture changed?

Settling the Great Plains

From 1865 to 1900, the land west of the Mississippi was settled. Before the Civil War, no one wanted the Great Plains. The area between the Mississippi River and the Rocky Mountains was called the "Great American desert." Settlers just wanted to get across it on their way to California and Oregon. But after the Civil War, people began moving onto the Great Plains to stay.

In 1862, the Homestead Act helped open up the Plains. This law gave free land to settlers. All they had to do was live on the land and work it for five years. Many farmers quickly claimed their land. With it, they claimed a very hard life. They built houses made of prairie sod. *Sod* is soil held tightly together by the roots of grass. The settlers lived through bitter winters and blazing-hot summers. They had to struggle to plant their fields, for the prairie sod was very tough. Sometimes, farmers would have to chop the sod with an ax before they could plow the soil underneath. And then grass fires, locusts, or a hail storm could wipe out a year's work in a few days.

Farming on the plains was best done by big machines that could easily turn over the tough sod. Many farmers could not afford such machines. Without them, they could barely

A family of settlers pose in front of their sod home.

At the end of the drive, cowhands herd longhorns into boxcars.

There were many black cowhands in the West. One was Nat Love, a sharpshooter who was known as "Deadwood Dick."

raise enough to stay out of debt. Little by little, the small farms were combined into larger ones. Some "sodbusters," as ranchers called the farmers, gladly sold out and moved to the cities for decent jobs and a better life. But farming was established on the plains. Before long, much of the prairie was planted in wheat and corn.

In the Southwest, cattle ranching became important in the 1870s. Texas *longhorn* cattle, which were tough, half-wild animals, were a main source of beef for Eastern markets. These cattle could be turned loose to feed on the millions of acres of unclaimed grassland. Ranchers didn't have to pay for feed. They didn't even have to build shelters for the cattle. Every spring, the cowhands would round up the animals. Then they would start the long drive north to the railroad towns in Kansas. The cowhands took their time. If the drive moved slowly enough, the cattle often gained weight on the way to market. In Kansas, the cattle were sold. Then they were herded on trains and shipped east to stockyards in Chicago, Kansas City, or Omaha. After spending most of their pay, the cowhands would head for home, ready to do it over again the next year. The days of cowhands and cattle drives did not last long. By the 1880s, this way of life had almost disappeared. The invention of barbed wire was the most important reason.

With barbed wire, farmers could fence cattle out of their fields. Before long, even old cattle trails were blocked by fences. The open range was mostly closed. Cattle raising changed. Ranchers, too, used barbed wire—to fence their cattle in. Penned in small areas, the cattle could be fattened with grain from the prairie farms. Ranching was more expensive than in early days. It became a big business. This helped to make life in the West more settled.

Cities and towns grew up. They attracted more and more people. In 1850, there were only half a million people living west of the Mississippi. In 1890, there were almost 9 million.

The people who settled the Great Plains were different from each other in some important ways. But they also had some things in common. Although some were foreign immigrants, they came to share a common language—American English. They shared many beliefs about what was good and right. They shared beliefs about the land. For example, they agreed that the land should belong to someone, and that it should be used for something.

There were people living in the West who did not share many of these beliefs. These were the native peoples of the plains. The plains peoples were among the last of the Native Americans to lose their freedom and their old ways.

TO DO

1. Name two kinds of people who settled the Great Plains.
2. How did the Homestead Act help settle the prairies?
3. Why were the plains a good place for cattle ranches?

ON YOUR OWN

4. Why do you think people began moving onto the Great Plains after the Civil War?
5. Why did the ranchers call the first farmers on the Great Plains "sodbusters?"

The People of the Plains

On the plains between the Mississippi River and the Rocky Mountains lived many different groups of Native Americans. The *Comanches* (kə man'chēz) lived in Northern Texas. The *Kiowas* (kī'ə wāz) and Southern *Cheyenne* (shī an) lived in Kansas and eastern Colorado. The *Pawnee* (pô'nē), *Crow*, Northern *Cheyenne*, and several *Sioux* (sü) groups lived in Nebraska, the Dakotas, Wyoming, and Montana. These were only some of the Native Americans living on the plains.

The plains peoples depended on the buffalo to live. In early days, they had to hunt these huge animals on foot. They did not yet have horses. Spanish explorers first brought horses to North America. Some horses escaped and became wild. As the years passed, herds of wild horses grew and wandered over the grasslands. By the early 1700s, the plains peoples had learned to capture and ride them. From then on, hunting was easier. The vast buffalo herds had to move in order to eat. They also moved south or north during certain parts of the year. With horses, the plains peoples could follow.

Disguised in wolfskins, Native Americans move in for the kill.

They could stay close to the animals that provided almost everything they needed.

Zona Thunderhawk is a Sioux teacher at the Standing Rock Reservation in North Dakota. Here she describes how the Sioux used the buffalo:

"Our braves hunted the buffalo because it had plenty of meat. They never killed for sport. The men shot the buffalo and brought it to camp. Then it was mostly up to the women to do what they had to do. The older women taught the younger ones to prepare everything for the year.

"First, we skinned the buffalo. We staked out the hide and dried it on the ground. We then removed all the meat off the bones. Some we ate fresh. But most of it we dried to eat in the winter. We even used the muscles —the muscles of the leg that people throw away today. We cut them into long strips and dried them. And even the windpipe, we cut and dried that, too. Because we never knew when we might be without food in the wintertime. We always prepared for the long winter months.

"When the hides were dry, we sewed them together to make into tents. We boiled the muscles and the hoofs and spread the slimy stuff on the tents. This hardened, and kept the rain out of the teepee. Our clothing was made from hides as well. For thread we used sinew (sin'yü), the stringy part of the buffalo's muscles. Sinew was also used for rope and bowstrings.

"We used the tail of the animal. We put it in the pot until all the meat was cooked off the bones. The little bones we used as playthings. There are holes in them. We laced them and gave them to the children to play with. The horns of the beast were carved into spoons, chisels, and other tools. Other bones were cut into pieces and boiled. We made a kind of bone grease out of this. This lard was then stored in a pouch made from the buffalo's stomach.

On the treeless plains, Native Americans took shelter in tepees made of buffalo hides. The poles, made from tall slender trees, were brought from far away. A set of lodge poles was a valuable possession.

"We scraped all the fur from the hide. The longest hair from the front of the buffalo was saved for mattresses. Tanned buffalo skins were sewed and stuffed with this fur. It made a soft mattress.

"We used everything. I mean everything. When we ate, if there was grease on our hands or on our lips, we wiped it off and put it on our hair. It oiled our hair. It made our hair grow thick and long.

"But the buffalo was hard to catch. Our chief would go up on the high hills to fast and pray for food for his people. Our chief was guided by mighty spirits. He always put the widows and fatherless children first. They are first. Braves and their families got their share later."

The railroads dealt the first blow to the culture of the plains peoples. Railroad workers needed food. Hunters like Buffalo Bill Cody were hired to shoot the buffalo to feed the workers. After the railroads were built, settlers came to the plains in great numbers. They wanted protection from the native plains peoples. The Army quickly saw that killing the buffalo was one way to control the plains peoples. So the slaughter of buffalo was encouraged. Passengers shot the animals from train windows just for sport. Millions of buffalo were killed for their hides or their tongues, which were

Special trains were run just for buffalo "hunters."

shipped back to Eastern restaurants. The *carcasses* (kär′kəs əz), or dead bodies, were left rotting on the plains.

In the early 1800s, there were about 60 million buffalo. Sometimes, a single herd would cover the plains from horizon to horizon. About 100 years later, only a few were left, in a national park. The native peoples of the plains found themselves without the mainstay of their culture. Soon, they would also be without their land.

TO DO

1. What was the most important thing in the plains people's way of life?
2. True or false: (a) There were many different groups of plains peoples. (b) The Sioux hunted for sport. (c) The plains peoples always had horses.
3. List five things the Sioux got from the buffalo.

ON YOUR OWN

4. Why do you think the settlers slaughtered the buffalo as they did?
5. Compare this with the way the Sioux killed buffalo.

Whose Land?

Not all the plains peoples were friendly with one another. For example, the Sioux were given that name by one of their neighbors. *Sioux* comes from a word meaning "snake in the grass." The Sioux call themselves Dakotas. *Dakota* means "allies" or "friends."

Plains groups often fought over the right to hunt, plant, or travel across a certain territory. Each tribal group tried to protect some areas of land for the group members. But all the members of a tribe had equal rights to the land. The idea of *owning* the land was completely strange to these people. For many people in Europe and the United States, land was something to own, as one owns a tool or a house. Land belonged to the person who bought it or claimed it. The owners could do whatever they wanted with it. No one could come on their property without permission.

This difference in values caused many misunderstandings. Often, settlers would offer to buy some land from Native Americans. They would give gifts, usually blankets, guns, coffee, or whiskey. The Native Americans thought they were allowing the settlers to use the land. The settlers thought they were buying it. Too late, the Native Americans discovered that they could no longer move freely on the land. They began to realize what the idea of ownership meant.

The title of this painting is "When Sioux and Blackfeet Meet." Does this tell you more about the plains peoples?

The Pawnee, a plains group, at a treaty council in 1820.

Chief Joseph

Some Native Americans would then "sell" land used by other groups. They knew that no individual could sell or even give land away. They knew that no other Native American had to honor such a sale. Settlers did not understand this. They became angry when other Native Americans continued to use the land. They went to court and to the Army to get support.

Until the 1880s, many fierce battles were fought between the U.S. Army and the plains peoples. These battles were followed by treaties with the United States government. In these treaties, the plains peoples agreed to stop fighting. They also agreed to give up some of their lands. In return, the government promised to protect the rights of the Native Americans to the lands that remained.

The treaties were broken again and again by settlers. The settlers were backed up by the United States government and the Army. The Native Americans fought hard. But without food or freedom to hunt, the people of the plains could not resist much longer.

In 1877, a band of *Nez Perce* (nez′ pėrs′), led by Chief Joseph, was struggling to escape from the Army into Canada. Chief Joseph had a handful of warriors and several hundred women, children, and old men. Finally, after they journeyed almost 1600 kilometers (1,000 miles), the Army trapped them.

When Chief Joseph surrendered, he said this: "I am tired of fighting. Our chiefs are killed. The old men are all dead. It is cold and we have no blankets. The little children are freezing to death. My people, some of them, have run away to the hills, and have no blankets, no food. No one knows where they are—perhaps freezing to death. I want to have time to look for my children and see how many of them I can find. Maybe I shall find them among the dead. Hear me, my chiefs! I am tired. My heart is sick and sad. From where the sun now stands, I will fight no more forever."

Native Americans in different parts of the country had been struggling with settlers for over 270 years. With the settling of the Great Plains, the struggle was almost over.

TO DO

1. Native Americans and settlers disagreed about (a) what to do with the land, (b) the idea of owning land, (c) how much money the land was worth.
2. True or false: (a) The settlers believed that land could be owned. (b) The Native Americans believed people could only use land. (c) Plains peoples always let other groups share the land they used.
3. Which of the following was *not* a result of the settlers' ownership of the land?
   (a) The plains people lost most of their land.
   (b) The plains peoples often fought over territory.
   (c) The plains peoples could hunt and move freely as they always had.

ON YOUR OWN

4. Are the rights of private ownership different from the rights we have in parks and other places that belong to the public? If so, what are the differences?

CHAPTER REVIEW

1. When were the Great Plains settled?
2. How did farming and ranching on the Great Plains change?
3. How did the killing of the buffalo change the culture of plains people?

309

4
NATIVE AMERICANS TODAY

What has life on the reservations been like? What are some differences between different groups of Native Americans? What are some of their contributions to North American life?

Reservations

As the United States grew, Native Americans steadily lost their lands. Settlers pushed west, starting farms and founding towns. It was the job of the United States government to protect the settlers and to see that they got the lands they wanted. To do this, the government had to deal with the Native Americans. Until 1871, Congress treated Native American groups as independent nations. After 1871, Congress said the Native Americans were no longer independent nations. But they were not United States citizens, either. It was not until 1924 that they became citizens, with the right to vote.

In 1824, the government established the Bureau of Indian Affairs (BIA). The **BIA** was set up to manage the *reservations*. These were the areas of land set aside for Native Americans. The **BIA** sent agents to the reservations. They were supposed to see that the Native Americans had enough food, warm clothing, and other necessities. The Native Americans needed such help because reservation land was often poor and difficult to farm. The Native Americans could not grow good crops or hunt for food. They had to rely on white traders for food and other goods. Often these traders cheated the Native Americans. Many agents from the **BIA** cheated them, too.

The government set up schools on the reservations. In the schools, Native American children were often not allowed to use their own language. They were taught to read and write only in English. They studied the same subjects that other children in the United States did. The schools wanted to make the Native Americans more like white people. They wanted them to live as other people in the United States did. Then, it was thought, Native Americans would fit in. They would not be unhappy. They would not be a "problem" anymore. In fact, this idea lay behind most government programs and laws. Here is an example:

In 1887, the government passed a law to divide up land that was owned by whole tribes. Smaller pieces of this land

NATIVE AMERICANS TODAY

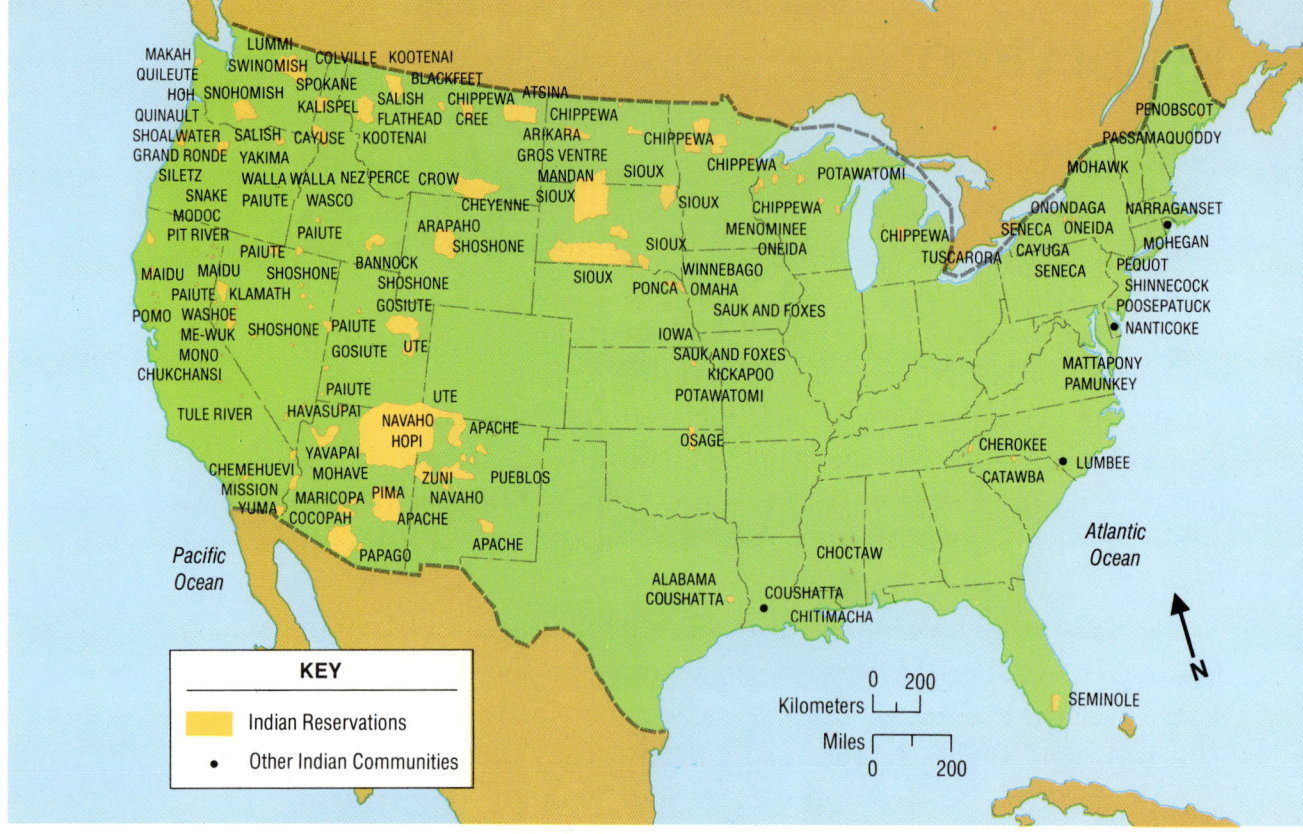

would be owned by individual Native Americans, instead. The government hoped this would make Native Americans want to become farmers. Then they would be more like whites. But many Native Americans did not want to be farmers. They wanted to hunt and gather their food, as they had done in the past. Besides, owning land individually and plowing up the earth went against their beliefs. Confused and bitter, many Native Americans sold their little plots of land. When the money was gone, they had nothing. In a period of about thirty years, Native Americans lost or sold about 90 million acres. This was about two-thirds of the land they had owned.

In 1934, the government again allowed whole tribes to own reservation lands. In some cases, it provided groups with loans to buy back reservation land that had been sold. It tried to improve education and medical care. It also allowed Native Americans to practice more of their old ways.

Today, there are about 275 reservations in the United States. About three out of every five Native Americans still live on reservations. There, much of their way of life is like that of other people in the United States. But the old cultures are still alive. They are being passed on to new generations with pride. Children are learning their people's customs and beliefs. They learn traditional tribal songs and dances. They study ancient arts and crafts. And they, in turn, will pass this culture on to their children.

Still, life for most Native Americans on reservations is not as good as it should be. Many people are poor and cannot get good jobs. They do not have good medical care. And many, in spite of the schools, do not have good educations.

One of the most important things you can learn about Native Americans is this: Any statement that begins "All Native Americans are" is probably false. It is almost impossible to make good general statements about Native Americans. There are too many cultural groups. There are too many differences among them. For example, there are nearly one hundred different Native American languages and religions.

Today, there are about 800,000 Native Americans in the United States. Separate communities can be found in almost every part of the country.

---

1. Native Americans became United States citizens in (a) 1871, (b) 1824, (c) 1924.
2. The idea behind most government programs for Native Americans was
    (a) to make them more like white people.
    (b) to make them like independent nations.
    (c) to help them keep their traditional cultures.
3. What is the name of the main government agency set up for dealing with Native Americans?
4. How many Native Americans live on reservations today? (a) all, (b) 3 out of 5, (c) 1 out of 5.

---

5. Why did the government's plan to make the Native Americans into farmers fail?

Native American Contributions

Native Americans have made many contributions to North America and to the world.

The early settlers in Plymouth and Jamestown might have starved to death if the Native Americans had not given them food.

The native peoples of North America introduced settlers to corn, beans, squash, melons, pumpkins, and other fruits and vegetables.

From the native peoples of Central and South America came sweet potatoes, white potatoes, peanuts, tomatoes, chocolate, avocados, and many more agricultural products.

Try to imagine what your life would be like without even some of these things. Corn, potatoes, and beans are very important foods. Today, millions of people throughout the world depend on these basic foods.

Native Americans influenced the early settlers in other ways, too. While the United States was still a colony of England, the Iroquois tribes had an advanced form of government. It was called the League of the Iroquois, or the Six Nations. There were representatives from all the tribes. They took part in decisions that affected more than one tribe. In 1754, Benjamin Franklin wrote to colonists who were thinking of forming a union. "It would be strange," he said, "if Six Indian Nations can have a union like this and we can't. They have made it work. We need such a union. . . ."

Native Americans have also made contributions to medicine. For hundreds of years, they have used plant roots and herbs as medicines. Many of these were used by European settlers. Willow bark is a good example. What we know today as aspirin is made from an ingredient the Native Americans got from willow bark. Willow bark was used for hundreds of years by several groups. At least fifty-nine drugs, including quinine (kwī′nīn), have come from wild plants that Native Americans used as medicines. Quinine is used in the treatment of malaria (mə lãr′ē ə).

European settlers learned about corn from Native Americans. Today, corn is one of the most important crops in the United States.

The rubber ball came from Native South Americans. Native North Americans invented lacrosse, a popular sport.

We now use many other things the Native Americans invented, and we often use the native names for them: canoe, kayak (kī′ak), hammock, toboggan. We also use parkas, snowshoes, rubber, pipes, and cigars—all from the Native Americans.

The ancestors of these Native Americans invented canoes many centuries ago. This family is using a modern canoe.

315

The English language is full of Native American words. Many animals are called by their native names. Chipmunks, skunks, moose, opossums, and raccoons are just a few such animals. Many tree names, such as hickory, catalpa, and pecan, are also Native American. Words as different as *pow-wow*, *hurricane*, and *totem* have their roots in Native American languages.

States, towns, lakes and rivers all over America have Native American names. There are so many of these names, and they are so familiar, that we tend to forget where they came from. Ohio, Chicago, Kansas, Miami, Milwaukee, Mississippi, Omaha, Peoria, Seattle, Tallahassee, Tucson, Tulsa, and Wichita are Native American names. So are Canada and Mexico.

We can see Native American contributions in almost every part of American life. These contributions have not stopped. There are still things we can learn from Native Americans. Today, some traditional Native American values, such as respect for the land, may be especially important for all Americans.

TO DO

1. Name two contributions Native Americans have made to our (a) food (b) medicine (c) language.
2. Look at a map. Find at least five places that have Native American names.

ON YOUR OWN

3. How is the government of the United States like the League of the Iroquois?

CHAPTER REVIEW

1. Why did the United States government establish a Bureau of Indian Affairs?
2. What are some differences among Native American peoples?
3. What are some of the contributions that Native Americans have made to American life?

5
BETWEEN TWO CULTURES

What are some traditional Navaho beliefs, values, and kinds of behavior? How do people learn? What things are the Navaho people learning?

Who Are the Navaho?

The Navaho (nav′ə hō′) are the largest single group of Native Americans. There are about 100,000 Navaho people in the United States today. Most live on the largest reservation in the United States. It covers over 5 million hectares (hek′tārz) (14 million acres), which is about the size of the entire state of West Virginia. The Navaho reservation covers parts of Arizona, New Mexico, and Utah. Some of this land is mountainous, but most of it is dry and desertlike.

The Navaho people migrated from the north about 500 years ago. At first, they hunted and gathered food. They learned farming, stock raising, and weaving from the nearby Pueblo people and from the Spanish. The Spanish called them *Navaho* from the name of a pueblo they lived near. The Navahos' name for themselves is *Diné* (də nā), meaning "The People."

In the 1860s, the Navaho were defeated by the Union Army and placed on reservations. This was a terrible time for the Navaho. But, unlike some other groups, they were able to keep their way of life. Many of their beliefs, values, and traditional customs are alive today.

The family has always been at the heart of Navaho culture. Today, as in the past, most Navahos live in family camps instead of towns. A camp is made up of two or three

The reservation land is better for raising sheep than other animals. Most of the herding is done by children.

The women of an extended family help each other prepare meals.

hogans (hō′gonz). A hogan is the traditional earth-covered home of the Navaho.

Most Navaho families are *extended* families. They consist of grandparents, other older relatives, the mother, the father, their young children, and their married daughters with the daughters' families. Members of the extended family build their hogans within shouting distance of one another. They help each other with chores and farming. They help share the costs of tribal ceremonies.

Sometimes two or more extended families form a group called an *outfit* in English. Members of an outfit can be separated by several miles. But they cooperate for certain purposes, such as planting, harvesting, and large religious festivals.

Many Navaho beliefs, values, and norms are different from those shared by most people of the United States. The Navaho language, for example, is very different from English and from other European languages. Words that pack many ideas together, such as *culture* or *education,* are rare in the Navaho language. When you speak Navaho, you mainly talk about things that can be touched or seen.

Navahos believe that it is dangerous to do anything too much. Most activities are "wrong" only if they are done too much. For example, an ordinary activity like weaving becomes bad if you weave for more than a few hours at a time.

Navahos believe that it is dangerous to finish some things. They must leave some little part out of a design or a sand painting. If you look closely at a Navaho rug, you will see that the pattern is not quite finished.

Navahos believe that nature is more powerful than people. They believe it is foolish to try to change the land or rivers. Trying to control floods, or to kill insect pests, or to stop the soil from wearing out is thought to be useless. If crops fail, or the soil gets poor, it is because the Navahos are forgetting their ways and their songs.

Among the most important Navaho values are health and strength. Health and strength are things that the Navahos want very much. Many of their religious songs and ceremonies are designed to bring them these things.

To Navahos, it is important to have possessions. One should have jewelry and clothing. One should also know songs. A person is thought to be poor if he or she knows no songs, chants, or Navaho stories.

Among Navahos, success, in the sense of getting ahead, is not highly valued. Parents never say, for example: "If you study hard, work hard, and are smart, you could become a millionaire or be president." A good Navaho is one who works hard, is helpful and generous, and never becomes angry with others. A bad Navaho is one who is lazy, stingy, or says cruel things or one who tries to make decisions for a group.

1. What are two things that the Navahos consider dangerous?
2. What are some things the Navahos value?

3. Compare some of the Navaho values with your own. In what ways are these values different? In what ways are they the same?
4. What is an extended family? Is this way of living different from the way your family lives? Would you like to live in an extended family? Why?

How People Learn

The Navahos and other Native Americans have passed on their ways of life from generation to generation for hundreds of years. They have done this by teaching each new generation the beliefs, values, and norms of the group.

We say that people have *learned* when they are able to do something that they couldn't do before.

When you were younger, you could not ride a bicycle. If you can now, then you have learned to ride a bicycle. Can you think of other things you have learned?

People learn in different ways. One way is called *trial and error*. This means trying something, making a mistake, then trying it over again until it is done right. Navaho children learn some Navaho ways by trial and error. The Navahos also teach their children by showing them how to do things. They also tell the children stories about the Navaho way of life. These are *models for learning*. A model for learning is an example of something to be copied. Older Navahos are models

Navaho children learn to make jewelry by watching a model.

for language, clothing, food, sheepherding, weaving, and many other things in Navaho life. The children watch and listen. Then they try to copy what they have seen and heard.

Watching a model is not always enough. Simply watching bread being made does not mean you will learn how to make bread, yourself. Listening to a storyteller does not mean that you will remember the story. An important part of learning from a model is that you must want to copy what is being done. If you want to learn what is being done or said, you will watch or listen very closely.

Anyone who provides a model for learning is a teacher. A teacher may be a parent or other adult. He or she may be a friend, a sister, or a brother. People tend to pay attention if they respect or like the teacher. They will also pay attention if the teacher makes the new learning seem interesting.

It is easier to learn something that is like something you already know. The closer the new thing is to what you already know, the easier it is to learn it.

Many of the things the Navaho children learn are familiar to them. They have watched adults bake bread many times.

A medicine healer is a respected teacher.

Sheep-herding, weaving, and making jewelry are not new to Navaho children. They have seen other Navahos do these things before.

It is very important to have a chance to practice what you have learned. In learning to play baseball, the more times you practice batting, catching, and fielding, the better you will be at these things. You will also remember how to do them for a longer time. The Navaho children practice many of the things they are taught. They enjoy doing them. They believe that they should do them because other members of the family do them, too. The children know that members of the tribe think it is very important for them to learn the Navaho way of life.

There is another reason why Navahos have been successful in passing on their way of life. While young children are being taught, they are given help and praise. People will learn something faster if they are given support for doing it. You may know how to do something. But you probably will not do it very often if your family or friends do not want you to do it. People usually do the things they have learned when there is some reward for doing these things. Praise and encouragement are rewards.

1. What do we mean when we say that someone has learned something?
2. Who do you think has a better chance of learning to knit: someone whose parents knit, or someone whose parents do not knit?

3. What are some of the models you have learned from? Think of something you do well. Why do you think you learned it?
4. What are some of the things people do or say when they praise someone? Do you think this is a good way of teaching? Do you think it is enough to praise someone? Or do you think people should also be scolded when they make mistakes?

Navaho Teachers and Navaho Models

Grandparents and medicine healers are very important people in Navaho culture. It is their job to teach young people history and values. They help preserve Navaho culture.

Grandparents over the years have taught Navaho children through stories. Navaho people believe that with age comes wisdom. The older people, with their many years of experience, are therefore qualified to teach the young. Elders are highly respected among the Navaho.

Grandparents sit on the floor of the hogan telling stories. They tell children the stories they learned from their own grandparents. Years later, these children will tell the stories to their grandchildren.

Medicine healers use very special songs and methods to cure sickness. They also use certain roots and herbs. The

A medicine healer teaches his son about roots and herbs.

medicine healers must know the long songs perfectly. They believe that if they make one mistake, the sick person will not get well. Medicine healers know a great deal about Navaho history and culture. They must remember the places from which the Navaho came. They have to remember how the Navaho lived in the past. They must know the traditional Navaho beliefs. They are often wonderful storytellers.

For Navaho children, as for most children, the most important models are usually provided by members of the family.

Let's look in on a Navaho family:

"Kee, get up and chop some wood," Francisca Cohoe (Kō′hō) says. "If we don't get a fire started, we'll be eating cold beans this morning."

"Ummmmmmmmmmm," mumbles her grandson. Kee Lope's (Lō′pā) parents live in a house next to the Cohoe's hogan. Sometimes, Kee Lope sleeps at his grandparents'.

"I've taught that boy everything he knows," says Francisca Cohoe, "and he still doesn't know anything! I taught him how to chop wood and feed the chickens, and all he can do is sleep!"

When Kee Lope comes back with the wood, Francisca Cohoe starts the fire. She peels some potatoes and opens a can of baked beans. Then she starts making the dough for the fry-bread.

"You have to make the dough carefully," she explains to her granddaughter, Maria Lope. "It must be round and thin if you want good fry bread. And the lard must be hot, but not too hot. You learn to tell the difference by experience."

Francisca Cohoe and her daughter, Sharon Lope (Lō′pā), spend much of their time teaching the young children. Chores are important, but so are special skills, such as weaving and cooking.

"I was taught to weave by my mother," explains Sharon Lope, "and now I must teach my own daughter. Navahos have been taught weaving for hundreds of years, and mothers have always taught their daughters. That's how we learn."

A mother watches as her daughter practices weaving.

"And fathers have always taught their sons, too," answers Joe Cohoe, Sharon Lope's father. "You can make a lot of money selling rugs. But I make money selling jewelry, too. When Kee Lope grows up, he's not going to earn enough as a farmer. He's going to have to make jewelry, too. And I'll see that he's good at it!"

Joe Cohoe also spends a lot of time teaching Kee Lope about farming. They have a tractor, and Joe Cohoe taught

This father is a model for his son.

Kee Lope how to drive. He also explains about the soil and seeds. He tells Kee Lope the best time of year to plant.

"Nowadays," Joe Cohoe complains, "they try to teach the kids at schools. But it's not the same."

"I saw a class once," adds Sharon Lope, "of old women learning how to weave. They had lived like white people so long that they never learned the Navaho ways. They had to go to school to learn how to weave."

"I know there's a lot the children can learn at school," says Kee Lope. "Somehow, it's not the same. The family is still the best place in which to learn."

1. Name four things Francisca and Joe Cohoe teach their grandchildren. How do their grandchildren learn these things?
2. What are some of the things that medicine doctors use to cure sickness?

3. What kinds of things have you learned to do in your family? Are these the same things that Navaho children learn to do? Can you do all the things Navaho children can?
4. Do you agree with Kee Lope's statement that the best place to learn is in the family? Explain your answer.

Confusing Models

Schools also provide models for Navaho children. Many schools have been built on the reservations by the United States government. In these schools, Navaho children are taught the ways, languages, and customs of other Americans. The difference between school and family teaching often makes growing up difficult for Navaho children.

Navaho children do not always know what they are supposed to learn. Before there were schools, they only had to learn what their parents and older members of the group wanted them to learn. The children were encouraged to learn traditional Navaho skills and knowledge.

Now, the schools want these children to learn to read, write, and speak in English. They want them to learn mathematics. They want them to learn how to get along in non-Native American communities. Some Navaho children are taught trades, such as carpentry and plumbing. Others are encouraged to be teachers, doctors, or lawyers.

These pictures are from a Navaho mural about learning. What things are being modeled? Who are the models?

Sometimes, non-Navaho teachers do not understand all the Navaho ways. Here are examples of things that often happened years ago.

A five-year-old child brings a toy to school. A visitor sees it and offers to buy it. The non-Navaho teacher urges the child to sell it. She says, "Your family can use the money. They will make you another toy." This surprises and frightens the child. Navaho parents would never try to influence the child's behavior in such matters. The child's decision is final, and only the child can make it.

Or, a non-Navaho teacher gives a test and then posts the grades for everyone to see. The students who did well are embarrassed. For Navahos, it is bad manners to call attention to someone's success or failure.

Many schools have changed today. Non-Navaho teachers are better trained in Navaho ways. There are also more Navaho teachers.

Navaho children often learn and remember some Navaho and some non-Navaho ways. The Native American children of today have learned to do some things their ancestors never did. But these children may not have learned all the old Navaho ways. Customs they have not learned cannot be passed on to their own children. There are many benefits in learning new ways of living. But the costs may be that some of the old ways will be gone forever.

Some young Navaho children who live near schools go there by bus each day. These schools are called *town schools*. Non-Navaho children go to these schools also. But many children on the Navaho reservation live quite far from any school. They live in family camps far from town. Such children usually go to *boarding schools*. These schools are run by the Bureau of Indian Affairs for Navaho children only. Students live at these boarding schools. They come home only on weekends and vacations.

Children who go to town schools often learn new things from their non-Navaho classmates. They learn that sometimes many people want to get something, but only one person succeeds. Trying to win something that other people are also trying to win is called *competition*. Most Navaho children do not learn to compete in their families. This is something they are learning in the town schools. One teacher tells this story about a town school:

"'*Errand*,' I say slowly. 'Can you spell *errand*, Mark?'
"'A-I-R-A-N-D,' answers Mark.
"'Theresa, can you spell *errand*?' I ask again.

Students at a boarding school read stories after class.

"'E-R-R-A-N-D,' she says with a smile. The girls on her team clap their hands and jump up and down.

"A spelling bee may not seem special to you. But it is special for the Navaho child. Did you see how excited the girls became when they won? A spelling bee is an example of competition. There are two teams, with one winner and one loser. In many parts of the Navaho reservation, a spelling bee would be impossible. The traditional Navahos are very cooperative people. They believe competition creates bad feelings between people.

"Last year, I taught at another school. It was a boarding school. It was not a town school like this one. I tried to have a spelling bee. As long as the children spelled the words correctly, everything was O.K. But when a child misspelled a word, all the other children misspelled the word, too. No one wanted to embarrass the child who couldn't spell the word. Embarrassment is the worst possible punishment for most Navahos."

Navaho children today are growing up in a white world. The schools are trying to help them compete in that world. But the Navahos don't want their children to forget who they are. They live in the United States. They know that they must learn the ways of the majority culture. But the old ways must not be forgotten. At some schools, teachers try to help the children remember.

TO DO

1. What are some of the new ways that Navaho children are learning in school?
2. What is the difference between a town school and a boarding school?

ON YOUR OWN

3. What do you think are some of the advantages of learning new ways of living? Are there any disadvantages?
4. Do you agree with the Navahos that competition creates bad feelings between people? Why do you feel the way you do?

Two-Culture Schools

Today, some Navaho schools try to solve the problems faced by children growing up between two cultures.

The Rough Rock School is one of several schools that try to give children models from both Navaho and non-Navaho cultures. The government pays for the school. But the school is run by the Navahos, themselves. Navahos pick the teachers. They also decide what will be taught. A Navaho teacher at Rough Rock tells about this special place:

"Take our youngest students. Each class at Rough Rock has a teacher, an aide, and a parent or grandparent. We try to get people from the community involved in the educations of their children. Classes are held in the Navaho language. Children learn to read and write Navaho before they learn to read and write English."

One can see what this teacher is talking about just by looking at the classrooms. Every room, for example, has a weaving loom in it. Parents and grandparents teach students how to weave. Weaving rugs is a way for Navaho people to earn money. It is also a part of Navaho history and culture. Rough Rock is a school where traditions are passed on from generation to generation.

In a classroom at Rough Rock are models from both the Navaho and non-Navaho cultures.

There are other examples of Navaho culture in the rooms. There are pictures of Navaho people on the walls. Navaho words and the Navaho alphabet are on the chalkboard.

"Every other week, a medicine healer visits each class," the teacher continues. "He talks to the children about Navaho culture by telling stories about the past. These stories help explain our religion, our values, and our history. Some of the medicine healers and grandparents don't like to tell stories in the classroom. So we built a hogan on the playground for them. Many people prefer to tell stories there, just as in the old days.

"Mornings, we have language studies, mathematics, geography, and other academic subjects. In the afternoon, children can learn to weave, make baskets, or cook. They can learn almost anything they want. We have some children learning carpentry and Spanish.

"We don't want our children to forget who they are. We are Navahos and must not forget our own ways."

1. What do people usually learn when they see two models that are very different from one another?
2. What contributions do Navahos make to the Rough Rock School?

3. Navahos at the Rough Rock School try to get people from the community involved in the education of their children. Why do they want to do this?

1. List three Navaho beliefs that are very different from your own.
2. Explain what it means to learn by "trial and error."
3. Explain what it means to learn by "copying models."
4. Tell in your own words why you think your text says the Navaho children have confusing models.
5. Tell if you think the school at Rough Rock has found the answer to the learning problems of the Navaho children.

UNIT REVIEW

What Do I Know?

1. List these events in the order they happened.
   - seven Southern states seceded from the Union
   - cotton gin invented
   - cannons fired at Fort Sumter
   - Abraham Lincoln elected President of the United States
   - Jefferson Davis elected President of the Confederacy

2. Copy these statements about the North and the South. Write an *N* next to each one that tells about the North. Write an *S* next to each one that tells about the South.
   - (a) People in this part of the country believed in a strong federal government.
   - (b) Most of the people in this area were farmers.
   - (c) Manufacturing centers were located here.
   - (d) People here did not want a tariff on European goods.
   - (e) Most of the battles of the Civil War were fought here.

3. The Underground Railroad, the Freedman's Bureau, the Thirteenth Amendment, the Fourteenth Amendment, and the Fifteenth Amendment all helped blacks. Briefly explain how.

4. Tell what each of these men invented. Then tell why each invention was important for the growth of our country: Eli Whitney, Cyrus McCormick, Samuel Morse, Alexander Graham Bell, Thomas Alva Edison.

5. People learn by trial and error, copying models, and receiving rewards. Match one of these terms to each of the following examples:
   - (a) A Navajo man and his son are going hunting. The boy watches carefully and tries to do everything his father does.
   - (b) A Navajo child made a piece of jewelry that has been sold for a good price. The child now wants to make more jewelry.
   - (c) A Navajo girl is learning to weave a blanket. She tries it over and over again until she gets it right.

What Can I Do?

1. This graph shows the number of immigrants entering the United States between 1906 and 1910. Study the graph. Then answer the questions below.

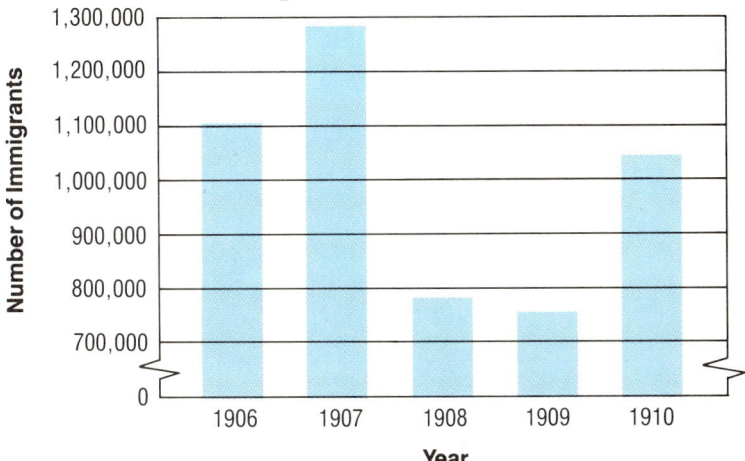

   (a) In which year did the most immigrants come to the United States?

   (b) In which year did the least immigrants come to the United States?

   (c) Approximately how many immigrants arrived in 1906?

   (d) Why is it difficult to tell exactly how many immigrants arrived in these years?

2. Pretend you are an immigrant coming to the United States in the early 1900s. Tell why you left your country. Give your reasons for choosing to come to the United States. Describe three problems you had when you arrived.

What Is Important?

1. In 1863, Abraham Lincoln issued the Emancipation Proclamation, which freed the slaves. How would your life be different today if he had not issued it?

2. During the Civil War, members of the same family often fought on different sides. What would you do if you and your brother or sister held different values on an important problem?

UNIT FIVE
The Modern World

1
INTO THE TWENTIETH CENTURY

What was the United States like at the turn of the century? Who were the reformers? When did women get the vote?

The United States at the Turn of the Century

At the turn of the century, the United States was a rapidly growing nation. Industry was growing. Business was growing, and so were the cities. Huge numbers of immigrants came into the cities, as did many people leaving the farms. Many black citizens left farms in the South to seek a better life in Northern cities.

This movement of people to different areas in the same country is called *migration*. City governments had to spend large sums of money to provide services for all these new arrivals. At that time, people needed to live near where they worked, because it was cheaper. This meant that they had to live in the heart of the city. Builders then had to construct higher buildings to house everyone. Taller buildings were also constructed to house business offices.

As the cities grew larger and more crowded, new means of transportation came to be used. Many people bought cars, and city streets soon became crowded with traffic. Construction became an important industry. Skyscrapers, bridges, and tunnels were built. Streets had to be paved as more people rode on buses and trolley cars. Tracks were built in tunnels underneath some cities for trains that were called subways. As crowds of people, cars, and buses filled the streets, a new problem arose. This crowding of vehicles and people on city streets is called *congestion* (kən jes′chən).

In the early 1900s, there were few laws telling people in the United States how to run businesses. Because of this, there were many abuses. Children worked in factories long hours because their work was needed to help support their families. Sometimes, huge companies drove smaller companies out of business by cutting prices. Sometimes, large companies sold spoiled food to stores that sold it to the poor. What is more, many people were not treated justly. Women could not vote. Blacks, Native Americans, and other minority

Until laws were passed in the early 1900s, children often worked long hours in factories or mines.

groups were treated as less than full citizens. Such conditions caused some people in the United States to protest. The protesters were called reformers.

TO DO

1. Name two things cities had to do to take care of the new arrivals.
2. What is congestion?

ON YOUR OWN

3. Tell about two conditions today that compare with conditions you read about in this lesson.
4. What advantages, if any, do you think there are in having a nation made up of people from many different backgrounds? Are there any disadvantages?

The Reformers

There are many advantages to being an industrial nation. More goods are produced, which are sold at a lower cost. Many people in an industrial society are able to buy things that in earlier times only the very rich could afford.

But industrialization in the United States had some problems, as well. There were people in this country who wrote about those problems and about the things they thought were wrong with the country. These people were known as *muckrakers* (muk'rā'kər). One of these muckrakers was Ida Tarbell. She was concerned that some businesses and industries were becoming too big. She feared that big business would be able to control society and take advantage of the people. Ida Tarbell wrote a book about this problem. The book told about the Standard Oil Company. Standard Oil had become so big it forced many other oil companies out of business. The company was then able to force people to pay whatever price it asked for its oil. The book also explained how the oil company used other businesses to make itself even larger. Standard Oil was run by John D. Rockefeller.

Ida Tarbell

In this famous cartoon, the huge companies, called trusts, are shown dominating the United States Senate. At that time senators were elected by state legislatures, where members could be influenced by rich companies located in that state.

Another muckraker was Lincoln Steffens. He wrote a series of magazine articles that became known as "The Shame of the Cities." In the series, Steffens wrote about how politicians helped big businesses take unfair advantage of other businesses. He also described how these politicians were cheating the people in order to help industries grow and prosper.

Other muckrakers wrote about different kinds of unfair conditions. While the rich built palaces, other citizens had barely enough to eat. Factory workers were at their jobs twelve hours a day, six or seven days a week. They seldom earned more than 15 cents an hour. Some children began working when they were eight or ten years old. Here is a description of the unfortunate conditions at one factory that used child labor:

"I shall never forget my first visit to a glass factory at night. It was a big wooden structure, so loosely built that it had no protection from draft. It was surrounded by a high fence with rows of barbed wire stretched across the tops. The foreman of the factory explained to me the reason for the fence. 'It keeps the young imps inside once we've got 'em for the night shift,' he said. The young imps were, of course, the boys employed. There were about forty, at least ten or whom were less than twelve years of age."

Poor people on farms lived no better. In the South, blacks and whites had to rent land in order to farm. Often, most of their crops went to the landlord as payment for use of the land. These farmers then did not have enough money left over to pay for good food and housing for themselves.

Muckrakers were responsible for making the nation aware of many bad conditions. Thanks to them, people in the United States learned that the meat they ate and the medicines they bought were often unhealthful or even poisonous.

In the early 1900s, a group of people started a movement to correct some of these injustices. These people were known as *Progressives*. The Progressives did not want to destroy United States business. They understood that big business is important because it is the way by which most wealth is produced. But the Progressives wanted to make sure that everyone was treated fairly by the law. They wanted the poor people to have a voice in government. They also wanted to make sure that everyone had a chance to earn a good living.

The Progressives were able to bring about important reforms because a President of the United States, Theodore Roosevelt, came to support many of their views. Roosevelt understood some of the problems of the poor. He tried to fight injustice and to make the government work for all the people.

Roosevelt's program became known as the "Square Deal." Under his leadership, the government acted to stop

Theodore Roosevelt was a colorful leader. His administration began the government's efforts to conserve this country's natural resources.

many harmful business practices and to end some of the poor living conditions of that time.

In 1906, Roosevelt and the Progressives in Congress were able to get the Meat Inspection Act passed. Under this law, the government could inspect all meat transported between states. It could stop any bad meat from being sent. In the same year, the Pure Food and Drug Act was passed. It kept businesses from selling, manufacturing, or transporting medicines and foods that might be harmful to people. Roosevelt was also concerned about saving the United States' natural resources. He ordered that 150 million acres of forest land which belonged to the government be set aside and not sold to private businesses or individuals. These lands were to be used as national parks and forest preserves.

Another leader of the Progressives was Florence Kelley. Florence Kelley was one of the leaders of the National Consumers League. She brought public attention to the hardships and unhealthful conditions of child labor. She worked to help women receive pay equal to that of men. Kelley also worked against businesses that had dangerous or unsanitary working conditions. Today, women are still fighting for some of the things Florence Kelly wanted. They especially want to receive equal pay for equal work.

1. Name two important muckrakers of the early 1900s.
2. Match the following people with their achievements:

   Florence Kelley   wrote book about an oil company
   Lincoln Steffens   leader of National Consumers League
   Ida Tarbell   wrote "The Shame of the Cities"
   Theodore Roosevelt   tried to save natural resources

3. How, in your opinion, does a practice like muckraking control the power of big business?
4. What were some of the factors that brought about changes in unjust business practices? Why do you think they were effective?

Women Get the Vote

Efforts to improve social conditions in the United States and to correct injustice had been made for many years. Laws had been passed to limit the power of big business. Other laws protected children from being used as cheap labor. There were reforms in law and in government. The Declaration of Independence had stated that all men were created equal. But half the country's citizens were still not considered equal—the women. Until 1920, most women did not have the right to vote. In the nineteenth and twentieth centuries, women in the United States fought for reforms. They demanded the equal rights that they had long been denied.

Women demonstrating to get the vote.

During the 1800s and early 1900s, the role of women was the subject of much heated discussion. People had been taught to believe that a woman's place was in the home. Girls were often told that they were too weak in mind and body to go to college.

But some women proved that these beliefs were not so. Through great determination, a few did go to college. They went on to become doctors, lawyers, scientists, and business managers. And women did many other things that people believed only men could do. Maria Mitchell discovered Mitchell's Comet in 1847. She was later professor of astronomy at Vassar College. In 1849, Dr. Elizabeth Blackwell graduated from medical school at the head of her class. She was the first woman in the United States to earn a medical degree. In 1879, Mary Baker Eddy founded the Church of Christ, Scientist. She also started her own newspaper, the *Christian Science Monitor*. In 1926, Gertrude Ederle swam the English Channel. She broke all the earlier records set by men. And, in 1932, Amelia Earhart became the first woman to fly a plane across the Atlantic alone. She was also the first person to fly alone from Honolulu to California.

From 1914 to 1918 a great war, called World War I, was fought in Europe. You will learn more about this war in a later lesson. World War I brought many women the opportunity to work outside the home. More women than ever before were taking those jobs that were open to them. Gradually, more and more women entered the business offices of the nation as secretaries and clerks. Some held jobs as bank tellers, nurses, teachers, and factory workers.

But, for the most part, women were kept from the more important, better paying jobs. Many men believed that if women wanted to work, they should do so before they settled down to raise families. And many women agreed.

Women sometimes disagreed with each other about whether or not women should hold jobs. But most did agree that they should have the right to vote. Women began to battle for women's suffrage, or the right to vote. The movement had started in the early nineteenth century in Seneca

Susan Anthony, Carrie Chapman Catt, Julia Ward Howe, Alice Paul

Falls, New York. There, a group of women declared that all men and women are created equal. Later, in 1872, a brave suffragist named Susan B. Anthony was arrested for casting a vote in the Presidential election. By the early 1900s, the women's suffrage movement had grown larger. Women began to win limited voting rights in some states. But at that time, almost all men and even many women were opposed to giving women the right to vote. Over the years, the efforts of such women as Susan B. Anthony, Elizabeth Cady Stanton, Julia Ward Howe, and Carrie Chapman Catt won the support of a growing number of women as well as men.

The millions of women who worked in the United States wanted better jobs. They wanted higher wages and better working conditions. These women believed that the vote would give them the power to bring about the changes they wanted. They realized that, with the right to vote, they could correct some other injustices, too. During much of the 1800s married women, for example, were not allowed to own any property in most states. Even those who worked did not really own their earnings. In the eyes of the law, everything a woman had belonged to her husband. One of the injustices which had led to the American Revolution in 1776 was the colonists' complaint against taxation without representation. Yet, 125 years later, working women in the United States had to pay taxes even though they were not represented in the nation's lawmaking bodies.

Some women, such as Alice Paul, told people about their causes by leading marches and demonstrations. Often the women who took part in these demonstrations were laughed at and insulted. Some were beaten and jailed. But they did not stop fighting for their rights. Finally, in 1920, the Constitution was changed. This new law gave women across the country the full right to vote in national elections. This important law was the nineteenth amendment added to the Constitution.

Winning the right to vote brought women closer to the United States' ideal of equality for all. But it did not solve all their problems. It did not change the attitudes of many people. Women could vote, but few were elected as representatives. And many other opportunities, such as important jobs, were still denied them.

TO DO

1. Name three leaders of the women's suffrage movement.
2. What was the name of the law that gave women the right to vote?

ON YOUR OWN

3. Why did women feel so strongly about having the right to vote? How do you think this right could improve women's lives?
4. Many people believed that if a woman wanted to work, she should do so before she settled down to raise a family. How do you think this attitude kept women out of the more important, better paying jobs?
5. Why do you think more women got jobs outside the home during World War I?

CHAPTER REVIEW

1. What were two problems facing the people of the United States at the turn of the century?
2. List three problems that the reformers attacked in the early 1900s and tell what was done about each problem.
3. Tell in your own words why women fought to get the vote.
4. What was President Roosevelt's program called?
5. What were two important laws passed in 1906 to protect people in the United States from bad meat and drugs?

The 1920s

The ten years between 1919 and 1929 were thought of as good years for the United States. Many people were making money. Business was booming. It seemed that the day would soon come when every United States citizen could live in comfort.

New products were being manufactured. Radios offered exciting home entertainment. Refrigerators were introduced that used electric motors instead of blocks of ice. People bought electric vacuum cleaners and washing machines. Many of these new products made housework much easier.

Henry Ford started manufacturing cars on an *assembly line.* The assembly line made it possible to build more cars at a faster rate, since each worker put on one part as the car moved down the line. Ford lowered prices until many more people in the United States could afford to buy a car. More cars meant more jobs for workers. More cars meant that more and better roads were needed. Dirt roads were paved with concrete and asphalt. Motels were built to give travelers a place to sleep along the road. Families now could easily travel longer distances to visit each other. People no longer had to live near their work. Many people moved from the city to the *suburbs.* A suburb is a place just outside a city where people live who work in the city.

In the 1920s, advertising became an important new business. Advertising told people about new products. Advertisers tried to persuade people to buy products. Much advertising said that the more people bought, the happier they would be.

It did seem as though people were happy in the 1920s. These years have been called the "Roaring Twenties" or the "Jazz Age." For example, a law was passed in 1919 making it illegal to drink or sell alcoholic beverages. This law was known as *Prohibition.* But many people did drink alcoholic beverages anyway. They wanted to live daringly. And people were shocked as many young women began wearing short

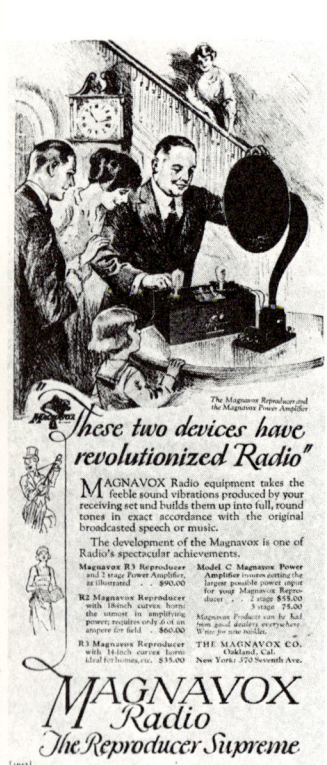

People were happy to have electric refrigerators. They no longer needed to buy ice for their ice boxes.

skirts. Before, women's skirts had covered their ankles.

During the 1920s, an area in New York City known as Harlem became a center for black artists, musicians, and writers. Harlem jazz clubs became popular and famous throughout the country.

But the good times of the 1920s did not reach all the people in the United States. In some industries, such as coal mining, workers often did not have jobs. Farmers' earnings did not rise. Most factory workers continued to be underpaid. Very few people in this country were well-off.

In 1929, the bubble burst. The good times that people thought would go on forever began to come to an end. Factories began to slow down production of goods. Workers had to be laid off. As people lost their jobs, they bought fewer goods. This made food prices drop and more factories close. People had to take their savings out of the banks in order to live. Many banks then had to close because they soon had no money left. This period was known as the *Great Depression*. It lasted for almost twelve years. It was one of the most difficult periods in United States history.

There were many reasons for the Great Depression. During the 1920s, many people bought stocks. Stocks are shares in a company. The prices of stocks kept going up. People thought this would continue forever. They put all their money into stocks. Then, in 1929, the price of stocks began to fall. Many people who bought on credit could not pay. They sold stocks at lower and lower prices. Whole fortunes were wiped out.

Other business owners became frightened. Factory owners closed their factories. Store owners ordered fewer goods. And the more people who were out of work, the less money people had with which to buy.

These were terrible times for the country. To make matters worse, in 1933 there was a terrible *drought* (drout) in the Great Plains. A drought is a period of no rainfall when land and crops are ruined. Dust storms destroyed land, livestock, machinery, and homes. Thousands of people had to leave their farms and go to the cities to look for work. But there was no work.

1. What were two causes of the Great Depression?
2. Name three new products that were invented in the 1920s.
3. Why did automobiles become important in the 1920s?

4. What was Prohibition? Do you think it was an effective law? Why, or why not?

World War II

The Depression that hit the United States in the 1930s was worldwide. Nations everywhere felt its effects. The Depression years caused great changes, especially in Germany.

In World War I, between 1914 and 1918, Germany, Austria-Hungary, and Turkey had fought on one side. France, Great Britain, Italy, Russia, Japan, and most other European nations had fought on the other. The United States entered the war in 1917 against Germany. This was partly because Great Britain and the United States were friendly. It was also because German submarines were sinking United States ships. In 1918, the Germans and their allies were defeated. After the war, all the nations met at Versailles (ver sī'), in France, and drew up the Treaty of Versailles. This treaty took land and resources from Germany. It made the Germans pay more money than they could afford to the winning nations. It also set up a democratic government in Germany. Germany had not had a democratic government before.

But the German people were angry and resentful. During the 1920s, the German government could not solve the people's problems. The Depression was especially bad there.

Adolph Hitler used huge rallies to stir up the patriotism of the German people.

Benito Mussolini came to power in Italy in 1924. He ruled till near the end of World War II.

Adolph Hitler became a powerful leader in Germany. He told the German people that they were better than any other people in the world. He told them that all of Germany's problems were caused by the Jewish people and by the way Germany had been treated by the Treaty of Versailles. Hitler told the Germans that the solution to their problems would be to obtain more land in Europe and to get rid of the Jews. Some German people were unhappy and so badly off that they believed what Hitler told them.

Hitler was able to take over the government in Germany. He became a *dictator*. This meant that he and his political party, the *Nazi Party*, controlled everything. Under a dictator, people no longer have the rights they had in a democracy.

In Italy, another dictator, Benito Mussolini, had seized power. Conditions in Italy were also bad. The Italian people thought that the Treaty of Versailles did not give them a large enough share of land. So Italy decided to take over lands in Africa.

Hitler and Mussolini joined forces in order to wage war against other European countries. Their partnership was called the *Axis*. Germany was better prepared for war than other countries. The war began in 1939. Between 1939 and 1941, Germany conquered most of Europe. The German army had taken over Poland, Norway, Czechoslovakia, Denmark, the Netherlands, Belgium, and France. Great Britain stood alone against the Nazis. Soon the Nazis started bombing British cities.

Throughout Europe, Hitler built special prisons for the Jews and other peoples he was trying to destroy. These prisons were called *concentration camps*. Many people died in them. By the time the war ended, Hitler had succeeded in killing 6 million Jews. He also killed countless thousands of other people who opposed him.

At first, the United States wanted to stay out of the war. Many people felt that the country should worry only about itself and not get involved with the problems of other nations. Such a policy was called *isolationism*. But by that time, isolationism was no longer practical. United States businesses were trading with other countries, so they were affected by events in those countries.

During the 1930s, the Japanese were trying to build an empire in Asia. They, too, were becoming an industrial nation. They needed raw materials, markets, and new territories. They wanted to control lands in Southeast Asia that had rich resources of oil and food. Japan went to war against China in 1931. In 1937 and 1938 Japan controlled all the coastal provinces of China.

But the United States did not want Japan to control China and Southeast Asia. The United States wanted these territories to remain open to United States trade. The Japanese would not have permitted that. Relations between the countries became worse.

Many citizens demonstrated against the war.

U.S. Navy ships burn in Pearl Harbor after the Japanese attack.

On December 7, 1941, the Japanese made a surprise attack against the United States Navy base at Pearl Harbor, in Hawaii. Thousands of Americans were lost. Many American ships were destroyed. The next day, the United States declared war on Japan.

The United States then joined forces with the Soviet Union and Great Britain to fight Nazi Germany. This group was called the *Allies*. Once again, a war reached around the world. This war was called World War II.

The United States and the Soviet Union had not been friendly for some time. This was because the Soviet Union had become communist in the 1920s. The United States did not trust the communists. Later, you will learn more about this.

During the war, the bravery of Soviet soldiers changed many United States ideas about the Soviet Union. When Hitler's army attacked the Soviet Union in June, 1941, the Soviet Armies were nearly defeated. They retreated as far east as Moscow, before they finally stopped the Germans. Although millions of Soviet Union citizens died, the Nazis could not get the Soviet Union to give up. United States citizens thought less, then, about communism and more about courage. Many in the United States hoped that, after the war ended, they could remain friends with the Soviet Union.

Soldiers from the United States and the Soviet Union shake hands when they meet after the defeat of the Germans.

By 1945, the Allies had defeated Germany and were preparing to invade Japan. The new President of the United States, Harry Truman, wanted the war to end quickly so that fewer United States troops would die. By this time, the United States had built the most powerful weapon the world had ever seen, the atomic bomb. Truman decided to use this weapon against Japan.

On August 6, 1945, the United States dropped the atomic bomb on the Japanese city of Hiroshima (hir′ə shē′me). Over 100,000 people were killed immediately. Three days later, a second bomb destroyed the city of Nagasaki (nä′gə sä′kē). Japan surrendered, and World War II was over.

TO DO

1. Who were the Axis Powers? Who were the Allies?
2. Why did the United States enter the war against Japan and the Axis?
3. Name two dictators who ruled European countries during the war.

ON YOUR OWN

4. Why did many people in the United States change their minds about the Soviet Union during World War II?
5. Why did Japan want to build an empire?

The Home Front: Effects of War

During World War II, almost everyone in the United States contributed to winning the war.

While millions of men were fighting in Europe, women stepped into important jobs in industry at home. They proved that they could do the work as well as men. Some women became welders. Others drove trucks, worked in construction, and did thousands of other jobs. Women also joined the armed forces in great numbers. There were thousands of women in the Army and the Army Air Corps. After the war ended and the soldiers came back to their jobs, industry in the United States was different. Women still worked in many jobs previously filled only by men. There were two reasons for the change. During the war, women were needed as workers. And many women wanted to work outside the home.

During World War II, factories stopped producing other goods so that they could manufacture guns and war materials. Automobile manufacturers began building airplane engines, tanks, and army trucks. Textile manufacturers were developing new materials, such as nylon. People in the United States were learning to do without many of the things they had been used to having. The government told people that they must cut down on buying goods such as meat, butter, and gasoline. Such goods were rationed. The government gave out ration coupons. Each family could buy only a limited amount of rationed goods.

The United States gave the Allies many of the weapons and supplies they needed to fight Germany and Japan. In 1944, the United States built over 60,000 planes and 45,000 tanks. Many citizens went overseas to fight in the war. Over a million of them were killed or wounded.

During World War II, many of the soldiers who fought and lost their lives for their country were black citizens. Yet

 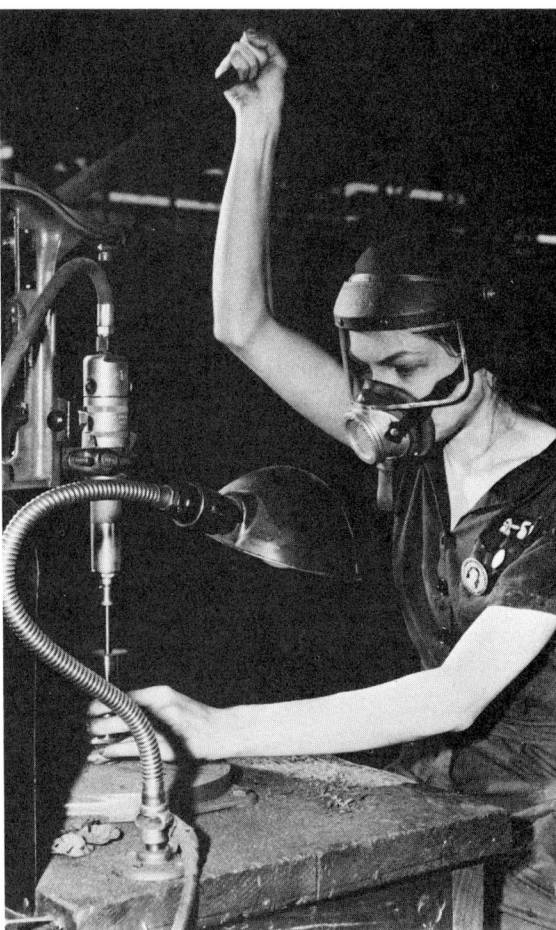

Many black soldiers fought bravely in World War II, just as their ancestors had fought in all the wars since this nation was founded.

During the war, women took many jobs that were previously closed to them as the above, right picture shows.

the blacks still did not have all the rights and freedoms that other United States citizens had. Even in the army, black soldiers had to live in separate barracks and fight in separate units. After the war, President Harry Truman integrated the armed forces. He did not want the armed forces segregated by race.

Because of the war with Japan, some people in the United States began to distrust Japanese Americans. People suspected the Japanese Americans of being spies for the Japanese government. In 1942, the United States government ordered thousands of Japanese Americans to be taken from their homes and placed in special prison camps. These were called *relocation camps*. They were located far from the

Japanese Americans at a relocation camp. Japanese in other parts of the United States were not put into camps.

West Coast. Men, women, and children were imprisoned in these relocation camps. This was a harsh and unfair way to treat the Japanese Americans. Yet they continued to be loyal and good United States citizens. In fact, 8,000 Nisei (nē'sā')—children born in the United States of Japanese parents—joined the armed forces and fought bravely for their country.

United States scientists were also working for the war effort. They developed the atomic bomb in 1945. It was the most powerful weapon the world had ever seen.

TO DO

1. Give two reasons why women in the United States went to work in large numbers during World War II.
2. Why did the government issue ration coupons to families during the war?
3. How did black citizens participate in World War II?

ON YOUR OWN

4. Why do you think President Truman integrated the armed forces after World War II?
5. Why do you think Japanese Americans were put into relocation camps? How do you think they felt about this treatment?

The Atomic Age

By the end of World War II, the Soviet Union and the United States had many disagreements over other countries. The Soviet Union, for example, wanted a communist government in Poland and in other countries in Eastern Europe. The United States wanted democratic governments there.

The Soviet Union and the United States became involved in a civil war in China. This war was fought between Chinese Communists and Nationalists. The Soviet Union supported the Communists, who were led by Mao Tse Tung (mä′ō dzu′ dung). The United States helped the Nationalists, who were led by Chiang Kai Shek (chyäng′ kī′ shek′). But Chiang's government was weak. It did not have the support of most Chinese. Partly for this reason, the United States began withdrawing its support of the Nationalists in 1948. In 1949 the Communists won.

By 1949, the Soviet Union, too, had developed an atomic bomb. The United States was no longer the only nation in the world with this weapon. Both countries realized that if they fought each other now, they could destroy much of the world in a few minutes. They began to wage a new kind of war—a war without fighting. It was called the *cold war*.

Communism grew stronger in many parts of Europe and Asia. Soviet soldiers helped Communists take over the governments in Eastern European countries such as Hungary, Bulgaria, and Rumania. Poland and Yugoslavia also fell under communist rule.

The United States wanted to stop the Communists for several reasons. The Communists believed in an economy controlled by the government. The United States believed in an economy run by private businesses. The Communists wanted to overthrow *capitalism*, which is what the United States economic system was called. Communist governments also denied their people many rights and freedoms that the United States believed were very important.

In the 1950s and 1960s, the United States became involved in wars in different parts of the world. In Korea in the 1950s, the United States supported South Korea, while China supported the Communists in North Korea.

There was also a civil war in Cuba. There, the Communists, led by Fidel Castro (kas′trō), won in 1959. Some United States citizens were frightened to have a communist country only 144 kilometers (90 miles) away.

In the 1960s and early 1970s, the United States fought in Vietnam. The United States supported the South Vietnamese, while the Soviet Union and China supported the North Vietnamese. In 1974, the United States pulled out of Vietnam. This was because the war became unpopular here.

In recent years, people in the United States have started thinking differently about the cold war. Under President Richard Nixon, the United States became more friendly with the Soviet Union, China, and Cuba. Many people in the United States think it is more important to have friendly relations with nations on all continents. But others still fear that Communists want to destroy other nations.

In 1976, Jimmy Carter was elected President of the United States. He has continued to try to be friendly with all the nations of the world. But he has also insisted that nations respect their people's human rights. This has caused some nations to become less friendly with the United States.

1. Name one Communist and one Nationalist leader in China.
2. What was the cold war?
3. Name two wars the United States became involved in after World War II.

4. Why was the United States so eager to fight Communism? Does it make any difference if another country is Communist or not?
4. What advantages, if any, do you see in the decision of the United States to have friendly relations with the Soviet Union, Cuba, and China?

Justice for All

United States citizens who pledge allegiance to their country tell of a nation that believes in liberty, equality, and justice for all. These are the values that the United States stands for. These values have been called the "American Dream." They are, like a dream, the type of nation the United States wants to be.

Many citizens live with pride, opportunity, and dignity in the United States. These people feel that they share fully in the American Dream, whether they are poor or rich.

Other citizens do not feel that they share fully in the American Dream. These people suffer from *discrimination*.

For many years, blacks had to use separate facilities throughout many parts of the United States. This black airman is at a bus station.

Martin Luther King was a great leader of black people in the United States. He is shown above with Rosa Parks.

This means that they are not allowed to have the same opportunities as other people. They are denied good jobs, a good education, and decent housing.

Blacks in the United States have always been victims of discrimination. For years, many states had laws that forced blacks to attend separate schools from whites. When blacks rode on public buses, they were forced to sit in the back. In many parts of the nation, blacks were prevented from voting in elections.

In the North, there were no laws establishing segregation but segregation existed all the same. Landlords would rent apartments to blacks only in separate black neighborhoods. Discrimination against blacks existed in employment, too. It was difficult for a black to get a good job. Often, they were the last people hired in good times, and the first people fired in bad times.

During the 1950s and 1960s, black leaders fought against the segregation laws in the South. In 1954, they succeeded in getting the Supreme Court of the United States to declare segregation in public schools illegal.

Rosa Parks, a black woman from the South, started a movement to end segregation on public transportation. A black minister from Montgomery, Alabama, Dr. Martin Luther King, Jr., led many demonstrations against the unjust treatment of black citizens throughout the South. In 1955, he organized the blacks in Montgomery. He got them to stop riding the city's buses as a protest against having to sit in the back. This kind of protest is called a *boycott*. One year after the boycott started, the owners of the buses gave in and allowed the blacks to sit wherever they chose. Martin Luther King, Jr., was honored for his effort. He won the Nobel Prize for Peace in 1964.

In 1964 and 1965, Congress passed civil rights laws. These laws made discrimination illegal in jobs, education, voting, and public facilities.

Over the next years, blacks made more progress. Many ran for public office. Some became mayors and members of Congress. Blacks continued to fight discrimination.

There are other groups in the United States who faced discrimination. They, too, have struggled to gain equality.

Daniel Inouye, United States Senator from Hawaii, is a Japanese American who fought in World War II.

Puerto Ricans in New York demanded a voice in decisions about the city's schools, hospitals, and other services. Native Americans asked the federal government for payment for the land that had been taken away from them in broken treaties many years before. Mexican Americans worked in the Southwest to force schools to use both Spanish and English in classrooms. In California, Cesar Chavez led workers on lettuce and grape farms in a struggle for the right to form a union. They hoped that a union would help them earn higher wages and have better living conditions.

Herman Badillo, a Puerto Rican, represented a poor part of New York in Congress. In 1978, he became a Deputy Mayor of New York City.

Many injustices also existed in the way that women in the United States were treated. Women were often denied jobs just because they were women. Even when women did the same jobs as men, the women were usually paid less. Often, women were not given promotions. Unmarried women could not get loans from banks even if they had high-paying jobs. This was not the case for unmarried men.

Since the foundation of the nation, women in this country have been fighting for their rights.

Women began to unite in order to fight discrimination. The National Organization for Women (NOW), founded by Betty Friedan and others, helped make people and the government more sympathetic to the struggle for women's rights.

There have been many changes in social conditions in the United States. But many more reforms are still needed. The struggle for equality and justice for all continues.

TO DO
1. Name two black leaders from the South.
2. Name three ways in which blacks are discriminated against.
3. Who is Betty Friedan? Cesar Chavez?
4. Name two ways in which women are discriminated against.

ON YOUR OWN
5. What do you think are some good ways people can end discrimination?
6. Why do you think groups of people who share a common problem often join together, or organize, in order to solve the problem? What advantages are there in this?

Challenges for the Future

On July 4, 1976, the United States celebrated its 200th birthday. This birthday was called the *bicentennial*. This was a day of many celebrations. It was also a time when many United States citizens looked at the many new challenges facing the United States.

Honesty in government is one concern of the nation. The muckrakers in the early 1900s made the nation aware of politicians who were not dealing fairly with the people. In

In 1973, for several months, certain countries stopped selling oil to the United States. This resulted in a shortage of gasoline, as these long lines at a gas station show. In the 1970s, the United States became more and more dependent on foreign oil.

the 1970s, some politicians were still behaving dishonestly. Some people who worked for President Richard M. Nixon broke into an office in the Watergate building complex in Washington, D.C. They were trying to spy on the candidate running against President Nixon in 1972. Newspaper reporters found out about the spying. This caused many people to become suspicious of the President and of others in the government.

President Nixon tried to help his friends. He wanted the people to believe his friends did nothing wrong. But this made people even more suspicious. They felt that perhaps

he, too, had done something illegal. The people did not feel that a President of the United States should have the right to break the law. Congress thought about removing Nixon from the office of President. Before they could do that, he chose to resign. This event came to be known as *Watergate*.

A nation with as much industry as the United States faces another challenge. It needs *energy* to keep everything running. Energy means power. Electricity is a form of energy. It makes light bulbs, refrigerators, record players, televisions, and air conditioners work. Gasoline is another form of energy. It powers our cars, trucks, and airplanes. Coal is another form of energy. It is used to heat many homes and factories and to make electricity.

The United States is a land rich in natural resources. Some of these resources, such as water, oil, and coal, have been used to produce the energy the country has needed. But as the United States grows larger, it needs more and more energy. Many people see now that the oil in the United States cannot provide as much energy as the nation needs.

The United States has begun to buy more than half the oil it needs from other countries. These nations demand very high prices for their oil. Many people in the United States cannot afford to pay those prices. The United States must think of ways to make sure that its people can get the energy they need at a price they can afford to pay.

Some people think that atomic reactors, like the one shown here, should supply much more of our energy needs.

Many people fear that too much development will destroy much of the natural beauty of our nation.

The natural resources of the United States give its people more than just energy. The air the people breathe and the soil from which food grows are also resources. Other resources are the mountains, forests, rivers, and valleys that make this country a beautiful place in which to live.

People in the past had always acted as though there were no end to the forests and other resources of the land. Generations of settlers had burned or cut the forests down to make room for farmlands. There always seemed to be plenty of forests left. But by 1900, this was no longer true. The people of the United States now know that if they use up too many resources, there will soon not be any left.

They have also learned that some ways of using resources can destroy the environment as well as the people living in it. For example, coal mining is dangerous work. Coal miners often suffer from an illness called *black lung* disease. Many have died from it. Very often, too, the methods used to take the coal from the earth destroy the land. This is a great danger to the environment.

There are other dangers. When automobiles and factories burn gasoline and coal, certain chemicals get into the air. These chemicals can cause disease and illness. Filling the air we breathe with poisonous chemicals harms our environment. And this endangers our health.

Governments in all areas of the United States are trying to stop water pollution.

Some factories throw their waste products into nearby rivers and streams. These waste products often contain harsh chemicals which kill the fish and plants that live in those rivers and streams. These waste products contain harsh chemicals which *pollute* the water, killing fish and plants. Birds and other animals who feed and drink in these polluted waters also die. Many people are afraid that there may soon be no fish, plants, or animals left. Protecting our natural environment is an important challenge for the future.

The United States has business and other interests all over the world. Whatever happens in distant lands now affects people here at home. The entire world has become one very large community. There are many world problems that affect the people of the United States.

Many people in the world suffer from hunger and poverty. The people of the United States must decide what they want to do to help those people. Wars in distant countries make world wars possible. The people of the United States must help to find ways of bringing all wars to an end. In Africa, a few countries are still trying to overthrow colonial governments and to become independent, just as the United States did in 1776. The people of the United States must decide how much help they can give these countries.

President Jimmy Carter spoke to the people of the United States about the right of people everywhere to live in freedom. This will be one of the greatest challenges in the future. How can the people of the United States help peoples all over the world to find freedom? How can they bring about complete freedom and equality in their own country?

1. What is meant by the bicentennial?
2. Who was the President that resigned from office because the people thought he had broken the law?
3. What are some causes of pollution?

4. Why do you think its people feel so strongly that even the President of the United States should not break the law? Isn't the President a special person with special privileges?
5. What are some of the things that might happen in the United States if we ran out of energy?

1. List three reasons that the 1920s were considered good times for many people of the United States.
2. What was the Great Depression? What caused it?
3. What were four causes of World War II?
4. Why did the United States fight in World War II?
5. How did the role of women change as a result of the war?
6. Why did the United States want to stop communism after World War II?
7. What groups in the United States fought for their rights in the 1960s and 1970s? What right were they fighting for?
8. Tell about two important challenges you see for the United States in the future.

UNIT REVIEW

What Do I Know?

1. Match the terms on the left to their correct meanings on the right.

   suburb
   empire
   isolationism
   tenement
   nationalism
   dictator
   suffragist
   migration
   muckraker
   discrimination
   cold war

   (a) crowded apartment building
   (b) war without fighting
   (c) movement of people within the same country
   (d) system where one country controls other countries
   (e) person who takes over a government
   (f) giving some people more rights than others
   (g) person who wrote about problems of industrialization
   (h) not getting involved with other countries' problems
   (i) person who fought for women's right to vote
   (j) place outside the city where workers live
   (k) great pride in one's own nation

2. Answer *true* or *false* to the following statements.
   (a) The Pure Food and Drug Act gave the government power to inspect meat.
   (b) The Nineteenth Amendment gave women the right to own property.
   (c) Prohibition made the sale of liquor illegal.

3. Relations between the United States and the Soviet Union have changed over the years. Number these events in the order they happened.
   (a) The United States and the Soviet Union begin the cold war.
   (b) The United States becomes more friendly toward Communist countries.
   (c) Both countries support different sides in Viet Nam.
   (d) The United States and the Soviet Union are allies.

What Can I Do?

1. This graph shows the number of women and men that were working in the years 1966 to 1970. Study the graph. Then answer the questions below.

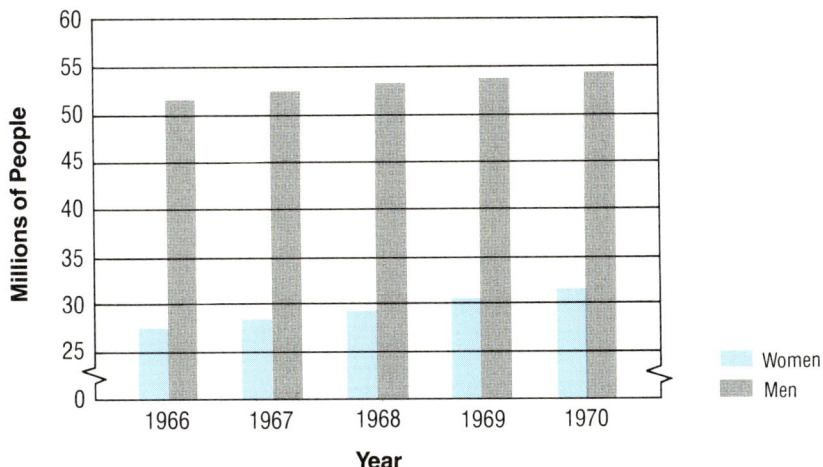

   (a) Were there more women or more men working in these years?
   (b) Does the number of working women seem to be increasing or decreasing? Give one reason why.
   (c) How do you think a graph for the year 1965 would look compared to the other years shown?

2. Pretend you are a child living during the Great Depression. Tell what changes you and your family had to make. How have these changes affected your life?

What Is Important?

1. At the end of World War II, the Allies forced the Germans to give up many things. Do you think the Germans were treated fairly? Why? How do you think losers of war should be treated? Should the winners help the losers rebuild their country?

2. The United States faces many challenges for the future. If you had the power to solve just one of these problems, which one would it be? Why? How would you solve it?

GLOSSARY

abolitionist: person who wanted to do away with slavery. (page 259)

amendment: a change in the Constitution. (page 187)

barrio: a neighborhood of Spanish-speaking people. (page 221)

belief: thinking something to be true, good, or right. (page 50)

benefit: anything we hope to gain by choosing one alternative over another. (page 132)

bilingual: being able to speak, read, and write in two languages. (page 227)

Black Codes: laws passed by Southern states which prevented blacks from voting, serving on juries, and carrying guns. (page 279)

border: a boundary between nations or states. (page 236)

capitalism: an economic system, as in the United States, in which the means of production and distribution are privately owned and businesses are free to compete on an open market. (page 361)

climate: the weather on an average day or over a long period of time. (page 21)

colony: a group of people who settle in a distant land, but are still ruled by their parent country. (page 83)

competition: trying to win something that other people are also trying to win. (pages 329–330)

compromise: an agreement in which each side in an argument gives in a little, thereby granting part of what each side wants. (page 182)

Congress: lawmaking branch of the United States government. (pages 35, 184)

cooperation: the act of working together with others to achieve a common goal. (page 128)

cultural group: people who share the same culture. (page 45)

cultural identity: a feeling of belonging, or togetherness, among members of a cultural group. (page 217)

cultural pluralism: different kinds of behavior, different languages, and different beliefs found within the same country. (page 53)

culture: the behavior, beliefs, and language that are shared by members of a group. (page 45)

elevation key: a table or chart which tells how high or low a place is in relation to sea level. (page 11)

executive branch: the part of the United States government headed by the President which carries out the laws. (page 183)

federal government: the national government. (page 182)

federalists: people who were *for* the Constitution. (page 183)

House of Representatives: the lower house of Congress to which each state elects representatives every two years according to its population. (page 185)

immigrants: people who leave their country and settle in another. (page 288)

international boundaries: lines on a map that divide one nation from another. (page 13)

judicial branch: the part of the United States government which settles questions about what the laws mean. (page 184)

landforms: kinds of structure or shapes of land a country or continent has. (page 11)

legislative branch: the lawmaking branch of the United States government, called Congress. (page 184)

migration: movement of people to different areas in the same country. (page 339)

norm: a shared belief about how the members of a group should behave. (page 50)

nuclear families: a family consisting of parents and their children. (page 223)

political map: a map showing divisions of government—national, state, or local. (page 30)

population-density map: a map which shows how many people live in a certain area. (page 31)

precipitation: water that falls from the air as rain, snow, or fog. (page 21)

Reconstruction: a plan to rebuild the South after the Civil War. (page 278)

representatives: people who are chosen to speak or act for a group. (page 90)

reservations: areas of land set aside for Native Americans. (page 311)

revolution: a war in which the people of a country overthrow the government and start a new government. (page 153)

secession: means to withdraw from something. (page 269)

segregation: term used to describe separating blacks from whites. (page 280)

Senate: people elected every six years to represent their state in one of the two bodies of Congress. (page 185)

tariff: a tax placed on goods brought into the United States. (page 266)

temperature: how much heat is in the air. (page 21)

time lines: lines which show important events in the order in which they happened. (page 61)

unconstitutional: a law declared not fitting in with the ideas and purposes of the Constitution, and thereby does not have to be obeyed. (page 186)

urban areas: towns and cities with more than 2,500 people in them. (page 31)

values: beliefs about what is important. (page 51)

weather: the condition of the air at any one moment or on a particular day. (page 21)

wetlands: areas of land covered with shallow water. (page 14)

INDEX

abolitionists, 259–263, 267, 273
Adams, Abigail, 167, 170*
Adams, John, 159, 166*–167, 170, 179
Adams, Samuel, 159, 169
Adventure, 114
Africa, 72, 73, 103, 256, 354, 373
Alabama, 14, 79, 194, 269, 281
Alaska, 31
Allende, 220, 225, 244–247
Allies, 356
amendments, 187, 280, 348
American Revolution, 153–165*, 273, 347
    cause of, 153–158*
Amish people, 113–147
Amistad Dam, 41
ancestors, 11, 35, 76–77, 210
Anthony, Susan B., 349
antifederalists, 183
Appalachian Mountains, 11, 14–15*, 17, 193, 199–201
Appomattox, 275, 278
Arctic, 34
Arizona, 68, 205, 210, 318
Arkansas, 79, 274
Arnold, Benedict, 162
Articles of Confederation, 178
Asia, 62–63, 72–73, 289, 361–362
assembly line, 350
Atlantic Coastal Plain, 11, 13–14
Atlantic Ocean, 23, 41, 73, 94
atomic bomb, 357, 360–361
Austria, 173
Axis, 354
Aztec people, 66–67, 76–77

Baja, 42
Baltimore, 286
Banneker, Benjamin, 260
barrio, 221–222
Beckwourth, Jim, 203*
Belgium, 354
beliefs, 28–29, 171
    cultural pluralism, 53

*Also denotes photograph

Bell, Alexander Graham, 297
Berkeley, William, 106
Bethlehem, 218
bicentennial, 368
bilingual, 227–228
Bill of Rights, 187–190
bills, 185
Black Americans, 255*–281
    after the Civil War, 276–278
    against slavery, 260–263*
    Black Codes and, 279
    in Civil War, 273*
    in colonies, 255
    discrimination and, 364–365
    education and, 256, 276–278, 280
    Freedman's Bureau, 278
    Harlem and, 351
    migration of, 339
    rights and, 339–340, 359
    segregation, 280–281
    voting and, 256, 279–280, 364
Black Codes, 279
Blackwell, Dr. Elizabeth, 346
Boone, Daniel, 192
Boston, 100, 155, 157–159, 166, 267
Boston Tea Party, 156*, 167
boycott, 157, 167
Bradford, Cornelia, 110
Bull Run, Battle of, 172
Bunker Hill, Battle of, 159–160
Bureau of Indian Affairs, 311, 329
Burgoyne, General, 162
Byler family, 126–128

Cabot, John, 75
California, 18, 42, 205, 207–210, 243, 300
Calvert, George, 106
Canada, 11, 13–15, 20, 316
Canadian Shield, 11, 20
Cape Cod, 94
capitalism, 361
Carnegie, Andrew, 281, 297
carpetbaggers, 279–280
Carteret, George, 106

Carter, Jimmy, 373
Catholics, 106, 217–219, 293
Catt, Carrie Chapman, 347
cattle, 14, 16, 17*, 20, 93, 102, 195, 205, 264, 301*–302
census, 31
Central America, 63, 216, 314
Central Lowlands, 11, 15–16
Charleston, 270
Charter of Liberties, 106
Chavez, Cesar, 366
Cherokee people, 201–202*
Chesapeake Bay, 106
Cheyenne people, 303
Chiang Kai-shek, 361
Chicago, 15, 41, 264, 288, 290, 293, 296, 301, 316
Chichén Itzá, 65
Chief Joseph, 308–309
child labor, 339–340*, 344
China, 72, 361
    immigrants from, 289–290, 293–294
Christian Science Monitor, 346
Church of Christ, Scientist, 346
Cincinnati, 264
cities, 14, 15, 17, 23, 31, 64*–66, 79, 109*–112*, 264–265, 285, 288, 294, 296–298, 339
Civil War, 271*–275
Clark, George Rogers, 164
Clark, William, 199–200*
Cleveland, 15
climate, 33, 38, 91
coal, 15, 121, 288, 351, 370–371
Cochise people, 68
Cody, "Buffalo Bill," 305
Cohoe family, 325–327
cold war, 361–362
colonies,
    English, 83, 85*–116
    Jamestown and the South, 86*–93
Colorado, 303
Colorado River, 23, 40
Columbia River, 41
Columbus, Christopher, 71*, 72–75
Comanche people, 303

Committee of Correspondence, 166
Common Sense, 168
communication system, 28
Communism, 216, 356, 361–362
communities, 113–147, 213*–247, 318*–333
Concord, 157–158
Conestoga wagon, 203*–204
Confederate States of America, 269–270
Congress, 35, 169, 178–179, 182–183, 201, 266, 294, 311–313, 344
Connecticut, 100
Constitution, 181*–190, 187–190, 280, 348
continent, 11–13, 40–42
Corbin, Margaret, 160
corn, 15, 63, 65, 68, 93, 102, 108, 195, 243, 259, 264, 285, 301
Cornish, Samuel E., 260
Cornwallis, General, 164
Coronado, Francisco, 79
Cortez, Hernando, 76
cotton, 63, 66, 91, 195, 201, 205, 264, 271, 286
cotton gin, 266, 285
crops, 11, 14–15, 88, 91–92
Crow people, 203, 303
Cuba, 73, 216, 362
Cuban Americans, 45
Cuffe, Paul, 260
culture, 44–45, 197, 209, 293
   behavior and language, 46*–49*
   bicultural zone, 243
Cumberland Gap, 192
Czechoslovakia, 354

Daughters of Liberty, 167
Dawes, William, 157
decision making, 129–131, 166–172
Declaration of Independence (1776), 161, 169, 260, 345
Delaware, 105, 108
Delaware River, 161
Democratic Party, 267, 286
De Soto, Hernando, 70, 79
Detroit, 15, 41, 290
discrimination, 363*–367*
District of Columbia, 30

Douglas, Frederick, 260–261*
drought, 352
DuBois, W.E.B., 277*–278, 281
Dutch, *see* Netherlands

Earhart, Amelia, 346
East Indies, 74
Eddy, Mary Baker, 346
Ederle, Gertrude, 346
Edison, Thomas Alva, 297–298
education, 53
Eighth Amendment, 190
elevation, 11–13
Emancipation Proclamation, 273
England, 72, 314
   colonies and, 83, 85*–116
   Dutch and, 106
   slaves and, 266
   World War II and, 354–356
English Channel, 346
Ericson, Lief, 72
Esh family, 124–125
Eskimos (Innuit), 34
Estevanico, 78
Europe, 35, 37, 64, 361
   explorers from, 71–84
   immigrants from, 288–294
   World War II and, 353–357
executive branch, 184–185
exploration,
   of English, 82–84
   of French, 80–81
   Portuguese and, 73
   of Spaniards, 76–79
extended family, 223, 319

factories, 19, 27, 35, 173, 179, 257, 271, 351
farming, 14–15, 18, 63, 113–116, 140–141, 195, 208, 302, 351, 352
federal government, 182–183
   branches of, 184–186
federalists, 183, 187
Ferdinand, King, 74
Fifteenth Amendment, 280
Fifth Amendment, 187
Finland, 108
First Amendment, 187
First Continental Congress (1774), 157
Florida, 77, 79, 216, 269
food, 121, 242*–243, 258–259

Ford, Henry, 350
forests, 11, 20, 35, 203, 371
   preservation of, 344
Forten, James, 260
Fort Sumter, 270
forty-niners, 207–208
Fourteenth Amendment, 280
Fourth Amendment, 187
Fox people, 193
France, 72, 80–81, 154, 162–165, 199, 354
Franklin, Benjamin, 111–112*, 159, 169, 314
Freedman's Bureau, 278
Freedom's Journal, 260
French and Indian Wars, 154, 159
French language, 35
Friedan, Betty, 367
frontier, 192, 199–202
fur trade, 81, 105, 203

Galveston, 77
Garrison, William Lloyd, 267
George III, King, 165
Georgia, 14, 90, 269
Germany, 108, 111, 175, 289–290, 354–357
Gettysburg Address, 274
gold, 63, 66, 74, 82
Gould, Jay, 296
government, 29, 95, 106, 192
Grand Banks, 72, 80–81
Grand Canyon, 79
Grant, Ulysses S., 272, 274–275
"Great American desert," 300
Great Basin, 11, 17
Great Britain, 153–165, 173–176
Great Depression, 352–353
Great Lakes, 23, 40–41, 68, 81
Great Plains, 11, 13, 15–16*, 40, 201, 285, 299*–309
Great Salt Lake, 17
Greece, 291
Greenland, 72
Guatemala, 64
Gulf Coastal Plain, 11, 14
Gulf of Mexico, 15, 68, 77, 236

Hanukkah, 218
Harlem, 351
Hawaii, 31, 356
Henry, Patrick, 175

379

hieroglyphics, 64
Hiroshima, 357
Hispaniola, 73
Hitler, Adolph, 353*, 354–356
Homestead Act (1862), 300
Hopewell Culture, 68
House of Burgesses, 90
House of Representatives, 185
Houston, Sam, 205
Howe, General, 162–163
Howe, Julia Ward, 347
Hudson Bay, 20
Hudson, Henry, 81, 105
Hudson River, 81
Hungary, 361
Huntington, Collis P., 296
Hutchinson, Anne, 99–100

Iceland, 72
Illinois, 199, 267
immigrants, 288–294, 302
 in cities, 289–290, 343
 problems of, 292*–294
indentured servants, 84, 91, 255
independence, 159*–176
Independence, Mo., 204, 205
India, 27, 72, 74–75
Indiana, 194
"Indians," 74
indigo, 91, 92
Industrial Revolution, 288–298
industry, 42, 260
 big business and, 295–298, 341–343
Innuit (Eskimos), 34
international boundaries, 13
International Joint Committee, 41
International Peace Garden, 36
Ireland, 108, 289, 293
Iroquois people, 314
irrigation, 68
Isabella, Queen, 73–74
isolationism, 355
Italian Americans, 45
Italy, 291, 354*

Jackson, Andrew, 202
Jackson, Thomas "Stonewall," 272
James River, 86
Jamestown, 86*–93, 314
Japan, 291, 294, 355–357
Japanese Americans, 45, 359–360

"Jazz Age," 350
Jefferson, Thomas, 159–160, 175, 179, 260
Jesus Christ, 217, 263
Jews, 291, 354–355
jobs, 53, 297, 350, 352
 blacks and, 276–278, 364
 immigrants and, 288–293
 Mexican Americans and, 211
Johnson, Andrew, 278–281
Jones, John, 260
judicial branch, 184–186
jury, 106, 189

Kansas, 68, 77, 301, 303, 316
Kansas City, 301
Kelly, Florence, 344
Kentucky, 193–194
King, Dr. Martin Luther Jr., 364*, 365
Kiowa people, 303
Kosciusko, Thaddeaus, 175

Lafayette, Marquis de, 175
Lake Erie, 41
Lancaster County, Pa., 114, 117–147
landforms, 11, 13–20
land speculators, 192–193
language, 44, 79, 199, 201
Lapp family, 122–123, 126
Lee, Robert E., 271, 274–275
legislative branch, 184–185
Lewis, Meriwether, 199–200*
Lexington, 157–158
Liberator, The, 267
Liberty Tree, 167
Lima, 79
Lincoln, Abraham, 267–270, 272–273, 278
London, 88
Loredo, 243
Los Angeles, 243
Louisiana, 269, 274
Louisiana Purchase, 199–200*

Magellan, Ferdinand, 75
Manhattan, 105
Manitoba, 36
Mao Tse-tung, 361
maps,
 climate, 21
 elevation, 11–13
 political, 30
 population-density, 31

Marshall, James, 207
Maryland, 90, 105–106, 262
Mason, George, 93
Massachusetts, 96–100, 157, 166, 179
Massachusetts Bay Company, 95–96
Maya people, 64–65, 70
Mayflower, 94
Mayflower Compact, 94
McClellan, George, 272
McCormick, Cyrus, 285
Meat Inspection Act (1906), 344
Memphis, 79
Mennonites, 145
mestizos, 38, 210
metric system, 240–241
Mexican Americans, 210–212*, 214–247, 366
Mexico, 11, 13, 63, 68, 316
 Allende, 220, 230, 244–247
Mexico City, 19, 66, 78–79, 205
Miami, 21, 316
Miami people, 193
Middle Colonies, 105*–116
migration, 339
Miller family, 124*–125
Milwaukee, 290, 316
minority, 210, 339–340
missions, 79
Mississippi, 79, 194, 269, 316
Mississippi River, 23–24, 66, 70, 79, 192, 193, 274, 300, 303
Missouri, 204, 205
Missouri River, 15–16, 23–24
Mitchell, Maria, 346
Montana, 303
Monterrey, 220, 230, 243
Montezuma, 76–77
Montgomery, 365
Montreal, 81
Morelos family, 216, 220*–223, 227–228
Morse, Samuel, 286–287
Moscow, 357
muckrakers, 341*–342, 368
Mussolini, Benito, 354*

Nagasaki, 357
Narvaez, Panfilo de, 77–78
Natchez people, 70
National Consumers League, 344
Nationalist Chinese, 361

National Organization of Women (NOW), 367
Native Americans, 11, 34–37, 62–63, 81, 86–88, 90, 94–95, 99, 162, 175, 178, 192–193, 199–200, 203–204, 303–309, 311–316
natural gas, 15, 35
natural resources, 35, 344, 370–371
Navaho people, 45, 318*–333
Nazi Party, 354
Nebraska, 303
Netherlands, 81, 105–106, 108, 354
New Amsterdam, 105
New England, 94–104
New England Primer, 101–102
Newfoundland, 75
New Hampshire, 100
New Jersey, 105–106
New Mexico, 62, 68, 205, 318
New Netherlands, 105
New Orleans, 199
New World,
  discovery of, 71–75
  exploration of, 73–84
New York City, 109, 162
  draft riots in, 273
New York State, 68, 346–347
Nez Perce people, 308–309
Nineteenth Amendment, 348
Ninth Amendment, 190
Nixon, Richard, 362, 369–370
norm, 50, 135–136, 319
North America, 17–18
North Carolina, 90
North Dakota, 36, 303, 304
North Korea, 362
North Vietnam, 362
Norway, 72, 354
Nova Scotia, 72
Nuevo Laredo, 243
Nuevo León, 230

Ohio, 194, 288, 316
Ohio River, 23–24, 68, 192
oil, 15, 35, 41, 295–297, 341, 355, 370
Old Copper Culture, 68
Omaha, 301, 316
oranges, 14, 18, 244
Oregon, 200, 203–204, 300
Ottawa, 35

Pacific Coastal Region, 11, 13, 18
Pacific Ocean, 75, 199–200, 236
Paine, Thomas, 168*, 175
Parks, Rosa, 365
Parliament, 35, 153–154, 157, 165
patroon system, 106
Paul, Alice, 348
Pawnee people, 303
Pearl Harbor, 356
Pennsylvania,
  Amish people in, 113–147
  as a colony, 105, 108
  founding of, 108
Pennsylvania Dutch, 121
Penn, William, 106–108, 113
People's Republic of China, 27
Peru, 79
Petersburg, 275
Philadelphia, 109*–112*, 161–163
Philadelphia Mercury, 110
Philippines, 75
Pilgrims, 94–96
pioneers, 192, 200
plantations, 264
  blacks on, 258*–259, 264, 276
  life on, 91*–93
pluralism, 53
Plymouth Colony, 94, 314
Pocahontas, 86, 88
Poland, 291, 354, 361
Poor Richard's Almanac, 111
Poor, Salem, 160
pollution, 41–42, 371–372
Portugal, 72–73
potatoes, 63, 65, 289, 314
Powhatan people, 86–87
precipitation, 21–22
President, 185, 370
Prince Henry "The Navigator," 73
Princeton, 161
Progressives, 342–344
Prohibition, 350
Protestants, 106–108, 293
pueblo, 245
Pueblo people, 68, 318
Puerto Rican Americans, 216, 366
Puerto Rico, 31, 73, 218
Pure Food and Drug Act (1906), 344

Puritans, 83, 94–104

Quakers, 106, 109
Quebec, 35, 80–81
quinine, 314

railroads, 15, 27, 207, 271, 285–286, 290, 295–297
Raza Island, 42
reaper, 285
Reconstruction, 278–281
religion, 79, 99, 106–108, 113, 125, 145, 187, 319–320, 346
  Puritans and, 83, 94–95, 97–100
  Roman Catholic, 217–219
relocation camps, 359–360*
Republican Party, 267
reservation, 304, 311–313, 318, 329
Revere, Paul, 157
revolution, 153, 156*–158*
Rhode Island, 99, 100
rice, 14, 91, 92, 264
Richmond, 272
rights, 339–340
  Bill of Rights, 187–190
Rillieux, Norbert, 260
Rio Grande, 23, 40, 41, 205
rivers, 17, 23–25, 92, 283, 371
"Roaring Twenties," 350–352
Rochambeau, Comte de, 175
Rockefeller, John D., 297, 341
Rocky Mountains, 11, 17, 24, 40
Rolfe, John, 88
Roosevelt, Theodore, 343*–344
Rough Rock School, 332*–333
Rumania, 361
rural areas, 31
Russia, *see* Soviet Union
Russwarm, John, 260

Sacajawea, 199–200
Sacramento River, 207
St. Lawrence River, 23, 41, 80
St. Lawrence Seaway, 41
Samoset, 94–95
Sampson, Deborah, 160
San Antonio, 205, 216, 217, 220–221, 225, 243
San Francisco, 205, 209*, 217
San Salvador, 73
Santa Barbara, 217
Santa Fe, 215

Saratoga, 162
Sauk people, 193
scalawags, 280
Schmidt, Calvin, 142–144
Scotland, 108, 297
Seattle, 316
secession, 269
Second Amendment, 187
Second Continental Congress (1775), 159, 161, 170
segregation, 280–281, 364–365
Senate, 185
Seneca Falls, 346–347
Seventh Amendment, 190
Shays, Daniel, 179
sheep, 16, 93
Shoshone people, 199
Shurtleff, Robert, 160
silver, 20, 66, 77
Sioux people, 303–305, 307
Sixth Amendment, 189
slavery, 178, 182–183, 255*–281
   abolitionists and, 259–263*, 267, 273
   blacks against, 260–263*
   "slave" v. "free" states, 264–270
   in the South, 92*–93
   Thirteenth Amendment and, 280
Smith, Captain John, 86–87, 94
Smith, Dr. James McCune, 260
Society of Friends, 106–109
Sons of Liberty, 166–167
South America, 63, 75, 205, 216, 314–315
South Carolina, 90, 269
South Dakota, 303
Southeast Asia, 355
Southern Colonies,
   Jamestown, 86*–93
   plantation life, 91*–93
   slavery in, 92*–93, 103
South Korea, 362
South Vietnam, 362
Southwest, 202–210*
Soviet Union, 27, 291, 296, 356
Spain, 214, 318
Spanish language, 38, 222, 333
   Hispanic, 214
Spanish-speaking people, 210–247, 366
Spice Islands, 75

"Square Deal," 343–344
Stamp Act (1765), 153–154, 169
Standard Oil Company, 341
Standing Rock Reservation, 304
Stanton, Elizabeth Cady, 347
state's rights, 265–267, 271
steamboat, 207, 285–286
steel, 287, 295, 297
Steffens, Lincoln, 342
Von Steuben, Baron, 175
Stowe, Harriet Beecher, 267
Stuyvesant, Peter, 106
sugar, 103, 153, 260, 264, 286
Supreme Court, 185–186, 364
swamps, 14, 19, 86
Sweden, 108

Taino people, 74
Tallahassee, 316
Tarbell, Ida, 341*
tariff, 266
Tarrytown, 160
taxes, 76, 237
   American Revolution and, 153, 167, 169, 179, 185, 237
tea, 154, 156*, 167
telegraph, 286–287
telephone, 297
temperature, 21–22
Temple, Louis, 260
Temple Mound Culture, 68–70
Tennessee, 79, 192, 194
Tenochtitlan, 66
Tenth Amendment, 190
Texas, 62, 77–79, 205, 260, 210, 216, 243, 269, 274, 303
Thanksgiving, 95
Third Amendment, 187
Thirteenth Amendment, 280
thresher, 285
Thunderhawk, Zona, 304–305
time lines, 61
tobacco, 65, 74, 91, 105, 106, 266
Toltec people, 65–66
Toronto, 41
trade, 41, 42, 63, 66, 68, 72–73, 266, 355
traditions, 217*–219*
"Trail of Tears," 202*
transportation, 15, 27, 295*–298, 339
Treaty of Versailles, 354
Trenton, 161

trial and error, 321
trial by jury, 106, 189
Troyer family, 142*–144
Truman, Harry, 357, 359
Truth, Sojourner, 260, 262
Tubman, Harriet, 260, 262*
Tucson, 316
Tulsa, 316
Tuskegee Institute, 281

Uncle Tom's Cabin, 267
unconstitutional, 186
Underground Railroad, 262
unions, 366
United States,
   American Revolution, 163–176
   atomic age, 361–362
   bicentennial, 368
   birth of, 177*–190
   culture groups in, 44*–45, 53, 113–147, 213*–247, 288–294, 303–333
   environment, 10*–25
   regions of, 14–18
urban areas, 31
Utah, 318

Vaca, Cabeza de, 78
Valley Forge, 163
values, 51, 116, 130, 307
Vanderbilt, Cornelius, 296
Vassar College, 346
Veracruz, 19
Vespucci, Amerigo, 75
veto, 185
Vikings, 72
Virginia, 94, 159, 164, 170, 175, 272, 275
Virginia Company, 86, 88–90
vocational schools, 139
vote, 211
   Black Codes and, 279
   blacks and, 256, 279–280, 364
   Fifteenth Amendment, 280
   Native Americans and, 311
   women and, 261, 339

Wampanoag people, 95
War of 1812, 200, 273
Warren, Mercy, 167
Washington, Booker T., 280*–281
Washington, D.C., 30, 265, 272

Washington, George, 159, 161, 163–164, 171–172*, 175
Watergate, 369–370
weather, 14–15, 21–22, 230
West Indies, 103, 105, 108
West Virginia, 318
wetlands, 14
wheat, 15, 16*, 102, 106, 243, 300
Whitney, Eli, 266, 285
Wichita, 316
"Wilderness Road," 192
Williams, Roger, 99
Winthrop, John, 83, 97, 99
Wisconsin, 68

women,
  against slavery, 262–263, 267
  in American Revolution, 160*, 163, 167, 170
  Daughters of Liberty, 167
  on the frontier, 195*–198*
  in Jamestown, 87, 89
  jobs and, 346–348, 358, 366
  National Organization of Women (NOW), 367
  rights and, 262, 347–348, 367*
  voting and, 261, 339, 345*–348
  Women's Suffrage, 346–348

wool, 195, 283–285
World War I, 346
World War II, 353–360
  effects of, 358–360
Wyoming, 303

Yoder family, 119–121, 140
York, Duke of, 106
Yorktown, 162
Yucatán Peninsula, 19, 64–65
Yugoslavia, 361

CREDITS

Pictures listed clockwise from upper left, unless otherwise noted.

Bruce Roberts/Photo Researchers: **8–9**; Shelly Grossman/Woodfin Camp: **10**; Erich Hartmann/Magnum: **14**; Ken Foster/Photo Researchers: **15**; Information Canada Phototheque: **16**; John Running/Stock, Boston: **17**; Van Bucher/Photo Researchers, Georg Gerster/Photo Researchers: **18**; Craig Aurness/Woodfin Camp, Al Satterwhite/Image Bank: **19**; Dan Budnik/Woodfin Camp: **22**; Georg Gerster/Photo Researchers: **23**; Robert Phillips/Image Bank: **24**; J. H. Sullivan/Photo Researchers, Bryn Campbell/Magnum, Rene Burri/Magnum: **26**; Leonard Nadel/McGraw-Hill: **27**; Tim Eagan/Woodfin Camp: **28**; Jim Holland/Stock, Boston: **31**; National Film Board of Canada: **35**; Burt Glinn/Magnum, George Hall/Woodfin Camp: **36**; Cary Wolinsky/Stock, Boston, Rene Burri/Magnum, Albert Moldvay/Woodfin Camp: **38**; Carl Frank/Photo Researchers: **39**; Erich Hartmann/Magnum: **40**; Wally McNamee/Woodfin Camp: **43**; Culver: **44**; Toge Fujihira/Monkmeyer, Guy Gillette/Photo Researchers, Jim Amos/Photo Researchers: **46**; Peter Arnold/Peter Arnold Photo Archives, Daniel Brody/Stock, Boston, Oliver Rebbot/Stock, Boston: **47**; Bjorn Bolstad/Peter Arnold Photo Archives, Richard Avery/Stock, Boston, Peter Arnold/Peter Arnold Photo Archives: **49**; James H. Karales/Peter Arnold Photo Archives: **50**; Katrina Thomas/Photo Researchers: **51**; Mike Mazzaschi/Stock, Boston, Christa Armstrong/Photo Researchers: **52**; UPI: **53**; Bruce Curtis/Peter Arnold Photo Archives, Owen Franken/Stock, Boston, James H. Karales/Peter Arnold Photo Archives: **54**; United States Air Force: **55**; *Hope of Jamestown*, John Gadsby Chapman, Collection of Mr. and Mrs. Paul Mellon: **58–59**; American Museum of Natural History: **60**; Monkmeyer Press Photos: **64**; Dick Hufnagle/Monkmeyer: **65**; American Museum of National History: **67**; Martin J. Dain/Magnum, American Museum of National History: **69**; Culver: **71**; UPI: **74**; British Embassy, Mexico City: **77**; New York Public Library: **78**; *La Salle's Expedition*, George Catlin, National Gallery of Art: **80**; New York Public Library: **81**; © 1920 J. L. G. Ferris, © 1947 Ernest N. Ryder d.b.n.c.t.a. Renewal Wm. E. Ryder, by will UCC 1977, Archives of 76, Bay Village, Ohio: **85**; New York Public Library: **86**; Courtesy of American Heritage: **87**; Bettman Archives: **88**; *The Plantation*, Metropolitan Museum of Art, Collection of Edgar William and Bernice Chrysler Garbisch: **91**; Bettman Archives: **92, 95**; New York Historical Society: **96**; New York Public Library: **97**; Pilgrim Society: **98**; New York Public Library: **99**; Bettman Archives: **101**; New York Public Library: **103**; Bettman Archives: **104**; Museum of The City of New York, J. Clarence Davies Collection: **105**; The Historical Society of

Pennsylvania, Abby Aldrich Rockefeller Folk Art Collection: **107**; R. Campbell and Company: **109**; Bettman Archives: **110–112**; New York Public Library: **113**; John Neubauer/Photo Researchers: **114**; Jane Latta: **115, 117**; Mel Horst: **118**; Jane Latta: **120**; Grant Heilman/Monkmeyer: **122**; Mel Horst: **123**; Mel Horst, Jane Latta: **124**; Jane Latta: **126**; Mel Horst: **127**; Jane Latta: **128, 132, 133, 135**. Mel Horst: **136, 137**; John Launois/Black Star: **138, 139**; Perry Cragg: **140**; Perry Cragg, Mel Horst: **141**; Jane Latta: **142**; Vincent Tortora: **143**; Jane Latta: **145, 146**; Library of Congress: **150–151**; *Pulling Down the Statue of George III in New York*, William Walcutt, 1854, Gilbert Darling Collection, New York: **152**; Massachusetts Historical Society, The John Carter Brown Library, Brown University: **154**; Bettman Archives: **155**; New York Public Library: **156**; Connecticut Historical Society: **157**; Delaware Art Museum: **158, 159**; Bettman Archives: **160**; United States Naval Academy Museum: **162**; Indiana Historical Bureau: **164**; Bettman Archives: **165**; New York Public Library: **166**; Kennedy Galleries, New York: **167**; New York Public Library: **168, 169**; Culver: **170**; New York Public Library: **171**; The Metropolitan Museum of Art: **172**; *George Washington, Lafayette and Tench Tilghman at Yorktown*, Charles Willson Peale 1741-1827, Maryland Commission of Artistic Property: **172**; Bettman Archives: **175–181**; New York Public Library: **182**; Erich Salomon/Magnum: **186**; Robert Capece: **188**; UPI, Bettmann Archives: **189**; Washington University, St. Louis: **191**; Bettmann Archives: **193**; State Historical Society of Missouri: **195**; Bettmann Archives: **196, 198**; Montana Historical Society: **200**; Bettmann Archives, Museum of The American Indian: **201**; Woolaroc Museum, Oklahoma: **202**; New York Public Library, Bettmann Archives: **203**; The Butler Institute, Cincinnati: **205**; Bettmann Archives: **206**; Southwest Museum, Los Angeles: **208**; Bettmann Archives: **209**; Witte Museum: **211**; UPI: **212**; San Antonio Convention Center: **213**; Hella Hammid/Photo Researchers, Peggy Cromer, John Running/Stock, Boston, Gary Metz, Porterfield-Chickering/Photo Researchers: **215**; Gene Daniels/Black Star: **217**; Yorem Kahana/Peter Arnold Photo Archives: **219**; Michal Heron/McGraw-Hill: **220–239**; Porterfield-Chickering/Photo Researchers, Michal Heron/McGraw-Hill: **240**; Michal Heron/McGraw-Hill: **241**; Constantin Manos/Magnum: **242**; Michal Heron/McGraw-Hill: **244–247**; Metropolitan Museum of Art: **252–253**; The Veterans of the Seventh Regiment, New York: **254**; Culver: **255**; Bettmann Archives: **256**; The Granger Collection: **257**; Bettmann Archives: **258, 261**; Library of Congress: **262**; The Granger Collection: **263**; Culver: **267**; Library of Congress: **268**; Bettmann Archives: **269**; Museum of the Confederacy: **270**; Lynd Ward, *Soldiers Marching During the War*, in *America's Robert E. Lee*, Henry Steele Commager, Houghton-Mifflin, 1951: **271**; Library of Congress: **272, 273**; Photo by Charles Anderson, The Veterans of the Seventh Regiment, New York: **274**; Culver: **275**; Library of Congress: **276**; Bettmann Archives: **277**; Library of Congress: **278**; Culver: **279**; Bettmann Archives: **280**; Culver: **282**; Yale University Art Gallery, Collection of Mabel Brady Garvan: **283**; Culver: **284, 286**; Illustrated London News, Bettmann Archives: **289**; San Antonio Museum: **290**; Culver: **292**; George Eastman House: **293**; Culver: **295**; Bettmann Archives: **296**; Culver: **297**; Taft Museum, Cincinnati: **299**; Nebraska Historical Society, Collection of Solomon D. Butcher: **300**; Courtesy of William L. Katz, Union Pacific Railroad Museum: **301**; *Buffalo Hunt under Wolf Skin*, George A. Catlin, American Museum of Natural History: **303**; *Indians of the Plains*, A. A. Jansson, American Museum of Natural History: **305**; Bettmann Archives: **306**; *When Sioux and Blackfeet Meet*, Charles M. Russell, Gilcrease Museum: **307**; The Granger Collection, Bettmann Archives: **308**; Peter Dublin: **310**; United States Department of Agriculture, Joseph C. Farber: **315**; Michal Heron: **317**; Dennis Stock/Magnum: **318**; Magnum: **319**; Adam Woolfitt/Woodfin Camp: **321**; Michal Heron: **322**; Peter Dublin: **324**; Michal Heron: **326**; Peter Dublin: **327, 328**; Michal Heron: **330**; Peter Dublin: **332**; Fred Ward/Black Star: **336–337**; Bettmann Archives: **338–345**; Bettmann Archives, New York Public Library, Bettmann Archives, Daniel Kramer: **347**; Culver: **349**; Bettmann Archives: **350–356**; UPI: **357**; UPI, Bettmann Archives: **359**; Bettmann Archives: **360**; UPI: **363–367, 368–369**; Brookhaven National Laboratory: **370**; National Park Service: **371**; Bettmann Archives: **372**.